THE SUMMIT

THE SUMMIT

HOW TRIUMPH TURNED TO TRAGEDY ON K2's DEADLIEST DAYS

Pat Falvey | Pemba Gyalje Sherpa

Beyond Endurance Publishing

First published in 2013 by
Beyond Endurance Publishing
The Mountain Lodge, Beaufort, Killarney, Co. Kerry, Ireland
Tel: +353 64 6644181
www.thesummitk2.com
info@thesummitk2.com

In association with
The O'Brien Press Ltd.
12 Terenure Road East, Rathgar, Dublin 6, Ireland.
Tel: +353 1 4923333; Fax +353 1 4922777
www.obrien.ie
books@obrien.ie

ISBN: 978-1-84717-643-1

Typesetting and design by
Switzer Studios, Co. Kerry, Ireland
www.switzerstudios.ie

Printed and bound by CPI Group (UK) Ltd, Croydon, CR0 4YY

Front cover image, images for chapters two, five, seven, epilogue image, back endpaper image,
back cover images © Wilco van Rooijen; front endpaper image, chapter six image © Chris Klinke;
prologue image © Cas van de Gevel; chapter one image © McDonnell family; chapter three image ©
Oystein Stangeland; chapter four image © Norit expedition.

A CIP catalogue record for this book is available from the British Library

To the memory of those adventurers who have lost their lives in the pursuit of their dreams and to the families and friends they have left behind.

Often times, when somebody does lose a life, what went on is held up under the microscope. Some people might say they should have done this and they shouldn't have done that. Just because you survive a mountain doesn't make you an expert; I don't think it gives you any right to say that somebody made a mistake because, when you weren't there, you don't know. Only the mountain knows.

Ger McDonnell, mountaineer (1971-2008)
(The Summit/West Limerick Radio)

CONTENTS

ACKNOWLEDGEMENTS

There are many people around the world who helped to bring this book from a concept to a reality, and to whom we are extremely grateful.

This book would not have been possible without the heartfelt and honest contributions of many of the climbers on K2 in 2008 and members of their families who were interviewed for the award-winning documentary film, *The Summit*, and on whose interviews this book is largely based. Their candour and willingness to share their experiences are greatly appreciated – thanks to Tsering Bhote, Hoselito Bite, Marco Confortola, Chhiring Dorje Sherpa, Pasang Lama, JJ McDonnell, Eric Meyer, Lars Nessa, Damien O'Brien, Cecilie Skog, Annie Starkey, Fredrik Sträng, Cas van de Gevel, Wilco van Rooijen, Predrag Zagorac, and Alberto Zerain.

We are deeply grateful to our researchers and compilers, Bridget McAuliffe and Owen O'Shea, who embraced the project and who worked tirelessly to ensure that as complete an exposition as possible of what happened on the mountain could be presented here. Thanks are due to our book designer, Damien Switzer, for his creativity and energy.

Sincere thanks to all the staff at Image Now films and Pat Falvey Productions including Darrell Kavanagh, Olivia Leahy, Alan Torpey, David Torpey, Betty Baker, Katherine Kennedy, Gabriela Kavanagh, Lorraine Gordon, Niall Foley, Sylwia Cytrynska, Mary Healy, Chris Doona, and also to Ciara Foley for organising travel and flights.

A special thanks to Nick Ryan, director/producer of *The Summit*, for all his hard work and dedication, for giving his all in the making of the feature documentary and also for his contribution of images for the book.

Thanks to all those who provided photographs, including Mike Farris, Chris Klinke, Marco Confortola, Lars Nessa, Hoselito Bite, Wilco van Rooijen, and the McDonnell family. We are grateful to Mike Farris and Chris Klinke for permission to use the updates from their blogs.

Sincere gratitude to all the McDonnell family and to Ger McDonnell's partner, Annie Starkey; to Maarten van Eck of the Norit expedition for providing photographs, written material and comments on the narrative and for providing meteorological data from the Norit expedition's weather forecaster, Ab Maas; to Bjorn Sekkesaeter from the Norwegian team for additional information; to Shaheen Baig from the Serbian expedition who kindly agreed to be interviewed; to Chris Warner, leader of the Shared Summits Expedition to K2 in 2007, for his helpful insights; to Stephen O'Reilly for his contribution in bringing this project together; to Mick Murphy for his descriptions of Pakistan and the trek to K2 Base Camp; to Vito Missorici for his detailed translations; to Gloria Crispino, Giuliana Natale and Snigdha Dhunge who also assisted with translations; to Ang Rita Sherpa, Dawa Tenjing Sherpa and Sumba Ringi Sherpa for facilitating interviews in Kathmandu.

To the many other friends who read, contributed to and commented on drafts, including Brian and Patrick Falvey, Dr Clare O'Leary, Chris Horan, Hélene Philion, Breda Joy, Julie Galvin, Cliona McCarthy, Tina Gates, Johnny Lyons, Gerry Walsh, Joe O'Leary and Heather Irwin, our grateful thanks. A special thank you to Micheál O'Connell, Martin Harvey, Gordon Judge, Tim Falvey, and Martina O'Sullivan.

Finally, we would like to thank our families and friends for their support while this book was being written.

EXPEDITIONS & CLIMBERS

Norit K2 Dutch International Expedition (Cesen route)
Wilco van Rooijen *(leader)*
Gerard (Ger) McDonnell
Cas van de Gevel
Pemba Gyalje Sherpa
Court Haegens
Mark Sheen
Jelle Staleman
Roeland van Oss

Norwegian K2 Expedition (Abruzzi route)
Cecilie Skog
Rolf Bae
Lars Nessa
Oystein Stangeland

South Korean Flying Jump Expedition (Abruzzi route)
A team:
Kim Jae-soo *('Mr Kim', leader)*
Hwang Dong-jin *(deputy leader)*
Park Kyeong-hyo *(climbing leader)*
Go Mi-sun *('Ms Go')*
Kim Hyo-gyeong *('Little' Kim)*
Jumik Bhote*
Pasang Lama*

B team: **(Abruzzi route)**
Lee Sung-rok
Song Gui-hwa
Lee Won-sub
Kim Tae-gyu
Kim Seong-sang
Son Byung-woo
Tsering Bhote*
'Big' Pasang Bhote*

French-led K2 Expedition (Cesen route)
Hugues D'Aubarède *(leader)*
Nick Rice
Peter Guggemos
Karim Meherban*
Jehan Baig*
Qudrat Ali*

American K2 International Expedition (Abruzzi route)
Mike Farris *(leader)*
Chhiring Dorje Sherpa
Chris Klinke
Eric Meyer
Fredrik Sträng
Chris Warner
Timothy Horvath
Paul Walters

Serbian K2 Vojvodina Expedition (Abruzzi route)
Milivoj Erdeljan *(leader)*
Predrag Zagorac
Dren Mandic
Iso Planic
Miodrag Jovovic
Shaheen Baig*
Mohammad Khan*
Mohammad Hussein*

Singapore K2 Expedition (Abruzzi route)
Robert Goh *(leader)*
Edwin Siew Cheok Wai
Ang Chirring Sherpa*
Jamling Bhote*

Italian K2 Expedition (Abruzzi route)
Marco Confortola *(leader)*
Roberto Manni
Mohammad Ali*
Mohammad Amin*

Independent climbers
Hoselito Bite *(Serbia)* **(Cesen route)**
Alberto Zerain *(Spain)* **(Abruzzi route)**

French TGW K2 Expedition
Yannick Graziani
Christian Trommsdorff
Patrick Wagnon

Sunny Mountain Chogori Expedition
George Dijmarescu *(leader)*
Teodora Vid
Mircea Leustean
Rinjing Sherpa
Mingma Tunduk Sherpa

* Denotes high-altitude worker or mountain guide

GLOSSARY OF TERMS

Acclimatisation – the process by which organisms adjust and adapt to different climates, environments and altitudes.

Adze – the flatter end of an ice axe used for cutting footsteps and clearing ice.

Alpinist/alpine climbing – refers to a self-sufficient approach to climbing in which climbers carry all of their equipment and supplies as they ascend a mountain, often without recourse to fixed ropes, high-altitude workers or oxygen.

Belay – a method of securing a safety rope to an anchor point and feeding the rope through a crab to aid the safe progress of a climber.

Bivouac – an improvised temporary natural construction or shelter used for sleeping and often used to refer to sleeping in the open air.

Carabiner/crab – a spring-loaded metal loop or catch for attaching ropes to fixed lines.

Cerebral oedema – a condition resulting in the swelling of the brain tissue due to the presence of excessive amounts of fluid.

Chorten – a Buddhist shrine.

Couloir – a gulley or narrow passage, often used to describe the Bottleneck on K2.

Crampons – sharp spikes affixed to climbing boots to aid traction on ice and snow.

Death Zone – the name given to altitudes in the troposphere above approximately 8,000 metres in which human existence is unsustainable for long periods because of a reduced capacity to process oxygen.

Expedition/siege style – refers to a style of mountaineering which involves the setting up of fixed lines and stocked camps, usually with the assistance of high-altitude workers, in advance of a summit attempt.

Fixed ropes – ropes fixed to anchor points along dangerous surfaces or terrain and placed in advance of, or during, an ascent to provide safety for climbers.

Jumar – a device used to climb on fixed ropes which slides upwards and locks when any downward pressure is applied.

High Camp – Camp Four on the Shoulder on K2.

High-altitude workers – people who are employed to work at high altitude, sometimes referred to as high-altitude porters (HAPs).

Hypoxia – a condition in which the body or parts of the body are deprived of an adequate supply of oxygen and which often occurs at high altitude.

Ice axe – a tool used for climbing on icy surfaces, which can also be used as an anchor or a walking aid.

Ice screw – a threaded tubular device used to hold ropes in place during climbing and which can be used as an anchor point for fixed ropes.

Lama – a Tibetan cleric or head of a monastery.

Low-altitude porters – people who are employed to work at low altitude, sometimes referred to as LAPs.

Moraine – rock and ice debris on a glacier.

Névé – granular snow.

Objective danger – a naturally-occurring phenomenon, such as an avalanche, rockfall or icefall, which usually occurs without warning.

Piton – a metal spike used as an anchor.

Pulmonary oedema – a condition in which fluid accumulates in the lungs and which may be caused by high altitude.

Puja – a ceremony involving worship of a deity through song, prayer and invocation.

Rappel – controlled descent using a rope on steep terrain (also known as abseiling).

Serac – a large overhanging block or column of ice.

Sherpa – a member of, or referring to, an ethnic group in Nepal. The term Sherpa is also used generically for people from the Himalaya who work as mountain guides and high-altitude workers.

Sirdar – the head guide on an expedition.

PREFACE

The overwhelming yearning for adventure and exploration has forever been part of the human condition. The need to discover, to experience and to investigate the furthest reaches of the planet and its most desolate and inhospitable places has an innate and lasting allure that endures even when it seems there is nowhere or nothing left to discover. The longing remains because the human desire to pit oneself against nature and the impulse to push oneself physically, mentally and psychologically to one's absolute limits, continue to be incredibly potent and powerful forces.

Adventurers are always thinking of their next expedition, dreaming of the mountain, the snow and ice, the beauty and the challenge; some deep impulse keeps pulling us back to the outer limits of the natural world. When that impulse is satisfied and the next challenge has been met, thoughts of returning to the comforts of home are relished, only for the cycle to – inevitably – begin all over again, until time or death dictates otherwise.

Mountains are like cathedrals, places where, despite, or perhaps because of, the extreme physical demands, space emerges for climbers to be fully present in their own lives in the midst of the world's most pristine and most dangerous places. Extreme adventurers push the boundaries of calculable risk – often selfishly – to satisfy their aspirations and egos. Family members live with the worry that their loved one may never return; that, despite the most rigorous preparations, they are engaged in a game of Russian roulette. Yet, those at home feel compelled to support their loved ones in the pursuit of their passion and dreams.

High-altitude climbing has a distinctive appeal all of its own, one that keeps luring climbers back to the mountains despite all the obstacles, whether physical, emotional or financial. Reaching the summit of the highest peaks means that, for one moment in time, you are standing on a piece of hallowed ground that has been 250 million years in the making, a place that still has an elite membership, despite technical and scientific innovation.

What makes higher altitudes all the more demanding and lethal is that life-denying place above an altitude of 8,000 metres known as the Death Zone, where the body deteriorates rapidly, where brain cells become numb and logical thinking is compromised. In that rarefied atmosphere, strong men are weakened, some become manic, and even the most experienced climbers can crumple under the pressure.

In August 2008, on a seemingly perfect day, 11 climbers perished in the Death Zone on K2, the world's second highest mountain, and also its deadliest. Among the dead was the first Irishman to reach K2's summit, Gerard (Ger) McDonnell. Ger was on a number of my expeditions to the great mountain ranges of the world and I greatly admired his tenacity, warm personality and wonderful passion for climbing.

With Ger on K2 in 2008 was my good friend Pemba Gyalje Sherpa, who had been the sirdar on a number of my Nepalese expeditions, and who spent almost three days in or near K2's Death Zone, co-ordinating rescue missions and bringing climbers to safety. On Mount Everest in 2003, just 50 metres from the summit, in the Death Zone, both men came to my rescue when I became crippled by oxygen deprivation, oedema and loss of peripheral vision. Also among the victims on K2 in 2008 was my fellow polar explorer, the Norwegian Rolf Bae, a diligent adventurer who, along with Ger, had joined me on the 2006 Beyond Endurance expedition to Antarctica in honour of Ernest Shackleton.

The loss of life on K2 had a dramatic aftermath as the tragedy quickly became a controversy. Those who managed to return safely to Base Camp walked away from the devastation on the mountain directly into the turbulence of a media storm, fuelled by a litany of contradictions and inconsistencies, many of which were contained in the survivors' own accounts. The consequent fallout caused immeasurable pain to many of the families left behind.

My search for the truth led me on a five-year journey that has resulted in the publication of this book, along with a joint venture production of the feature-length documentary, *The Summit,* with director Nick Ryan and Image Now Films. Sources for both the documentary and the book include most of the climbers who were on K2 in 2008, some of their off-mountain team members and family members. Pemba Gyalje Sherpa collaborated fully in the chronicling of his version of events on K2 during the 2008 expedition, and his clear and forthright testimony provides the context for this telling of events. In many ways, this is Pemba's story.

There have been many accounts of what took place on K2 in the early days of August 2008, but such a tragedy, in such circumstances, deserves re-examination in an effort to get a clearer picture of how even the best-prepared climbers were challenged to the limits of their endurance on the world's second highest peak.

This is a story whose complexity and dramatic nature demanded a chronological telling so that the full tapestry of events could be displayed, drawing out the personalities and themes that make for a more thorough explanation of what drew so many different people to such a desolate, forbidding place, and how and why 11 of them failed to come home.

Setting these tragic events in a chronological context, informed by the eyewitness accounts of many of those who were there, and also with the first full testimony of Pemba Gyalje Sherpa will, hopefully, facilitate a new comprehension of how and why things happened as they did, and help readers develop a deeper understanding of what drives people to risk their lives in some of the most hostile and godforsaken places on Earth. This account also details the efforts of five other Sherpas from Nepal who remained in or near the Death Zone over the course of almost three days in their heroic attempts to save fellow climbers.

Few reports or investigations are ever conducted when climbers die on the mountains; instead, over time, a narrative emerges from various sources – shared stories, media articles, interviews, documentaries and books. It is hoped that this book will contribute to a greater comprehension of what happened.

What we can learn and begin to talk about is what can be done differently in the future – the need for enhanced training and preparation for high-altitude adventure, the ability to know one's own limits and capacities and, above all, the need to respect nature and the mountains.

The story of what happened on K2 during the 2008 climbing season will captivate many and shock even more, prompting questions about why men and women continue to be drawn to places where the dance between humans and nature, between life and death, is at its most passionate and fragile.

Pat Falvey

FOREWORD

I grew up surrounded by the Himalaya mountains on a farm near the village of Pankhongma in the Solukhumbu District in Nepal, 50 kilometres south of Everest, the world's highest peak. Several generations of my family earned a living from the land and from a young age I worked on the farm with my father.

My village was on one of the main trekking routes to Everest and climbers often stopped off there on the way, regularly camping in the grounds of my school. I was just a teenager when I first met Sir Edmund Hillary, who, along with Tenzing Norgay Sherpa, summited Everest for the first time in 1953. Hillary, the most renowned mountaineer of his generation, visited my school many times as his charitable foundation was supporting a number of educational projects in the region, including providing funding to our school.

Hillary returned on several occasions over the years to assess progress. He also spoke freely with me and my fellow students about mountaineering and his experience on Everest. I was captivated and greatly inspired by his stories.

At 14 years of age, I began my own career on the mountains, working first as a porter ferrying the gear and supplies of expeditions to the mountains around my home, and earning some money to support my family. I learned much from the older Sherpa climbers in my region, observing closely their methods and skills. After years of learning, training and researching, I became a full-time guide and mountaineer, eventually becoming one of the first Sherpas in Nepal to gain international professional accreditation.

Gradually, I enhanced my high-altitude experience by completing multiple climbs above an altitude of 6,000 metres and higher in the Himalaya. I have always believed that, for every expedition, thorough preparation is vital. So I have always encouraged high-altitude adventurers to gain sufficient experience at 6,000 metres and 7,000 metres, before progressing to the very highest peaks in the world. By 2008, I had summited Everest seven times in seven successive seasons and had been on 40 expeditions into the Death Zone, on both Everest and Cho Oyu.

Experience has taught me that all climbers come to the highest peaks in the world because of their love for the mountains and nature. But climbers have varying degrees of technical ability, skill and training. Those variations in capacity and experience are often the difference between life and death.

I have often seen climbers coming to the mountains ill-equipped and ill-prepared. But I have also seen how even the most able and experienced of climbers can collapse under the strain of conditions above 8,000 metres.

K2 has a deep resonance for climbers; it is magnetic. I always considered it a very technically challenging mountain, best suited to professionals only, and in my many years working on Everest and other mountains, I never considered climbing K2 as a guide. In 2008, I was invited to be a full and equal member of a Dutch-led expedition to the mountain. I decided to go because it was a chance to visit the Karakorum mountains and also because my Irish friend, Ger McDonnell, was on the team.

In *The Summit: How Triumph turned to Tragedy on K2's Deadliest Days*, I provide, for the first time, a full account of what I experienced during the almost three months I spent at K2 in 2008. I describe events from the time we arrived at Base Camp, through the days and weeks of acclimatisation and preparation, the summit attempt itself and subsequent efforts to rescue those who became stranded in the Death Zone.

In particular, I recount the devastating series of events that occurred between 1 and 3 August which saw 11 climbers lose their lives.

What I offer here is my story, alongside the first-hand accounts of others who were also on the mountain, which, I hope, will bring a greater clarity to what happened during those dreadful days.

Pemba Gyalje Sherpa

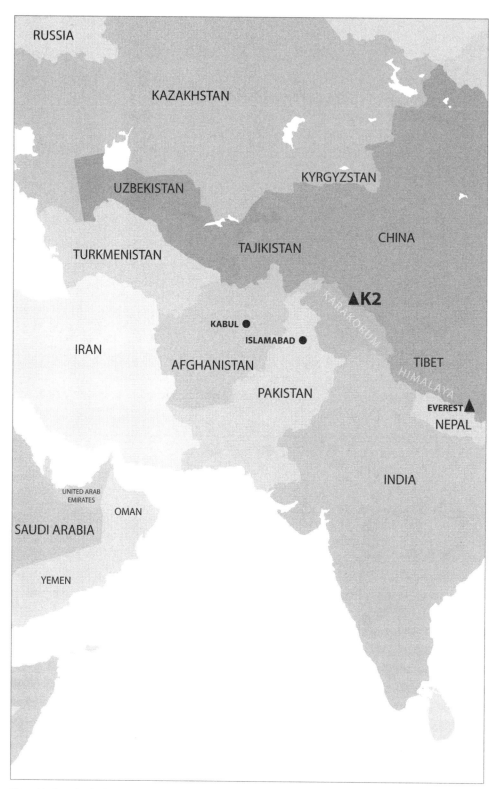

K2 and its location in Asia

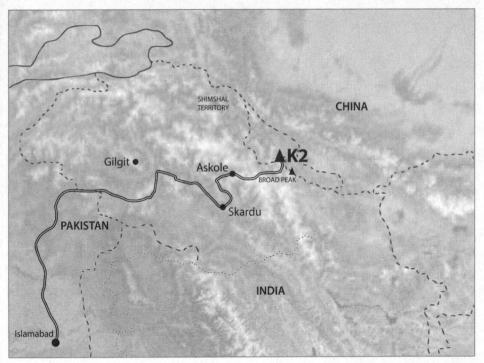

The route from Islamabad to K2

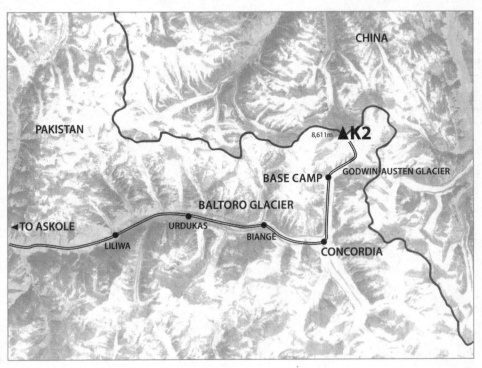

The route across the Baltoro glacier

Prologue

May 2008

The hardy, weather-beaten farmers from the foothills of the Karakorum mountains make their way to the small village of Askole in one of the most remote and inaccessible parts of northern Pakistan. Some walk for hours along crumbling roads and dirt tracks which wind their way through the parched and barren terrain deep in Asia's most mountainous region.

The men, mostly middle-aged but some not much older than teenagers, descend from their farms and homesteads around Askole in search of work. The climbing season is about to get under way and the dusty and featureless single-storey outpost is preparing to host a diverse assortment of international climbers in search of adventure on the ever-alluring mountains in the region.

Despite its remoteness, this part of northern Pakistan, situated along the border with China, has attracted explorers and thrill-seekers to the challenges of high-altitude adventure for over 100 years. Askole comes to life with the injection of people and revenue which the annual climbing season brings; the village is the climbers' final encounter with civilisation before several weeks, or maybe months, on the mountains beyond.

To launch their summit bids, the expeditions require hundreds of porters to ferry heavy loads of hiking gear, tents, clothing, foodstuffs and communications equipment to camps in the glacial valleys above, places far beyond the access of any motorised vehicle. For that service, the expedition members pay well, often enough to match several months of the regular earnings of their newly-hired staff. The expeditions' sirdars, the head guides responsible for mobilising and organising the porters, put the word about if any particularly large expeditions are due to arrive, news of additional short-term employment prospects rippling around the region.

As well as older men looking to supplement the meagre incomes they derive from farming in Askole's hinterland, younger porters, even a few college students, assemble, partly out of excitement at the prospect of a few weeks on the mountains and partly to earn some hard cash. The work is quite profitable by local economic standards. The sirdar negotiates remuneration for the porters, a daily rate of around $10, payable on arrival at Base Camp.

When all the hiring is done, rates agreed and cargo arranged, the porters wait in line, ready to tether to their backs and the tops of their heads boxes and containers full of high-tech clothing, satellite technology and new-fangled mountaineering gadgets, and carry them across the glaciers thousands of metres above.

The porters' routine has been a mainstay of the climbing season in the Gilgit-Baltistan district of Pakistan ever since outsiders first came to explore and survey the region, fascinated by the vast expanse of soaring mountains and gigantic glaciers which run from the Karakorum on the China-Pakistan border south-eastwards to the Himalaya which separate China from India.

The peaks form a vast phalanx of mountains, born millennia earlier when the Indian and Eurasian tectonic plates ploughed into each other, forcing volcanic ash and rock skyward, and forming a jagged, inhospitable and remote landscape of peaks and valleys. Historically part of the Silk Road trading route between Europe and Asia, the advent of colonialism and the expansion of the British Empire brought an increased commercial and geographical interest in the region from the West.

It wasn't until 1856 and the arrival of a British army lieutenant-colonel, Thomas Montgomerie, that the full breadth and dimensions of the mountain ranges in the region came to be known. As part of the Great Trigonometric Survey of India, Montgomerie took up a position on the summit of Haramukh in northern India, 200 kilometres to the south of the Karakorum range. From there, and with the aid of an angle-measuring theodolite, he charted and calculated the heights of the array of peaks along the horizon.

Thirty-two summits were visible, two of which jutted way above their peers. He sketched what he saw in his notebook. A simple nomenclature had to be found; Montgomerie decided he would call each of the peaks 'K' – shorthand for Karakorum – and then append a number to every one of the 32. And so was born the name of the world's second highest mountain, K2. K1 soon came to be known by its local name, Masherbrum, but the name given to the higher peak stuck.

For a brief period in the mid- to late-nineteenth century, the name Mount Godwin-Austen was used to refer to K2; the English topographer, Henry Haversham Godwin-Austen, is credited with being the first westerner, in 1861, to see the mountain close up from the top of the glacier which weaves its way towards K2's flanks on the Pakistani side. Godwin-Austen, instead, lent his name to the glacier on which he stood.

The Godwin-Austen glacier forms a corridor towards the peak from the south where it intersects with the massive Baltoro glacier, which, in turn, runs over 65 kilometres southwest towards Askole and civilisation. Chogori, a name used locally for the soaring peak, and deriving from the Balti words *chhogo* (big) and *ri* (mountain), never caught on. Montgomerie's original classification endured, and of his 32 'Ks' only 'K2' is still commonly used.

Climbers spend their last night in pre-mountain society in their tents in Askole, having made the long journey from the Pakistani capital, Islamabad, where permits are secured and other paperwork is completed before the 750-kilometre journey along the Karakorum Highway to the busy northern city of Skardu. The highway is the highest paved road in the world and is notoriously dangerous, often blocked by monsoon downpours and heavy snowfall. From Skardu, a heavily potholed and poorly maintained mountain road brings the expeditions to Askole.

Some of the expeditions have high-altitude workers travelling with them; men who will work as guides and helpers until the climbers leave the mountain. They assist in fixing ropes, carrying oxygen and other supplies, and leading their clients towards the summit. A handful are Sherpas from Nepal, thousands of kilometres away in the Himalaya, but most are from northern Pakistan and are generally hired based on their experience of the Karakorum mountains and their understanding and knowledge of high-altitude climbing.

Before the porters receive their allocation, the climbers check and re-check the inventory of their supplies, all bearing detailed labels to ensure foodstuffs rationed for the following two-month period are not dipped into any sooner than they should be. A precise catalogue of everything – from socks to spices, gas stoves to crampons, satellite phones to anti-inflammatory drugs – will have been calculated and formulated months before, based on a detailed daily allowance of items for the journey ahead.

As night falls, a sense of anticipation builds; tomorrow the climbers will begin the trek towards Base Camp where the expedition will begin in earnest, years of preparation and logistical planning finally realised. Ambition battles with fear, excitement with trepidation as a proper night's sleep proves elusive. The first group of porters will be gone by dawn to prepare camps and meals before the visitors even emerge from their tents.

As the climbers begin the ascent towards the icy moraine of the Baltoro glacier, they follow in the footsteps of the countless expeditions that have encroached upon the pristine landscape for over a century, each with varying degrees of success. One of the earliest expeditions was led by Aleister Crowley, the controversial English mystic, occultist, self-styled prophet and founder of the religious philosophy of Thelema.

With his friend, Oscar Eckenstein, Crowley made five failed summit bids in the space of nine weeks in the summer of 1902.[1] On the higher slopes, the expedition descended into near farce; at one point, a hypoxic and delirious Crowley – 'one of the strangest men ever to become a mountaineer'[2] – threatened a team-mate with a gun.

Seven years later, it fell to an equally flamboyant man, the Duke of the Abruzzi – grandson of Italy's first king – to attempt K2's summit. Fresh from expeditions to the Arctic and several mountains across the world, the renowned explorer arrived via the Baltoro glacier with a brass bed, camel hair-lined sleeping bags and other trappings of royalty. Despite being well resourced and having the best mountaineering equipment available, the duke and his team ascended no higher than 6,100 metres.

His hopes of a new high-altitude record were dashed but he later lent his name to the southeast ridge via which he attempted the summit, a name still in use today. The duke's expedition also gave the world some of the most iconic images ever taken of the mountain, which were captured by Vittorio Sella, the noted high-altitude photographer.

The elusive and mysterious K2 quickly captured the imagination of the small international mountaineering fraternity at a time when the conquest of mountains was a badge of glory, not just for climbers, but also for the countries from which they came. An American-led expedition in 1939 saw its leader, the well-known socialite, Dudley Wolfe, perish after several days stranded at the higher camps.

Three Sherpas died in an attempt to rescue him, the first recorded fatalities on K2.

After a decline in the number of expeditions to the mountain during the second World War and in its immediate aftermath, summit success finally came to a meticulously prepared Italian expedition in 1954. Just a year after Everest had been scaled by Edmund Hillary and Tenzing Norgay Sherpa, the 40-year-old Italian, Lino Lacadelli, and his fellow countryman, 29-year-old Achille Compagnoni, stood together at 8,611 metres on the snow-capped apex on the evening of 31 July. Nobody would set foot on the summit for another 23 years.[3]

The widely-celebrated Italian summit success was tinged with controversy, however, and their achievement was sullied by accusation and counter-accusation of selfishness and lies. Another member of the expedition, Walter Bonatti, had climbed towards Lacadelli and Compagnoni with supplementary oxygen to improve their prospects of success. Bonatti later accused Compagnoni of moving the highest camp, Camp Nine, to a location other than that agreed, forcing him and a Hunza porter, Amir Mahdi, to bivouac in the open air overnight.

The summiteers later retrieved the oxygen and Bonatti and Mahdi descended to a lower camp. Bonatti always held that Compagnoni didn't want him to share in the summiteers' success. Though Bonatti was considered fitter than Compagnoni, and had a real prospect of summiting, the latter was the favoured protégé of the team leader, Ardito Desio.

Bonatti's claims were largely written out of the official record of events although he eventually cleared his name in the Italian courts. However, there was never any reconciliation between him and the summiteers.[4] Half a century later, the Italian Alpine Club publicly acknowledged Bonatti as integral to the 1954 summit success.

The mountain continued to appeal to the more courageous and adventurous. In 1979, the South Tyrolean Italian climber, Reinhold Messner, climbed K2 along a route on the south face which he dubbed 'The Magic Line'. This success contributed to his record achievement of becoming the first person in the world to have climbed every one of the world's 14 peaks above 8,000 metres, known as the 8,000ers in the mountaineering fraternity.

It was 1986 before a woman set foot on the summit. Wanda Rutkiewicz, from Poland, saw her achievement overshadowed, however, by the deaths of two of her climbing partners, the French husband and wife, Maurice and Liliane Barrard, who died in a suspected icefall below the summit. That same climbing season became known as K2's 'Black Summer' when a total of 13 climbers perished in different accidents between June and August. As the number of expeditions arriving to K2 rose in the 1980s and 1990s, so, too, did the number of fatalities on what was rapidly becoming known as the 'Killer Mountain'.[5]

Unlike Everest and many other iconic peaks in the Himalaya and the Karakorum, K2 is relatively inaccessible, one of the many reasons it is climbed less often and has never gained the popularity and allure of its peers. Ahead of all climbers leaving Askole is a four- to seven-day trek to the foot of the mountain. Transporting tons of equipment across the Baltoro glacier, the mammoth ice field that leads almost all the way to the base of the mountain, is laborious, physically demanding and expensive.

The party of climbers and porters – up to 20 porters are required for every climber – move from an altitude of 2,500 metres to 5,000 metres over the course of the trek, traversing ice fields, gushing streams and rubble-strewn terrain. The neighbouring ice tributaries feed into the Baltoro – one of the longest glaciers outside the polar regions and two kilometres wide in places – giving an aerial view resembling the fronds of seaweed splayed out across the valley.

As the human caravan weaves its way up the glacial valley, the multitude of peaks which make up the Karakorum range comes into view, reminding the adventurers that each step is taking them closer to the mountain they have been thinking and dreaming about for years.

The Karakorum region is home to some of the most celebrated mountains in the world, each peak offering a different experience, its own tests and dangers and a distinctive and unique adrenalin rush. Gasherbrum I, II, III and IV, Masherbrum (K1) and Broad Peak (K3), along with an adventure park of climbing walls and cliffs of black granite, including the landmark Trango Towers, present a veritable smörgåsbord of some of the most exhilarating and best-known climbing challenges in the world.

But just one of the star attractions occupies the concentration of the chain snaking its way across the footbridges, boulders and snow: appropriately, K2 – dwarfing its neighbours – is the final destination on the route, the majestic terminus at the end of the rugged glacier.

The climbers come from different cultures and ethnic backgrounds, from different socio-economic groups and professions; they speak different languages and have different belief systems and approaches. They also have varying levels of experience and proficiency. Each will have left behind a family – parents, partners, perhaps a husband or wife, or young children – in their quest to explore not just some of the world's most majestic and dangerous places, but also to explore the limits of their physical and psychological capacities.

But the disparate group shares one thing in common – a passion for adventure, allied to a desire to achieve something few people on the planet ever will – overcoming the challenge of some of the most hostile but beautiful natural features in the world: its highest mountains.

For some, getting to Base Camp, or maybe one of the higher camps on the mountain, will be their 'summit'; for others, nothing less than the summit itself will suffice. But, for all, their love of climbing, being on the mountains and embracing the risks that presents, is the common bond they share, the stresses and strains of home, work and family fading with each step that takes them higher into the icy wilderness.

Despite the withdrawal of daily comforts and luxuries, the climbers begin to feel utterly alive, every sense more receptive and responsive to their surroundings. Whatever happens on this adventure, a new personal story is being written, one with which they will regale family and friends for years to come. Hope and fear battle for supremacy inside them as they prepare to test the limits of their abilities and defy their own mortality.

Before the 8,611-metre K2 is unveiled in all its glory, the climbers must continue their trek alongside the ghosts of Crowley, the Duke of the Abruzzi and Lacadelli. Up to eight hours of hiking each day takes its toll but they know that every kilometre brings them closer to the fitness levels which are required to mount a serious summit bid.

The low-altitude porters (LAPs) run with their cargo across parts of the more dangerous terrain, dodging and ducking beneath rock faces which are prone to shunting stones and boulders towards the ground at speed. By night, they rest in bivouac-style shelters while the climbers sleep in their expensive, high-quality tents.

For the entire footslog across the Baltoro, the climbers' target remains out of sight, hidden behind the gigantic peaks that stand sentry around it. It is not until they reach Concordia, the confluence of the Baltoro glacier and the much shorter Godwin-Austen glacier, that the expedition members get a first full glimpse of the imposing peak which has been in their thoughts and minds for years on end.

Though the mountain is still up to a day's walk away, this is a moment to pause in awe, to holler in relief at having come this far, to reach for a camera in a rucksack, to grapple with the extent of the mammoth task ahead. Reinhold Messner dubbed K2 'the most beautiful of all the high peaks'.[6] Most of his contemporaries would agree. Despite the close proximity of its peers, the almost-perfectly symmetrical diamond-shaped pinnacle stands out from the crowd, a pyramidal rock reaching upwards towards the heavens and resting imperially on the glacial plains below.

The first sighting of K2 also forces the climbers to confront another reality – its deadly reputation and status as the world's most dangerous peak. Names like 'Killer Mountain' and 'Savage Mountain', which locals sometimes dismiss as unjustified and unfair, have a certain ring of truth, at least when the statistics are examined.

Before the climbing season of 2008, just 278 people had successfully scaled K2, 66 of whom had died in the attempt – a fatality rate of 24 per cent. Out of every four climbers attempting the mountain, one will not come home. Thus, the mantra of 'one in four' has become a familiar refrain for those warning of the dangers of the world's second highest peak.

In stark comparison, one in 11 of those trying to scale Everest had lost their lives by 2008.[7] The fatality rate on Annapurna (8,091 metres) in Nepal – at one in three – was higher in the same period, but it has fallen steadily in recent years while K2's has remained stubbornly high. In many climbing seasons K2 can go unclimbed; even in a busy season it is often just a handful of climbers who make it to the top. In 2006, while hundreds successfully scaled Everest, just four people summited K2.

Less commercialised than Everest and despite its seniority in the pecking order of mountains, K2 has never lured climbers like its taller sister; its unpopularity, relative to its only superior, is reflected in the cost of the permit required to travel there. A Pakistani ministry of tourism permit for K2 in 2008 cost $10,000 per climber while one for Everest cost about $80,000, though the low fee for K2 was in part an attempt by the Pakistani government to attract adventurers in the wake of a number of terrorist incidents in the region.

Acute natural hazards and objective dangers, such as frequent ice avalanches and rockfall, make survival on K2 extremely precarious. Unstable and turbulent weather patterns are yet another deterrent. Impacted heavily by the jet stream airflow thousands of metres above sea level, the mountain has developed a reputation for climatic unpredictability rarely matched in the region. Weather forecasts, so detailed and comprehensive in modern meteorology, have to be taken with a liberal pinch of salt.

A moment of calm on K2's slopes can transform into a blizzard in minutes, a phenomenon that has put paid – sometimes with fatal consequences – to many attempts on its summit. K2 is over 1,000 kilometres further north than Everest, and consequently prone to lower temperatures and heavier snows.

The dozens of potential routes to the summit, a handful of which are now the most favoured, pose all those hazards and are only for those who are more competent and technically dexterous. But the summit is also only attainable by those who can overcome the crushing effects of high altitude which can render climbers incapable of even the most basic brain and bodily functions. In the Death Zone – the region above 8,000 metres – the bodily organs begin to fail, unable to metabolise or process oxygen as efficiently as required to sustain life.

Whatever its fatality rate, its natural hazards and its unpredictability, for many in the climbing fraternity, K2 is a thing of beauty which captivates them and which they consider the most significant prize in modern-day mountaineering. It is there to be climbed and, for many, a lifelong ambition remains unfulfilled until that challenge is undertaken.

In the 10 years to 2008, the summit had been reached in just five of them, but this proved no deterrent. In the summer of that year, its allure and appeal was no different to that experienced by the Duke of the Abruzzi and the countless others who had come before, some having tasted summit success, others having never returned.

A Nepalese climber named Pemba Gyalje was the first person to set foot at K2's base in 2008. He will never forget the first time he laid eyes on the mountain:

> I was face to face with K2. I felt it was a very steep mountain. It was a single mountain standing out, not like Everest which is surrounded by several other peaks. It did not remind me of anything else – this was just K2. I thought it was very beautiful.

The Waiting Game

28 May – 20 July

As Pemba Gyalje slid the rucksack off his back and onto the rocky ground, he breathed in the crisp air. Since two Kazakhstani climbers had reached K2's summit the previous autumn, the remote mountain region had lain pristine and untouched. Pemba, a Nepalese climbing Sherpa, was the first person to set foot on the pedestal of the world's second highest mountain that year. Behind him, applause echoed around the vast expanse.

The expedition leader, Wilco van Rooijen, had just told the 100 porters who had hauled the tons of equipment and supplies across the Baltoro glacier to Base Camp that, instead of being paid for seven days' work, they would be paid for 10. The porters were overjoyed; they had earned enough money to sustain their families and livelihoods for months. Bedecked in their much-prized special expedition peaked caps, which Wilco had printed up for them as a souvenir, the porters dropped the dozens of barrels and boxes of climbing gear and supplies on the glacial moraine and hurried away, back towards civilisation.

It was 28 May 2008 and Pemba was one of a team of eight supremely-equipped and rigorously-prepared climbers who were the first mountaineering expedition that summer to take up residence on the undulating plateau at the top of the Godwin-Austen glacier beneath the towering K2 – a place which would become their home for the next two and a half months. After weeks of arduous travel by airplane, bus, jeep and on foot, the Dutch K2 International Expedition had finally arrived to the spot where they pitched their tents and temporary auxiliary dwellings on the rock and ice for the weeks that lay ahead.

The eight climbers, including five Dutchmen, an Australian, a Nepali and an Irishman, comprised the members of the expedition which had been in the planning phase for almost two years. After a seven-day trek from the now-distant Askole, they reached a place nearly four kilometres beneath the summit where they set up Base Camp, home each summer to a menagerie of mountaineers from across the globe, compelled to come there by a shared passion and common goal.

It was a place without any precise geographical boundaries, no known address and no specific location on any map but it was the approximate point at which climbers seeking to conquer K2 could set up camp safely, out of the path of the rockfall, avalanches and turbulent weather episodes for which the mountain had gained a reputation.

Pemba and his climbing partners stood at an altitude of just over 5,000 metres above sea level, on a par with Turkey's Mount Ararat and Amarnath Peak in the Himalaya. The landscape was peppered with manifold boulders and debris, pushed down and aside by the massive glacier as it moved gradually across the valley. It was an inhospitable place, with scant vegetation and animal life, the terrain and environment anathema to the bare essentials and comforts of daily living. On every side of the barren plain, mountains soared towards the skies, none more daunting or impressive in Pemba's eyes than the highest peak in the Karakorum mountain range.

The silence at K2's Base Camp was almost deafening, in stark contrast to the ever-bustling Everest Base Camp from where Pemba had launched each of his seven successful summit attempts, one year after another. Often home to up to 1,000 people each climbing season, the encampment below the world's highest mountain was akin to a small town with people scattered across the plateau; at K2, there was no-one, something which spoke volumes in Pemba's mind about the mountain's reputation:

> When you see 1,000 people at Everest Base Camp from different countries – huge manpower and good service – you are thinking I want to climb Everest next year. K2 is different – at Base Camp there are minimal people, limited facilities, services, minimal manpower. There are only people who really want to do it.

Pemba paused for breath and surveyed the ground around him. There had been a recent heavy snowfall, its brilliant whiteness reflecting the rays of the afternoon sun. The expedition had the advantage of being the first to reach Base Camp; now they had plenty of potential sites to choose from, but finding a place to establish their temporary homes on what was an active, imperceptibly moving glacier was no easy task.

A minute shift in the moraine in the dead of night could be enough to collapse a tent, knock over barrels of foodstuffs or damage essential gear. Tents would have to be regularly adjusted and sometimes moved to accommodate the creeping, icy juggernaut beneath. Pemba brought his experience of establishing many Base Camps at Everest to bear on his first K2 expedition:

We chose the best camping site. It was the middle part of the major Base Camp area with less objective dangers from avalanches and glaciers, a safe Base Camp. The glacier was active, always changing. In many places there was no proper platform for the tent. For the first four days we worked every day, eight to 10 hours, to set up Base Camp. We had to dig out the ice, the snow and rocks for the tents. It was quite heavy construction on a bumpy surface. We used many stones and blocks. It is not easy to set up Base Camp on an active glacier.

Wilco van Rooijen directed operations with panache. The accomplished and ambitious Dutch mountaineer was in great shape after the week-long hike along the Baltoro. The terrain was manageable and acclimatisation to the new environment was under way. His team were bonding well, savouring the experience and relishing the prospect of tackling for the world's second highest point. He was feeling buoyant, the logistical preparations of the past two years realised, his emotions taut as he observed the landscape:

Humility, pride, wonder, fear and bravado all had a place in our cocktail of emotions. What a simply magnificent view. The area immediately around K2 is called the throne room of the mountain gods. It is easy to understand why.[8]

With the newly-arrived expedition were five ancillary staff, hired from the valleys of northern Pakistan. Their task was to tend to the team's eating requirements for the duration of their expedition. They had already started to unpack the essential items required for the first night on the mountain, rifling through rucksacks and barrels for the ingredients of what would be the expedition's first Base Camp meal.

Also present were a handful of international trekkers who had walked with the expedition from Askole; they were planning to go no further. Treks to K2 Base Camp were common, especially for the less experienced mountaineer intent on enhancing his or her experience; perhaps, next time, they would be settling into a tent at Base Camp, part of an expedition attempting the summit. Soon the climbers and their kitchen personnel were alone, staring at the seemingly endless mounds of climbing essentials piled against the boulders all around them.

The team moved swiftly to establish their miniature village of tents on the ice and rock, all well out of the path of potential avalanches and rockfalls. Everyone had their own tent, most of them orange, the colour reflecting the nationality of the majority of the team. Their thin-skinned domes, adorned with colourful flags and sponsors' bunting, were imaginatively partitioned into an invisible bedroom, kitchen and bathroom, with hiking gear stowed in one corner, a sleeping bag rolled up in another; the climbers mentally condensing their own homes into their new three by three-metre living quarters.

The expedition was being sponsored by the Dutch activated carbon producer and water purification company, Norit, and in the months and years afterwards, the Norit appendage became the shorthand description for the eight-man troupe. The company's logo was on almost every piece of clothing and headgear which the team had brought to the mountain. Among the items was a small Norit water purifier which looked like an office water cooler. It became the team's much-used 'tap' at Base Camp.

The toilet tent was pitched a good distance away, its placement so far from camp was a nuisance when required urgently in the cold dead of night, but the distance was essential for hygiene and preventing a contamination of snow which would be melted endlessly over the following weeks to supply drinking water for the climbers. Hydration at this altitude is essential, dehydration being one of the many enemies of a successful ascent. Glacial water supplied a tiny, red shower tent, to which the climbers paid chilly visits, trying to avoid slipping barefoot and partly clothed on the boulders and ice blocks en route.

Beard trims and haircuts were available on occasion from the kitchen personnel but some team members preferred to let their facial hair grow, if only to keep their faces warm. Pemba, a devout Buddhist, located the prayer flags he had brought from Nepal – they were strung between the tents to bring blessings and good luck to the expedition.

A large mess tent with fold-up tables and plastic chairs was used for eating, recreation, planning and blogging and became the main hub of activity. Above it, the cooks' Pakistani flag fluttered alongside the Irish tricolour, which a local tailor in Skardu had made for the Irish climber, Ger McDonnell.

Originally from the Solukhumbu district in north-eastern Nepal – a region synonymous with mountaineering tourism – Pemba Gyalje was on his first expedition to K2. Despite his passion for the mountains and his extensive experience of the Himalaya, many of his climbing friends and relatives were puzzled and concerned when he first announced plans to climb the mountain: they told him it was too dangerous, the death rate on K2 – one out of every four climbers attempting to scale the mountain dies in their effort – was too high, and they wondered why he wanted to risk those odds.

Pemba dismissed their worried queries. He had researched the region and studied any material he could find about K2. There was nothing he had learned about the mountain and its reputation that unduly unnerved him:

> Everyone says "Killer Mountain" and so the history makes people physiologically very uncomfortable. This is actually not really a killer mountain, this is a very beautiful mountain, the same as Everest and other 8,000-metre peaks. If people organise very well and use strong manpower like other 8,000-metre peaks, then the success rate will be high and it will be much safer.

Such confidence and self-belief were among the reasons that Pemba had been asked to join the Dutch expedition. And they were among the many reasons that Pemba's Irish friend and now team-mate, Ger McDonnell, had asked him to become a member. The two had first met on Everest in 2003 and from the moment they encountered each other, they seemed to bond, like kindred spirits. Ger had long been fascinated by the Sherpa way of life, their humble spirituality and sagacious approach to mountaineering.

He found in Pemba an articulate and exemplary exponent of Sherpa ideals and philosophies. In fact, the Irishman saw something special in him – a steely resilience combined with a pleasant and calming aura. Their experiences together had convinced Ger that Pemba would not just enhance the cohesion of the eight-man expedition to the mountain, he would also improve its chances of success.

Throughout their pre-expedition discussions, Ger was insistent that Pemba – whom he liked to dub 'Speedy Gonzales' – would join the team as a fully fledged regular member, with the same status as all the other climbers. He would be neither a mountain guide nor a high-altitude worker, a role the Nepali traditionally played on mountains like Everest and Cho Oyu.

Pemba mulled over his decision for several months. K2 had never beckoned him in the past, his focus was always on the Himalaya of Nepal and Tibet, but now he had an opportunity to explore Everest's deputy and a region he had never visited before. It would be a wonderful opportunity to visit the Karakorum mountains about which he had heard and read so much:

> Ger asked me and said if you are interested then you can join us, not like a high-altitude worker but as a member. He said they were trying to arrange the sponsors and other things and also that he would introduce me to the

expedition leader. We kept in contact by email and then I asked everybody ... I was thinking many times about K2 and the history and mountain terrain. Then, after three or four months, I said I would go.

When Ger had suggested Pemba's participation in the 2008 expedition to Wilco, the team leader welcomed him with open arms. Wilco admitted that the Netherlands, which has a very small climbing community, did not present rich enough pickings to form a strong and cohesive team with diverse skills and abilities.

He needed to look beyond his own country's boundaries to find climbers of sufficient professionalism and ability to enhance the expedition's prospects. Pemba came highly recommended and certainly fitted the bill; he seemed to exceed the expectations the Dutchman had of him:

> I knew a lot of Sherpas ... who didn't have an education, who are not so skilled in the mountaineering thing, bringing up or fixing the ropes and when Gerard was talking about him ... I could only dream about such a guy and when I met him it was unbelievable, he was really speaking English very well, he was trained ... He knew everything about safety ... it was his life. All year round he was busy with mountaineering.

The moment he arrived at the foot of any mountain, Wilco van Rooijen's mindset shifted completely from the outside world to a near-obsessive focus on the latest feat he was undertaking. Apart from the individual effort and sense of personal achievement, the 40-year-old relished nothing more than being the leader of a team of similarly dedicated climbers who had a shared passion, a common objective.

As he organised the tents and gas stoves, he looked at the team members around him unfurling their sleeping bags and down suits. Wilco felt very confident about their preparedness and ability. Everything had run smoothly so far – they were on schedule, all of the gear had arrived, safe and sound; the meticulous planning of every element of the trip had paid off:

> We were really on schedule because we were there at the end of May. We were the first expedition, so nobody was around and we were already working on the mountain, bringing up the ropes, working like hell in two

teams. We had a beautiful time, we had a lot of fun because everything worked very well, we missed nothing, everything was really well organised. We had good food, we had good cooks. And that gave such a good feeling, such a good relationship because if you are with such a small team and you dare ... to climb this huge and difficult mountain with all the risks, you are a really great climber from my point of view because the bigger the dream, the bigger the risks.

A Knight of the Order of Orange Nassau in his native Netherlands and an ambassador for Respect the Mountain, Wilco was a well-known climber within the relatively small Dutch mountaineering community. A no-nonsense adventurer, he did not suffer fools gladly but his attention to detail and skills on the mountains had won him plaudits with peers.

He glanced up at 42-year-old Cas van de Gevel who was helping the cooks to erect the kitchen tent. The pair had worked together for a time in construction and had become close friends, climbing some of the world's top peaks. A shy but congenial character, Cas recognised Wilco's leadership strengths and was happy to take a back seat and enjoy the expeditions he led. Another climbing fanatic, as soon as Cas had saved up enough money from his day job, he would take to the mountains on any expedition he could find, invariably with his friend.

He did not hesitate for a moment when Wilco asked him to join the 2008 expedition. For the carpenter from Utrecht, it was not about individual glory or success; it was about enjoying the experience with the team:

> I like to share the moment with somebody else, another climber or more climbers around me ... for me the team is very important ... A team doesn't have to be all the same kind of people. A team should be different kinds of people who have all their own speciality or strength. One is very strong physically; the other is a better thinker about tactics or what is to [happen] up the mountain. And altogether, we have to make one big team, have one goal and it is the summit of K2.

'It's good to be back here,' said Ger McDonnell as he craned his neck to catch a glimpse of the mesmerising peak. Ger first met Wilco on an expedition to K2 in 2006 and the two had become close friends. Despite many different character traits – Wilco the more blunt and abrasive climber who didn't pull his punches,

Ger the more conciliatory, jovial and mild-mannered – the pair recognised each other's respective abilities.

Ger admired the Dutchman's tenacity and methodical approach. A single common dream fuelled their companionship – reaching the summit of the world's second highest peak. Wilco had spent time climbing with Ger in Alaska in 2007 and their plan for a Dutch-led international expedition to K2 quickly took shape.

Growing up on a farm near the small County Limerick village of Kilcornan in the south-west of Ireland, Ger McDonnell had been passionate about climbing since he was a child. After qualifying from university with a degree in engineering, he moved to Alaska in 1997 where a tantalising panoply of climbing opportunities presented themselves. Ger became enthralled by the mountains of Alaska, particularly Denali (Mount McKinley), the highest mountain in North America.

He immersed himself in mountaineering and became a popular figure on the Alaskan social scene, playing the Irish drum – the bodhrán – with a local traditional music group, Last Night's Fun. He also met and fell in love with a fellow climbing enthusiast, Annie Starkey. A humble climber, the Irishman never spoke boastfully about his expeditions, something which endeared to him to others in the mountaineering community.

The other members of the Norit team included Roeland van Oss, who, like Court Haegens, had answered an advertisement in the Netherlands in 2007 which sought climbers to take part in an ascent of the world's second highest peak. Roeland was training to become a climbing guide and jumped at the opportunity to enhance his curriculum viate. Court was an experienced alpinist and had summited Gasherbrum II, further along the Karakorum range, in 2006.

Alongside them was fellow Dutchman, Jelle Staleman, who worked as a marine and who, despite his relative inexperience, impressed Wilco.[9] The final member of the octet was an Australian mountaineer, Mark Sheen, who had climbed the nearby Broad Peak in 2006 with Wilco and Ger, during which Mark had a lucky escape from the clutches of oxygen deprivation and frostbite.

Wilco was a shrewd team maker, ever conscious of the need to blend in his expeditions the right mix of skills, experience and, very importantly, temperament. Facing into several months of being in very close, daily contact with other climbers while exposed to subzero blizzards in one of the most desolate and lonely places on Earth, Wilco knew that he needed to be sure that all his team would get on with each other:

> Three months is a really long time especially when you have bad weather
> but, in these periods, it is very necessary that you have the right people in

the team because then you can survive these boring moments, especially if you have more than two or three weeks' bad weather ... then it is really necessary that you have social guys and, of course, a lot of fun.

Wilco's team was complete: 'A balanced group with "winners" at all positions. I am happy, more than happy.'[10]

There were other key components to a Wilco-led expedition. The team, like so many modern climbing groups, was heavily dependent on a network of off-mountain experts, advisors and specialists, each of whom provided essential support to the climbers from thousands of kilometres away. Among them, and probably as critical as the members of the team at Base Camp, was the expedition's webmaster, media spokesperson and IT specialist, Maarten van Eck.

From his houseboat in Utrecht in the Netherlands, Maarten maintained the expedition's website, kept in regular phone contact with Wilco, handled media queries and was the contact point for family members who found it difficult and sometimes impossible to speak directly to their loved ones on the mountain. He issued the daily expedition updates and supplied pictures or biographical information when required to the media.

Maarten's work was complemented by the team's weather guru and meteorologist, Ab Maas, who kept the team briefed by phone and email with the all-essential weather updates which would allow the climbers to plan their summit bid and, if lives were in the balance, to advise on when to desist. His efficient and reliable extrapolations from reams of meteorological data available from countless sources allowed him to send detailed weather forecasts to Base Camp. The projections carried a major health warning: they could not always account for the renowned capriciousness of K2's weather patterns, but they gave the climbers the information they required to chart their way forward.

Though the team did not have a doctor with them, Wilco made sure there was always one – in this case, Ronald Hulsebosch – at the end of a phoneline to advise from afar as required. Hulsebosch, who had worked in situ on previous expeditions with Wilco, could dispense medical advice in absentia via a satellite phone. Wilco believed how the off-mountain trio would perform and fulfil their obligations over the coming weeks and months would be critical to the success or otherwise of the expedition:

It's not the ordinary forecast that we know from sea level – you need a guy who is really monitoring this weather pattern for two, three months ... And the expedition doctor, it's really the same. It's not like just phoning and saying, "Oh listen, you have your medical kit and just take this medicine", or whatever, you need a lot of information in combination [with] the altitude of where you are and how it's doing every day by day. So the whole team, it was complete – maybe 10, 12 people ... [it] gives us a good feeling to take the risks and go to the max.

Before travelling to K2, Wilco had completed yet another important part of the expedition preparations by compiling a list of contact numbers and details for the next of kin of each of his climbers. As the expedition leader, he would leave nothing to chance in the event of something going wrong.

Historically, expeditions usually made provisions to alert a loved one if a climber had been injured or killed but, in the pre-telecommunications era, it might have taken days to relay any tragic news from the mountain to a relative back home, usually well in advance of the media getting hold of the information. Nowadays, however, it only takes seconds, a phone call or the click of a mouse, to distribute news of a fatality around the globe.

Wilco's emergency communications system could not account for the instantaneousness of social media and breaking news, especially where fatalities occurred, but the dutiful leader took every reasonable step to ensure that those bereaved would be the first to know. In a pre-expedition email to Pemba, Ger had reminded him to provide contact details for someone in the event of an emergency:

> Please read Wilco's message below. He is looking for contact details in case (God forbid) "the worst thing happens". We need name, address, phone number and maybe email of a person to contact in case of an emergency. Email would only be used as an update tool of course. Regards, Gerard.

Pemba relished the earliest days of an expedition when the foundations for a summit bid were being laid down through the efficient establishment of a well-stocked and homely Base Camp. He was beginning to settle in well at his new address on the Pakistan-China border. At his Kathmandu home two weeks earlier, he had bid farewell to his wife, Da Jangmu, and his four-year-old daughter, Jizmet

Dekye. Da Jangmu was happy for Pemba to make the journey to K2; he would be away for three months but this was normal in any given year for someone making a living on the mountains.

She was encouraged when Pemba told her that he would be an ordinary team member on this trip, not working as a Sherpa or high-altitude worker. Da Jangmu had watched as her husband matured and evolved into an established and highly-respected climber in his own right. She trusted in his experience and common-sense approach to the dangerous peaks in the region; K2 would be treated with the same cautious confidence and meticulous preparation as any other mountain.

Before leaving Kathmandu, as he did before he set out on any expedition, Pemba consulted his Buddhist lama at the nearby Boudhanath, one of the holiest Buddhist sites in the country, located about 11 kilometres from the Nepalese capital. The monk told Pemba that in 2008, 'You will have good things in June, July, August', and that he was to perform the puja prayer ceremony on specific dates and times while on the mountain. Five lamas came to Pemba's home to pray with him and his family for a successful expedition to K2 before he departed for Pakistan.

'Ta daa ... yeah we're here, K2 Base Camp,' declared Ger McDonnell in the first of his occasional but always upbeat and humorous blog updates from the bottom of K2:

> All very uneventful to date apart from the breathtaking views of the Trango Towers, Masherbrum, GII, Broad Peak etc and of course the one that we hope to befriend over the coming weeks. Last few days have been spent setting up base camp, sorting gear, food and catching up on sleep. The latter which we were denied en route by the nightly braying of a frustrated male donkey pleading with a mare more interested in the business of foraging. A common denominator there perhaps across the animal kingdom. Ha-ha![11]

Within days, the climbers had settled into a disciplined routine. Rising early, they enjoyed a hearty breakfast of porridge, toast, omelettes, chapattis and tea or coffee. Eating appropriately was a critical part of preparing for the physical toll their bodies were about to endure, so carbohydrate-laden foods like pasta and rice were always a feature of lunch and evening meals. Cas had brought along a cured Spanish ham which was sliced and served regularly.

Drinking water was sourced by melting snow from the surrounding glacier in what was a slow, never-ending process to which the mountaineers became unavoidably accustomed. Hours were spent daily either sorting gear or ferrying items to a temporary depot they established nearer to the base of the mountain, about a two-hour walk away.

After lunch, the climbers continued to prepare and allocate coils of rope for the fixing of lines which would soon begin, or they might wander out onto the glacier for exercise and some time to reflect. Evening meals, again laden with high-energy and nourishing ingredients, gave the team time to review their day, discuss the next and enjoy a game of cards, a book or magazine, or simply reminisce about their accomplishments and near-death experiences in the past.

Daily blogs and emails were dealt with in the evenings. The team had brought two satellite phones and two laptops for communication with the outside world and for the receipt of all-important daily weather forecasts. After up to 10 hours of hard work each day, the climbers were usually in their sleeping bags by 10pm.

In their earliest days at Base Camp, the cooks discovered that the expedition was not alone on the mountain. A mouse, dubbed 'Fred' by the climbers, had turned up in the kitchen, Ger noting that it looked 'very pregnant, much to the kitchen staff's chagrin'.[12] The team thought that 'Fred' might have made it to Base Camp in a barrel on the back of a Balti porter but they also spotted mountain cats and birds which were attracted by the presence of human life.

There was another, more macabre, attraction for animals in search of food – corpses and body parts were visible along the base of the mountain, forced downwards by gravity over many years, often dismembered and mangled by the force of an icefall or avalanche. Pemba noticed two mountain cats gnawing on some remains a few hundred metres above Base Camp. For the experienced mountain rescuer it was nothing new; he had become accustomed to the human detritus on the world's most unforgiving peaks:

> Within the ice glaciers, there is natural freezing and sometimes we saw very old dead bodies coming out from the glaciers. Also on Everest we can see that kind of thing, also around K2 Base Camp ... it doesn't bother me, but I don't know about other people.

Once Base Camp had been established, the team moved immediately to prepare for the difficult climb that lay ahead. Acclimatisation at higher altitudes was the immediate priority for everyone. The body would require time to adjust to a depleted oxygen intake and to cope with the rigours of altitude sickness. The climbers aimed to give themselves at least one month to acclimatise before attempting to summit so as to ensure that they could take the stress and strain of the higher elevations.

It is beyond the capacity of most human beings to ascend to high altitudes at speed without allowing themselves slowly adjust to the new environment, one in which it is more difficult to derive an adequate supply of oxygen for the organs and bloodstream. This is not because there is less oxygen available at higher altitudes; it is simply because the air pressure at those altitudes is lower, causing the density of the life-sustaining gas to drop.

Accordingly, with every inhalation, less oxygen is drawn into the body, stymieing metabolism, as well as physical and mental capacity. Like any organism in an alien environment, the human body requires a period of time before it can cope with different circumstances and climatic conditions.

It is no different at high altitude; once an appropriate adjustment period elapses the physiological processes adapt to a reduced intake of oxygen. Climbers often try to prepare physically for such eventualities before reaching the mountains; one of the smaller expeditions to K2 in 2008, a team from Singapore, spent weeks breathing low-oxygen air while on a treadmill under the direction of an exercise physiologist.[13]

Even the first successful K2 summiteers, a group of Italians who climbed K2 in 1954, were subject to primitive experiments in oxygen chambers to simulate the physical toll of high altitude.[14] But Wilco knew that there was no substitute for adjusting to the environment on the mountain in real time and he insisted that his team needed to be patient and methodical in their acclimatisation strategy:

> Air pressure at 5,000 metres is around 50 per cent of that at sea level and above 8,000 metres it is only one third. This effectively means the body is getting only one third the amount of oxygen at 8,000 metres in each breath than at sea level. This requires you to use energy wisely. It is as if the body is an emptying vessel. It is no longer able to absorb sufficient energy via the food consumed, partly because you lose appetite at altitude. Even if you force yourself to consume food, it is likely it would exit the body almost immediately. The body is in a state of alert and no longer focuses on digestion. It chooses to use the scarce oxygen for "more important" vital functions such as physical movement, heat regulation, thinking and

the organs. After a week at high altitude the climber must return to a lower altitude to allow their body to recuperate. The longer the time spent and the higher the altitude, the faster the bodily deterioration.[15]

The Norit team had decided not to use supplementary oxygen – one of the mottos for the expedition was 'K2: No oxygen' – because Wilco was convinced that it was only without oxygen that climbing occurred in its purest, most natural form. His experience had taught him that, whatever the merits of supplementary oxygen use, the consequences for the body if the bottled gas ran out while climbing were devastating, akin to an addict's withdrawal from drugs.

Having used a supply to get to a certain point on the mountain, 'coming off the bottle' can be crippling, as the body struggles with the rapid plunge from a more than adequate flow of the gas to the lungs, the brain and the bloodstream to about one third of that supply. On Pemba's first summiting of Everest in 2000, he had used oxygen on the way from the summit to High Camp at 8,000 metres. His team needed to spend a night at High Camp and he took off his oxygen for a few hours to see how he would cope:

> It was very uncomfortable, very painful, no headache or dizziness but I felt very uncomfortable. I felt my muscles cramp and there were problems with my breathing. It was like I was suffocating. I couldn't sleep even for a minute. I couldn't stay in one position; I needed to move and stretch. I kept fighting, fighting, fighting and only by 4am I felt a bit more comfortable.

The impact on the body of a depleted oxygen intake becomes all the more acute in the so-called Death Zone, a place above 8,000 metres where the air is so thin that human life quickly becomes unsustainable and the cells in the body begin to die. Apart from the rigours of a lower oxygen supply to the organs and the muscles, in the Death Zone cerebral and pulmonary oedema lurk with menace.

The altitude causes the brain and the lungs to swell with fluid, leading to a rapid and debilitating deterioration of bodily functions and mental capacity. A climber on K2 in 2008 described how the Death Zone envelopes humans in its icy grip:

> There is a struggle, there is a fight in every breath, in every thought and the time seems to stand still. Everything hurts, every limb, every cell is screaming "Oxygen". [In] that situation you start to lose the sensation in your body. You don't feel the cold anymore and everything becomes blurry. You don't think the same way; you start hallucinating and everything

becomes a fog and you're trying to keep yourself alive. It's like sinking through a hole and you know that when you hit the ground, you're going to die ... Then you're nodding and sleeping and you don't know how long for and then you wake up and you don't know if you are dreaming or if you are alive or if it's real and most of the time you don't know where you are. It's a terrible state.[16]

Within days of arrival at Base Camp, Pemba turned his mind to the performance of a ritual as old as the Buddhist religion from which it is derived. As a devotee of the Nyingma Buddhist tradition, one of the oldest branches of the faith, he was anxious to fulfil the direction of his lama in Kathmandu and to perform a puja ceremony before advancing any further up the mountain.

The lama had told him that 5 June was the most favourable date. Involving a prayerful worship of the mountain, respecting it as a deity which is due reverence and devotion, the puja is a custom known to any western climber who has ever been accompanied by Sherpas to the world's high peaks.

Pemba's belief system required a commitment to the philosophy that the mountain, like every object and element in nature, demands and deserves honour and deference. Unlike some puja ceremonies where a lama is present, such as happens at Everest Base Camp, on this occasion Pemba relied on recordings of mantras and chants which the lama had given him. It was a ritual full of symbolism and veneration:

> Puja is a religious ceremony to make the mountain happy and to make nature happy and we believe the mountain is a symbol of the gods. If we are going to do something on the mountain, then before that we have to make her happy, and that's why we make a puja before we climb ... The conclusion is, "Ok, now we are going to disturb your peaceful place, please protect us, let us do these things and give us your permission".

And so, just eight days following his arrival at Base Camp, Pemba rose at dawn to build an improvised altar, near the Norit camp, consisting of a small pile of stones to which prayer flags were affixed and on which offerings such as food and water were placed. The weather was fine and the flags fluttered in the gentle breeze. He played the music and mantras on his iPod and prayed as the other members of the expedition looked on. The chanting sounded as if it was emanating from the altar itself.

Pemba's beliefs did not allow him to ascend higher than Base Camp before the ceremony was performed, a wish usually respected by expeditions in the Himalaya, but he had not reckoned on his team leader's intentions to proceed with fixing ropes earlier than the Sherpa expected.

Wilco's team had settled in quickly and he was ready to begin climbing to install fixed ropes on the mountain, if only because the weather conditions were so favourable. Wilco suggested that the fixing of ropes begin on 3 June, two days before the date for the puja; it was time, he felt, to get going and avail of the good weather.

Pemba was more than happy for others to proceed but insisted that he could not begin work on the slopes until he had fulfilled the direction of the lama: 'I do not climb a big mountain before puja, because if I climb without puja, physiologically it is very uncomfortable for me.'

And so a situation arose that could have led to an early division in the Norit team; Wilco, Cas and Jelle were ready to fix ropes while Ger and Mark Sheen wanted to wait until the puja was complete. But Pemba was never going to insist that his non-Buddhist colleagues observe his traditions. He was shrewd enough to move quickly to defuse a situation which might potentially cause antagonism within the team:

> Wilco wanted to start climbing earlier, as soon as possible. He asked me if he could climb before 5 June, if possible. I actually cannot stop him because ... I feel I cannot disturb the people's interest, so I say, "Yes you can go on the mountain before puja".

The many expeditions that descended on K2 in the summer of 2008 had several options when it came to choosing a route to climb the almost four vertical kilometres from Base Camp to the summit. Two of those routes on the Pakistani side of the mountain have become popular in recent years and each has its own distinct advantages and disadvantages.

From Base Camp, at an altitude of 5,000 metres, the two principal routes up the south face of the mountain converge at a point almost three kilometres above at a narrow snowfield on a ridge known as the Shoulder from which almost every summit attempt on the Pakistani side of the mountain is launched.

The south-southeast spur, better known as the Cesen route, was named after the Slovenian climber, Tomo Cesen, who climbed it in 1986. Compared to the Abruzzi route, it presents a slightly longer climb to the highest camp, Camp Four, with greater degrees of steepness, but it is considered generally safer and less susceptible to ice and rockfalls.

The alternative path to Camp Four is the Abruzzi route, named after the colourful Italian, the Duke of the Abruzzi, who, in 1909, used the spur to reach 6,100 metres before being forced to turn back. It is considered the more hazardous of the two routes, liable to greater rockfall and icy terrain, although not as steep as the Cesen. Long before they had travelled to K2, the Norit team had chosen to use the Cesen to climb to Camp Four. But there was more to the decision than simply the merits of the route itself; it had much to do, too, with the horrendous experiences that two of the expedition members had on the Abruzzi spur in previous attempts at the summit.

Wilco van Rooijen had had a tempestuous relationship with K2. The mountain had embedded itself in his psyche ever since he first laid eyes on it in 1995. He and Cas van de Gevel had joined a Dutch expedition that year under the leadership of Ronald Naar at a time when a Dutch national had yet to stand atop the world's second highest peak. During their ascent of the Abruzzi route, Wilco was hit by heavy rockfall which slammed into his head and shoulders, leading to heavy loss of blood and a broken arm.

A helicopter took his battered body from Base Camp. His expedition was over but, in the years that followed, he devoted himself to enhancing his high-altitude experience, picking off peaks like Aconcagua, Denali (Mount McKinley) and Everest with little or no difficulty, all the while determined to return to face his adversary on the Pakistan-China border.

In 2008, Ger McDonnell was returning to K2 for the second time. He had devoured every written word about the mountain he could get his hands on, anxious to research thoroughly his latest climbing project. Despite making only his second trip to the peak, he and K2 already had a troubled history. During an attempted ascent in 2006, Ger had narrowly escaped death, having joined an expedition which included a fellow Irish climber, Mick Murphy, as well as Wilco van Rooijen.

Ger had climbed as far as Camp One on the Abruzzi route when, a short distance above the camp, a heavy rockfall narrowly avoided Wilco, who was just metres above Ger; however, a large rock crashed into the Irishman, catching him flush on the head. Though not knocked from his perch, his climbing partner, Mick Murphy, saw immediately that he was badly injured and concussed:

I could see him above when the rocks fell. Ger ducked down behind some rocks. One of them caught him right on the head. He came down to me and a porter from a Serb team and 'Banjo' Bannon from Northern Ireland. He was disorientated but the injury hadn't set in. There was a lot of blood. We bandaged him up and clamped his helmet on tight and that worked effectively to stop the bleeding. We knew very quickly it was concussion. He kept repeating himself. We clipped him onto Banjo and Banjo abseiled down the ropes and I lowered Ger down from above, six hours it took or something. He was able to walk a bit but he was being directed. There were boulders coming down continuously.[17]

Ger's subsequent experience in a hospital in Skardu was far from pleasant. He recounted being strapped down on a gurney for emergency medical treatment in a grubby operating theatre:

It looked like a slaughterhouse ... All the equipment was dodgy looking and filthy ... I didn't really begin to get worried until they started to strap both my arms and legs down. I immediately thought, "God, this is going to hurt"... The anaesthetist just started taunting me, mocking my request to have a CT scan done and he started saying stuff like "So where are your friends now?"[18]

Despite his experiences, Ger had a remarkable recovery and managed to make the long trip back to Ireland. Doctors there told him he had narrowly escaped being killed. Only for his toughened helmet holding a piece of his fractured skull in place, he would not have survived. But Ger knew that he would go back, drawn, like so many climbers, to both the singular beauty and the challenge of K2.

Since expeditions in the region had begun, over a century before, westerners have brought locals to the mountains to help guide them on the right path to a victorious outcome for their team or their country. Better accustomed to and able to cope with high altitude, and with an in-depth knowledge of the mountains in their local area, the guides have become an integral part of almost every expedition in the Himalaya/Karakorum region.

Though he was a regular and equal member of his climbing team, Pemba was also aware that much was expected of him given his experience on Everest and his reputation for success and competence on the mountains.

He was left under no illusion that he had been invited to K2 to enhance the expedition's prospects of success. This was nothing he had not experienced before, nor was he unaware of the financial pressure such expeditions were under; many of them had received significant backing from sponsors and some climbers had borrowed heavily to finance their trips. But, for those returning for the second or third time to the same mountain, the expectancy and reliance on Pemba was more acute:

> ... they had a big expectation of me because now they had one good Sherpa climber and maybe this time they would have a 98 per cent chance if the weather will be favourable ... And Wilco said ... "We need to try strongly ... you know, this is my third time and I don't want to come again to this mountain because of the time factor and big money". Directly they don't express those kinds of things but, internally, they have a lot of expectation.

Roping the Cesen route and setting up the higher camps which would provide team members with a series of essential pit stops en route to the summit was a labour-intensive and tedious process. But it also served another purpose – it helped the climbers to acclimatise and train their bodies for the physical demands required in a summit bid. Wilco rallied his climbers with near-soldierly discipline.

Two teams of four members would scale the Cesen in turn to place anchors and fix ropes along the ridge, ascending fractionally higher each day that the weather allowed until a permanent line was in place all the way to the Shoulder. While one team set ropes with ice screws and pitons, the other rested or slept.

A small depot full of additional equipment and supplies was installed at the bottom of the Cesen to obviate the need to always return as far as Base Camp for gear for the higher camps. From Base Camp, small red flags were placed along the path to the depot to aid the safe return of climbers in the event of a blizzard or a whiteout.

Over the course of the following month, hundreds of metres of rope were ferried up the ridge by this methodical and efficient relay system, which Wilco supervised with diligence:

Bringing up those ropes to 8,000 metres is a hell of a job so what we did the first four to five weeks, every day bringing up the ropes, fixing the ropes, 100 metre by 100 metre by 100 metre 'til we were finished bringing up from the Base Camp in one straight line 4,000 metres of rope, almost four kilometres.

Camps One (5,700 metres), Two (6,200 metres) and Three (7,100 metres) were placed at locations well established and preferred in recent mountaineering history. The camps, often perched on dangerously narrow ledges, would be essential, not just for the gradual ascent to the top, but also for the descent, particularly if K2's furious weather outbursts sent climbers scurrying for cover.

They also allowed the climbers the possibility to overnight at an interim point from where they could continue the following day, preventing the need to return to Base Camp each night. The camps were stocked with food, sleeping bags and stoves for melting snow.

Many of the team members experienced headaches and nausea as they ascended and descended but this was an inevitable part of acclimatisation. To compensate for their malaise, the higher they climbed, the more spectacular the views became, as both the vastness of the glacier below and the dramatic horizon of nearby peaks above moved breathtakingly into view. Clearly visible was the path carved out by the two glaciers which snaked around the bottom of the mountain – from on high they looked like vast dual-carriageways heading south to Concordia.

But the higher altitude also brought its own dangers. Though the team members avoided any serious accidents as they made their way between camps on the Cesen, they did witness occasional rock slippages. Owing to the rapid fluctuations in temperature on the slopes, stones frozen into the ice on the ridge sometimes came loose as the ice warmed. The incorrect placement of a crampon could send rocks hurtling down the almost vertical spur towards a team-mate just below. Immense concentration was required for every single movement.

Despite the often precarious ascents, Wilco was satisfied with the progress and the mood of his team. Pemba began to fix the lines on the morning he completed the puja ceremony, climbing as far as the location of Camp One in just three hours. There, along with Ger McDonnell, Mark Sheen and Court Haegens, he deposited items assigned for the first camp before returning to Base Camp.

By 12 June, Camp Two was in situ and, rather than return to Base Camp, the team spent the night in tents there, always with an eye to improving acclimatisation and conserving energy. At the second camp on the Cesen, at 6,200 metres, the air pressure was lower and this allowed their bodies to adapt to the reduced oxygen intake. Camp Three was established the following day but deteriorating weather conditions forced a return to Base Camp a day later.

Pemba felt that every aspect of the expedition so far was well organised and running according to plan. He maintained a daily record in his notebook, charting how high he had climbed and to which camps. The productive roping relay system augured well, he thought, for the summit attempt itself. But the installation of fixed lines was not without hiccups as Ger explained to the outside world in his blog:

> A little problem we've run into now though is that we're running short of fixed line. Once the shortage raised its ugly head more was ordered from Skardu. From the early onset one important (and expensive) roll of 200 metre five millimetre spectra [rope] went mysteriously missing somewhere between Islamabad and Skardu. Probably hidden accidentally under a seat of one of the many broken-down mini-buses en route. We were hoping that we could do without but when we alerted our local facilitating company, Jasmine Tours, of the lack of fixed line they went well out of their way to solve the problem. They promised a delivery within four days via an athletic Askole porter. We're not too sure how much this Skardu rope will weigh but that porter will end up carrying 500 metres of seven millimetres, some 85 kilometres in four days. Very impressive stuff and a substantial tip will go his direction.[19]

'We're still very strangely the only team here. To have this particular mountain all to ourselves since the 29th of May is a thrill – although it'll be a short-lived one. The hordes are surely around the corner,' Ger McDonnell posted on 7 June. And true enough, the mountaineering multitudes en route to K2 were not far away. The Norit team had been alone on the mountain for three weeks, the sole tenants at the base of K2.

The enjoyment of that reclusiveness came to a sudden end with the arrival at Base Camp, within the space of two weeks, of three large international expeditions, as well as several smaller teams and a number of independent climbers. Like a congregation assembling in their high-altitude cathedral, the climbers were coming to pay homage to the mountain, to worship at its altar and to ask for its blessing.

From a wide diversity of backgrounds and with diverging styles and approaches to high-altitude mountaineering, the men and women, most of whom had never met the other teams before, looked forward to sharing their passion with like-minded adventurers in the weeks ahead. Even if the summit did not give itself up that easily, the climbers had come to an exclusive outdoor explorers' club, far removed from the distractions of family and society, a place where they could immerse themselves, along with fellow enthusiasts, in the sights and sounds, hopes and fears unique to the fabled mountain.

By mid-June, teams from Serbia, South Korea, France and Norway had all arrived, laden down with tents, rope and climbing equipment, each fancying their chances of success on the infamous peak. On 9 June, the ExplorersWeb website reported a steady flow of expeditions arriving in Pakistan:

> Expeditions are flocking to Pakistan and early birds are already at work on Karakorum's giants. A Czech team is currently in GI/GII's C1, while on K2's Cesen route at 5,800 meters, Wilco van Rooijen's team watches avalanches roaring a bit too close to their path ... The Dutch-international team is the only one yet on the mountain ... [but] K2 is packed this season.[20]

On 11 June, a French team, made up of three climbers, Yannick Graziani, Christian Trommsdorff and Patrick Wagnon, joined the Norit expedition at Base Camp.[21] Days later, by far the largest of the 2008 expeditions, the 11-strong Flying Jump team, arrived from South Korea. It was a name that amused many, not least Ger McDonnell who blogged: 'Seems to coin images of *Crouching Tiger, Hidden Dragon* bamboo-scaling techniques. Seem like a lovely bunch though, although a bit too busy for an impromptu cup of tea and a chat. Understandably eager to get settled in.'[22]

Under the leadership of the ambitious Kim Jae-soo – who came to be known at camp as 'Mr Kim' – the group included their country's star climber and extreme sports enthusiast, Go Mi-sun, who was almost halfway through her quest to become the first woman to scale each of the world's 14 peaks above 8,000 metres. From Seoul, she was one of the best-known sportspersons in her country, a seven-time winner of the Asian X Games. She was heavily sponsored in her Karakorum exploits by the Kolon Sports company.

Kim guarded and shepherded his precious female star assiduously. The previous season the pair had claimed three 8,000ers, Makalu, Kangchenjunga and Dhaulagiri – the world's fifth, third and seventh highest mountains respectively – at breakneck speed in the space of just six weeks; K2 was now firmly in their sights.

The South Koreans' approach to K2 was rooted in the siege-tactics tradition which involved a painstaking, methodical and almost military-style conquest of the peak, as if the expedition was at war with the mountain. They adopted an attitude to summiting which invariably put national prowess and reputation ahead of personal ambition, the prospect of a South Korean flag fluttering in the summit breeze outweighing the personal kudos of any prospective individual achievement.

Taking additional risks to win glory for their country was not unheard of; modern mountaineers tell of how South Korean climbers often continue climbing in adverse circumstances when others have yielded to nature and the elements. On every mountain Pemba had encountered South Korean climbers, the summit was an overwhelming fixation, verging, he thought, on mania:

> I didn't climb with the Korean people officially on the mountains but I know the history of the Korean mountaineering in Himalaya. They are very keen for the summit. It's do-or-die; they want to do-or-die. Every mountain they want to summit, summit, summit. They are thinking only of the summit on the mountains and that is why there are so many accidents recorded about Koreans climbing in the Himalaya ... it's not a good idea working continually in this kind of environment of people.

The Flying Jump expedition was divided into two teams; the first including those who were stronger and more experienced and who would be more likely to succeed in summiting, the second comprising the less experienced who had lower summit expectations. There was no doubt to which team Go Mi-sun – dubbed 'Ms Go' by many at Base Camp and given the pet name 'Didi' by their Sherpas – would belong.

From the moment they arrived at Base Camp on 15 June, the South Korean flag flew prominently and proudly, a specially commissioned banner reading '2008 Flying Jump Korean K2 Expedition' in both English and Korean pinned upright beside their tents.

For several climbers, the K2 expedition was about a lot more than reaching the summit of the world's deadliest mountain – it would be an adventure and an end in itself. Unlike most of the climbers from abroad, many of the Sherpas who were journeying to the region for the first time would not have had the same access to published sources about the history and technical difficulties of climbing the mountain.

In regions without ready access to the internet or books, many of those now joining expeditions to K2 were reliant on the tales they had heard from their peers or seniors drawing attention to its deadly statistics and its reputation as the 'Savage Mountain'.

Sherpa Pasang Lama's family were not keen on his participation as a high-altitude worker with the South Korean expedition, such was that reputation. Though his father, Phurbu Ridar, had introduced him to climbing and had summited Everest with him in 2006, K2 was an entirely different prospect for the young mountaineer from Hungung near the Tibetan border with Nepal. For Pasang, however – with almost eight years of climbing, including Nepal's Annapurna, under his belt – the excitement was barely containable. This would be his first trip to Pakistan; it was the chance of a lifetime.

Leaving home in early May, he first joined the South Korean team on Lhotse, the world's fourth highest mountain, and his competent performance there secured him a place on their K2 expedition. Ms Go in particular had urged him to rejoin them on K2. He was one of five Nepali Sherpas with the group, but they were not just any Sherpas – the other four were all Pasang's cousins. Apart from Ngawang Bhote, a team cook, Pasang was to be joined on the 2008 expedition by 'Big' Pasang Bhote and brothers Jumik and Tsering Bhote, all from the same part of northern Nepal.

The involvement of so many relatives whom he knew well reassured Pasang's family. As soon as he met the South Koreans in the luxurious Hotel de l'Annapurna in Kathmandu, where payment and visas were arranged in plush surroundings alien to the Nepali, Pasang felt like he was on the most exhilarating odyssey of his life:

> It was my first time in a Boeing plane. That huge plane; we four were excited. I sat along with Tsering [Bhote]. I was looking forward to it. Everything looked just perfect. It was [a] completely strange place, the hotels were different.

Like Pasang, 21-year-old Tsering Bhote was driven into mountaineering by economic circumstances. He had been studying for a Bachelor of Education but, by 2007, his financial predicament compelled him to become a Sherpa guide, the chosen profession of several members of his family. He had minimal climbing experience before he travelled to K2 apart from a recent successful ascent of Lhotse with Pasang Lama and the same South Korean team who were now asking him to join them for their K2 expedition. Tsering made no secret of his lack of training and knowledge of high-altitude mountaineering:

I was new to this field ... a year's experience ... I had no idea about K2, I had heard about the accident; that a Nepali Sherpa had died [the previous] year. I knew it was the second largest mountain, other than that I had no other information.

Conscious of the young Sherpa's inexperience, the South Korean leader, Mr Kim, appointed Tsering to the second Flying Jump team which would attempt the summit after the first team's ascent. Tsering's brother, Jumik, had been to Everest and Shishapangma with the South Koreans in 2007, where he was cajoled by Ms Go not just to join their expedition to K2 the following year, but to become their lead sirdar. Though his wife, Dawa Sangmu, was seven months pregnant, Jumik knew he had to go; the K2 expedition would bring not just worthwhile experience, it would also help to cover the costs of a new addition to the family.

Pemba Gyalje's wife did not dwell on pining for him when he left for K2, accustomed as she was to his frequent absences on the mountains, but for Chhiring Dorje's wife, Dawa Sherpani, it was different. Chhiring was one of the most experienced Sherpas on K2 in the summer of 2008 but Dawa was perturbed about his first expedition to the 'Killer Mountain': 'My wife was worried about my interest as she knew about the danger that I had to face. I really wanted to ace that mountain ... without oxygen ... [it was] like a passion and a challenge.'

From Rolwaling in eastern Nepal, an impoverished rural area with limited sanitation, electricity and telecommunications infrastructure, the 34-year-old had started his mountaineering career as a porter but quickly realised the potential financial security and prosperity to be derived from becoming a skilled climber in his own right.

Chhiring had come to Kathmandu in 1990 with his uncle who encouraged him to climb. Between the early 1990s and his trip to K2 in 2008, he summited Everest several times, earning a reputation as a competent and resilient mountaineer. His talents were spotted at an early stage by an American doctor, Eric Meyer, who invited Chhiring to visit his Colorado home in 2007.

Eric, a regular visitor to the Himalaya, wanted Chhiring to join a team that he and Mike Farris, a fellow American, were putting together to go to K2 in 2008. Chhiring would not be a Sherpa on the American international team – he would be a full team member on an equal standing with all of the other climbers.

The experienced Nepali was trepidatious – he would be the only Sherpa with the group; he did not know K2; he hadn't been there before. But the prospect of a real shot at ascending Everest's elusive smaller sister whetted his appetite; in addition, he would be a regular team member surrounded by a talented group of adventurers. It soon became apparent to Chhiring that his medical friend was willing to put his money where his mouth was to get him to K2:

Eric was graceful to say that he would pay my expedition charge of $9,000. I agreed to it ... if I don't get a sponsor, Eric will pay for it. So, in 2008, after climbing Everest I paid my travel expenses and I went to Islamabad and there I met my team members including Eric Meyer. There I was informed that a wireless company had sponsored $20,000, [of which] $6,000 was for me to climb K2 ...

The American International K2 Expedition, under the leadership of biology professor, Mike Farris, reached Base Camp on 26 June. It was a diverse but highly organised team; apart from Eric Meyer and Chhiring Dorje, the team included Chris Klinke from Michigan, among whose first Base Camp observations was that 'the glacier has two sides, one is the bathroom side (outgoing) and the other is the ingoing or drinking water side'.[23]

Also on board was the exuberant Swedish adventurer Fredrik Sträng. The talkative Swede puzzled Pemba – he had come to the mountain with a glut of high-tech videography equipment. He was making a film about K2 and wanted to document 'this awesome mountain and especially the people behind it, the souls, the intentions, the reasons why they go there and go up there, because there are so many reasons to turn around and only a few reasons to continue and I wanted to pinpoint those reasons'. Pemba noticed that Fredrik was 'always with the big professional video camera. I never saw him without the camera at Base Camp', the omnipresent recording device an irritant for many, he thought.

Within days of their arrival at K2 Base Camp, Pemba Gyalje felt '100 per cent confident' about the American-led group, especially when he discovered that Chhiring Dorje would be part of their team. Pemba knew none of the other Sherpas on the mountain except for Chhiring, whom he knew well and held in high esteem. The Americans looked well equipped and physically fit and the fact that they had brought with them the only medical doctor on the mountain, which would be home to over 100 people for several weeks, reassured Pemba even more.

Equipped with their own mobile weather forecast station and a pharmacopoeia of drugs prepared by a medical institute in Subotica, the Serb K2 Expedition of 2008 comprised five adventurers from a country which had yet to celebrate a successful attempt on the summit, but they were an impressively organised group under the stewardship of their leader, Milivoj Erdeljan. He declared that his climbers were 'excellently prepared and they had not any problems either with the condition or with altitude sickness'.[24]

For Erdeljan, K2 was 'the greatest challenge of the alpine mountaineers, by no means for classic expeditions. We knew that it would be long and tiring and that we would need each experience which we gained in the previous five expeditions in Himalaya and Karakorum'.[25] Their trip to K2 was part of a wider project aiming to bring a Serb team to the summits of key Karakorum peaks including Gasherbrum I and II; Broad Peak had been claimed the previous summer without the use of supplementary oxygen.

The Serbs had gone through a rigorous training regime and sourced the latest innovations in energy gels and dehydrated foods in Hungary. While the Serbs were generally well received, the American team leader, Mike Farris, was not so keen on their presence:

> I was not pleased to see a Serb team on our route. I encountered one of these guys on Gasherbrum II. We called him the 'Flying Serb' because he claimed to summit on a terrible weather day and my friends in Camp 4 saw no footprints leading to or from the only route to the summit. Perhaps he'll fly to the summit of K2![26]

If the Serb climbers themselves lacked experience of K2, the same could not be said for two of the guides they had hired for their expedition. Pakistani guides Mohammad Hussein and Shaheen Baig had previously reached K2's summit in 2004; in fact, they were the only climbers at Base Camp who had done so, though it was something neither bragged about. Almost 40, Shaheen was one of the most competent guides in Pakistan; he had trained several climbers, including two of the high-altitude workers with the French expedition to the mountain that year.

Jehan Baig and Karim 'The Dream' Meherban had learned their skills from the widely respected guide in their native Shimshal Valley in northern Pakistan. Karim travelled to K2 at the invitation of Hugues D'Aubarède, a 61-year-old from Lyon in the south of France. The experienced mountaineering enthusiast was a distinguished-looking and affable figure at Base Camp. He loved talking about the Sherpas' way of life, their traditions and customs. He had hundreds of pictures of Sherpas from his other expeditions which he liked to show to Pemba. Despite the Frenchman's mature years, Pemba was not worried about his abilities; he didn't think age mattered much once one's physical condition was good.

Karim Meherban had climbed Nanga Parbat with Hugues in 2005 and the pair had been to K2 in both 2006 and 2007 but hadn't bagged the summit. Karim now joined Hugues for another attempt. Third time lucky, perhaps. Hugues' expedition – a 'motley crew' in Ger McDonnell's eyes[27] – also included a young Californian, Nick Rice, and Peter Guggemos from Germany.

Both D'Aubarède and Rice were prolific bloggers during their time on the mountain, sharing their photographs and updates with the outside world on an almost daily basis. Rice, from Los Angeles, hauled an array of IT and technical equipment to Base Camp with him, including a 30-kilogramme generator, to ensure his laptop, satellite phone, MP3 player and other electronic paraphernalia were kept fully operational. Pemba wasn't sure whether the American was there for a shot at the summit of K2 or as part of a profile-raising exercise:

> He was always with laptop, laptop, laptop, always with his generator which made a lot of noise every day. He was a very young man and there was something different about him: I felt he was not a climber, that maybe he was a journalist, or a kind of media person or researcher or something.

To remember those who had come the mountain before them but who had not survived, many of the climbers made a salutary visit to a rocky outcrop, a short distance from Base Camp, known as the Gilkey Memorial. It was named after the American adventurer and geologist, Art Gilkey, who died during an expedition to K2 in 1953.

On his approach to the summit, Gilkey had become disabled by blood clots in his leg and his team-mates struggled to lower him down the mountain. When they paused to rest, Gilkey, wrapped in a sleeping bag, slipped down the mountain out of sight of his would-be rescuers, possibly swept away by an avalanche, but prompting suggestions that he had taken his own life rather than put his friends' lives in jeopardy. His remains were eventually discovered in the glacial melt at the bottom of the mountain in 1993.

The pile of rocks that forms the memorial in his name is a place where many corpses and human remains have been buried over the years, with others interred in a nearby crevasse. Bones and fragments of clothing are clearly visible in the crannies between the rocks. The mound of stones is bedecked with prayer flags, photographs and nameplates – aluminium dishes inscribed with the names and dates of death of climbers who have perished on K2, the earliest plate dated 1939.

Many bereaved family members have made the pilgrimage to the memorial over the years to visit the place where their loved ones died; it gives them solace to visit a headstone of sorts. The memorial means different things to different people; for some, the Gilkey serves as a sobering reminder of the fragility of life in the face of the forces of nature, for others it is a place that brings unease and discomfort, but everybody shares a desire not to be responsible for the addition of the next nameplate to the decades-old cairn.

It is visible from K2 Base Camp from where many tried to avoid looking at it. However, for Chris Klinke from the American team, spending time at the Gilkey was an opportunity to confront his own mortality:

> So I'm sitting there and I'm staring up at K2, and I'm going, this is where people are spending eternity, looking out at their choice of climbing K2. It's a very grim reminder of what you are about to undertake. I actually ended up sitting down and allowing myself to cry and Eric and Fred were there with me. And I think that's where our bond really started to grow.[28]

Kneeling beside the Gilkey, Hugues D'Aubarède was reminded that this would be his last trip to K2. Not everyone was drawn to the memorial; Chhiring Dorje deplored the Gilkey as a place that reeked of death and Pemba Gyalje refused to set foot there until his expedition was complete:

> In Kathmandu I decided I would visit the Gilkey Memorial only after the expedition, just before I came back. Before that I don't want to go there because that is not comfortable for me psychologically. I don't mind on other mountains but the Gilkey Memorial is quite stressful psychologically for me.

Broad Peak Base Camp, a short distance from K2, was another popular destination for those looking for some time and space away from the routine of their own camps. The 8,051-metre peak was a popular training ground for those intending to scale its near neighbour and it was seen as a useful place to acclimatise before an assault on K2's slopes. There was a series of summitings on Broad Peak during the 2008 season and, one day, the climbers at K2 Base Camp spotted somebody paragliding off the side of the mountain.[29]

One of the climbers at Broad Peak was Alberto Zerain, a Basque adventurer who had picked off the summits of Everest, Makalu, Lhotse and Gasherbrum I and II in previous years. The Spaniard had joined a team which planned to summit Broad Peak but their attempt was scuppered by poor acclimatisation levels and altitude sickness.

Throughout the climb, Alberto was distracted by K2 further up the glacier, a magnetism compounded by meeting those who wandered over from K2 Base Camp and regaled him with their plans to claim the world's second highest peak. Eleven years earlier, he had been to K2 but was denied the summit by bad weather.

If Broad Peak failed to happen for Alberto in 2008, he would consider K2 and would climb it alone. It was the chance of a lifetime and there were mutterings about a weather window in the offing. K2 had captured Alberto's imagination like no other mountain:

> It has a kind of presence. It kind of weakens you of your strength, just having it near you ... I tried not to let it drag me towards it because that can create doubts in you, create fear.

He began to visit K2 Base Camp, becoming friendly with many of the teams there, particularly Hugues D'Aubarède and Nick Rice from the French-led expedition. Hugues offered him a tent spot in the higher camps on the Cesen route if he was planning to climb alone. Shaheen Baig from the Serb team also agreed to involve the personable and experienced newcomer if Alberto shared their workload on the Abruzzi, which the Serbs were using to reach Camp Four. The philosophical Spaniard had wrestled with his conscience while debating whether or not he should attempt the summit on his own:

> I was a bit reluctant to talk about my idea of doing a solo climb when I saw all the other expeditions with huge amounts of equipment and preparation ... when you see that you ask yourself maybe I am wrong coming here on my own. Maybe I am being a bit arrogant to face K2 on my own when I see other people who need a lot of means, a lot of equipment and the help of Sherpas and others.

Frictions between high-altitude workers and their clients are as old as mountaineering itself and tensions emerged when one of the teams at Base Camp was forced to fire their high-altitude workers following a series of unfortunate episodes. 32-year-old Jehan Baig was one of the high-altitude workers with Hugues D'Aubarède's multi-national expedition but he had not started the climbing season at K2 in the employ of the Frenchman.

Like so many Pakistanis working on the Karakorum mountains, Jehan was one of a large number of high-altitude workers trying to expand their portfolio of experience, building expertise and skills in the process. But Pakistani high-altitude workers had yet to win as much credibility as their Nepalese counterparts, whose reputation was more favourable. Jehan had learned much from his cousin, Shaheen Baig, and was hired to travel to K2 in 2008 by a Singaporean team, which was led by Robert Goh.

Along with two other high-altitude workers, Jehan was paid $4,000 to carry loads for the Singaporeans and set up each of the camps between Base Camp and Camp Four on the Abruzzi route and to strip those camps once the expedition was over. From the beginning of the ascent to the higher camps, however, Jehan experienced the symptoms of high-altitude sickness to the extent that it greatly affected his capacity to fulfil his duties.[30] On one trip to Camp One, he abseiled off a fixed rope with the gate of his carabiner open.

Two days later, at the same altitude, and complaining of headaches and loss of appetite, he and his fellow high-altitude workers were forced to hand over the items they were carrying to their clients, unable to climb any further. On another occasion, according to his employers, Jehan had refused to shuttle gear to Camp Two because of bad weather, insisting that avalanches were too prevalent on the ridge and that his life was in danger.

The incidents prompted the Singaporean expedition to post a dispatch on their website about their experiences 'which we want to share here to help others to be more prepared for their climbs':

> The HAPs [high-altitude porters] suffering from AMS (Acute Mountain Sickness) made no effort to further acclimatise upon their return to Base Camp. Two of the HAPs were not suitably acclimatised and were also not technically skilled. Mr Mehraban Shah, the HAP guide who recruited the other two HAPs did not ensure they were acclimatised on the mountain during free days. There was a lack of motivation to work in the interest of the expedition ... The HAPs would have jeopardised our climbs had we not brought along our Sherpa friends, for whom we paid full fees as climbing members on top of their salaries, but who load carried far more than the HAPs.[31]

Infuriated by his lack of acclimatisation and inability to perform at altitude, the Singaporeans fired Jehan Baig. But, fortunately for the Shimshal Valley native, Shaheen Baig came to his rescue, securing a position for Jehan on Hugues' team. Hugues paid him to carry oxygen bottles to an agreed place between Camp Four and the summit, at which point he could turn back and descend. A grateful Jehan accepted the offer readily.

Wilco and his team-mates felt aggrieved at the late arrival to camp of dozens of climbers weeks after they had done much of the groundwork for a summit bid. Ropes had been placed and higher camps had been set up on the Cesen route and it now seemed that several of the newly-arrived expeditions would seek to avail of those facilities without having so much as inserted an ice screw or fixed a rope on the face of the mountain.

Whether by accident or design on the part of the newcomers, their late arrival at camp in mid- to late-June jarred with Base Camp's first occupants. 'No, we were not really satisfied with those people because they did nothing on the mountain,' Pemba observed. What baffled Wilco even more was why so many experienced climbers from around the world were descending on Base Camp so late into the summer climbing season:

> We couldn't understand why they arrived that late because some climbers were just arriving at the end of June. It's amazing because if you see in history ... most of the accidents happen in August so we said, "Listen, we have to be ready in July because we want to quit the expedition at the end of July".

However, the majority of the expeditions were not planning to use the route that had already been almost fully fixed by Wilco and the others; they, including the South Koreans, intended to climb to the Shoulder via the Abruzzi route. It fell in the main to the South Koreans to spearhead the ferrying of ropes and equipment up the Abruzzi to higher camps, though they later had the help and support of the Serbs and Americans. The South Koreans undertook the task with military-like precision and unwavering dedication.

Other expeditions bartered and bargained to secure the use of their fixed ropes as well as those of the Norit team on the Cesen route. It is not unusual that smaller expeditions or latecomers to any Base Camp would make a payment for using ropes which have already been fixed by others; there is no point whatsoever in newer teams placing more fixed rope and having additional lines tethered alongside each other. If ropes are already installed, it seems only logical to use those facilities in return for an appropriate fee.

Teams regularly agree to share rope and rope-fixing duties but where the task itself is not divvied up, teams usually reach agreement on what should be paid to avail of the installations of others. How the system plays out in reality, however, often causes antagonism and tensions, a scenario Pemba was very familiar with:

> Generally everyone makes a contribution to this when they work together
> – these are the ethics. But, in reality, some people arrive late when they
> know the ropes and camps will be in place. This is a very unhealthy culture
> ... and leads to many clashes because some people become aggressive.
> They say we have already spent a lot of energy setting up ropes and you
> are here without anything so people ask if they can pay. Many climbers
> are selfish. They are opportunistic; they create only problems on the
> mountain.

Another phenomenon that annoyed many of the larger expeditions was
the presence of several independent, or solo, climbers, individuals who came
to camp, ostensibly without adequate supplies, climbing equipment or rope
and who intended to piggyback on the larger teams' resources en route to the
summit. The phenomenon of the independent climber is nothing new; climbing
mountains alone is completely absurd in the eyes of many but mountaineers have
long ascended peaks alone with limited supplies and occasionally no ropes.

It is only when those climbers seek to muscle in on the hard work of others
and try to avail of the equipment and provisions of larger expeditions that
problems arise. Mike Farris, the American team's leader, described individual
climbers who leech off larger expeditions – thereby, in his opinion, jeopardising
their own safety and that of others – as 'parasites' whom he abhorred on the
mountainside:

> ... We are providing our share of the rope and helping to maintain the
> [Abruzzi] route. I'll talk about parasites (as Messner called them) in a later
> post. These individuals use the ropes (and often tents, gear, gas, and food)
> of other climbers without contributing anything themselves. Luckily, there
> are few on our route this year.[32]

Solo climber Hoselito Bite, who had arrived at Base Camp in mid-June,
was a vivacious and animated 35-year-old; he came to K2 alone as his climbing
companion had taken ill a few days after leaving Askole, forcing him to abandon
his expedition. Though he was on his own, Ger McDonnell was prompted to call
Hoselito a 'team': 'You'd have to meet him to understand why I say "team".'[33]

Drawn by K2's legendary beauty and aesthetic allure, Hoselito paid little heed
to names like 'Killer Mountain', experience having taught him that it was the
actions of mountain climbers rather than those of the peaks they scaled which
led to the application of such epithets. He was enthralled on his first sighting of
the mountain: 'Shit, this is the summit. I have a feeling like it is not too big, every
step you are closer to the summit, the summit calls you ... "come on, come on,

come on" and this happens with people there ... It was magnetic.'

Only three French climbers and the Norit team were present when Hoselito reached Base Camp, and they were bemused by his airy persona and seemingly substandard climbing gear. Ger took the Serb under his wing, however, regularly visiting his tent, while Wilco eyed the newcomer suspiciously. They didn't get off to a great start, Wilco remembers: 'This guy was doing some stupid things because he was thinking, "I'm climbing with oxygen so I will bring two oxygen bottles to 7,000 metres and, after that, I will make a summit push with these bottles to the summit". I said, "Listen, you have to acclimatise to 8,000 metres, to the Shoulder, and then you can make a summit push".'

Hoselito began to exasperate Wilco. To the methodical, organised and efficient Dutchman, the Serb's approach was the opposite of what was required of a climber planning to take on K2. Time and time again, he warned Hoselito – who also planned to use the Cesen route – that he was ill-equipped, that his apparent lack of proficiency and acclimatisation could jeopardise not only his own summit plans, but also those of the Norit team.

Hugues D'Aubarède from the French expedition also recognised carelessness in the Serb, even with something as basic and precautionary as sun cream, essential in combating sunburn and UV rays reflected from the snow. Hoselito, Hugues wrote, 'had not had the courage to [bring] his cream from the bottom of his bag and was as red as a tomato'.[34] Wilco implored Pemba to try to talk sense into the solo climber; the latter understood his team leader's frustrations:

> Many times Wilco talked with Hoselito in Base Camp or during the climbing ... "You have no team, just yourself on the mountain, you have not enough equipment, not enough supplies on the mountain but you want to continue. It's not a good idea and if something goes wrong on the mountain we cannot help you." Wilco was not happy with Hoselito ... [he] kept climbing on the mountain with minimal supply ... Then sometimes Wilco would say, "Pemba, you have to advise Hoselito about the situation you know, he is on his own with minimal supply ... if something goes wrong on the mountain, he will make big problems for other people, especially for our team. I told him several times but still he didn't want to listen to me. Please Pemba, maybe he will respect what you say ... I cannot help Hoselito". I told him several times in Base Camp and on the way up, but he didn't listen to me.

Ger noticed how Hoselito cast the occasional 'sheepish look' towards the Cesen route, apparently daunted by its steepness and complexity.[35] A few weeks after settling in, he decided to broach the subject of using the Norit team's ropes with Ger; Hoselito did not have any ropes but he was willing to pay his way to use theirs to climb the Cesen. Ger relayed the message and Wilco agreed to think about it, still irked by the presence of such a poorly-prepared climber on such a treacherous mountain.

But Wilco knew it would be safer, for everyone's sake, to have the solo climber on secure ropes. He named his price and Hoselito agreed: 'After two or three days, when he came to my tent, he told me that I can go there and I will need to pay $500 for using the rope and I said, "Okay, it's no problem. I will pay that".'

Unfortunately for Hoselito, payment was not so straightforward. He surrendered $350 to Wilco, all the cash he had available, promising to wire the balance through his agent, but he quickly realised he might need the cash to buy food or other provisions at Base Camp, or pay a runner to go to Askole for supplies.

Abashed, he asked for the money back, promising Wilco that the entire sum was being arranged by his agent and would be sent to Wilco's bank account. When the Dutchman scowled and asked for verification that the money had gone through, the Serb felt he was being unfairly questioned and cast as a cheat, a slur which infuriated him:

> I was not a cheater. I am not that kind of person. I can't let somebody treat me like that ... I was very mad and I thought at that moment I will kick his ass, he will fly straight to the summit and he will be the first summiteer on K2 for that year.

Disagreements over the use of fixed ropes were not confined to the Cesen route. As soon as the South Korean expedition had established their living quarters at Base Camp in mid-June they set about placing fixed lines along the Abruzzi route. They had fewer problems with the other teams who were vying to avail of their lines to Camp Four, but some detected that Mr Kim seemed reluctant initially to accede to the requests of others. The Americans, who had chosen the Abruzzi from early on, opted for the path of diplomacy in dealing with the South Koreans. Humility and a bit of savoir faire seemed to work, Fredrik Sträng believed:

> So we were there a little bit later than many other teams ... and there was ... some arguments with the South Koreans who weren't too happy that we used their ropes etcetera. That's why you have to be diplomatic and be honest and you say, "Ok, sorry guys we came in late, how can we help

you guys?"... And it works out, it always works out. You just have to be smooth, you have to be human and be humble and it worked out very good in the beginning, definitely.

With the fixed ropes often buried under snow and ice, camps battered by high winds and climbers regularly rebuffed by heavy snowfalls, the Abruzzi route was living up to its reputation as a very demanding terrain, with ever-present and unpredictable objective dangers, including rockfall, icefall and avalanches.

Robert Goh and Edwin Siew Cheok Wai from the Singaporean team, along with their two high-altitude workers, had also chosen to use the Abruzzi route at an early stage in the expedition and they co-operated with the South Koreans, Americans and others in roping and stocking the route and the various camps on the way. 'K2 is no joke,' Robert reported. 'It's at least ten times harder than Everest ... so far. The terrain is relentless and exposed.'[36]

Goh and his team had employed the Singaporean National Environment Agency's meteorological division to supply them with detailed charts on wind speeds and temperatures at different altitudes around the Karakorum region, as well as pressure and precipitation readings and five-day weather forecasts. None were so accurate, however, as to predict the turbulence and dramatic changes in climatic conditions on the south-east of the mountain as they climbed. The spur was beginning to test the mettle of the rope fixers.

Beyond Camp One on the Abruzzi route, the terrain becomes steeper and climbers use an intricate web of ropes – which have been left behind by historical expeditions and are akin to a rope ladder – to climb the 100-foot wall of rock known as House's Chimney, named after the American, Bill House, who ascended there in 1938. Above Camp Two, another landmark, the overhanging Black Pyramid, looms, requiring a careful ascent with fixed ropes in an area prone to the sudden displacement of snow. From Camp Three, climbers usually ascend without fixed ropes, but avalanches are always a threat.

Chris Klinke from the American expedition, who was making his debut on the Abruzzi, marvelled at its beautiful but highly taxing topography and detailed the exhausting work involved in installing tents and supplies at Camp One, at an altitude of 6,200 metres:

> ... we spent the afternoon hacking a semi-flat spot out of the ice and rock
> so that we could have a secure platform for our tent. We arrived at Camp

One about 1pm and then spent the next four hours creating a platform for our tent. We secured it to the mountain with ice screws, and pitons, and 25 metres of rope. The snow chutes are used on the corners of the tent, you pack them with snow and then stomp down on them so that there is compression and snow melt, and then it becomes a bomber anchor.[37]

When setting ropes did not require their attention, the various expeditions had time to adjust to the naturally-occurring phenomena at Base Camp. Nighttime brought an eerie silence in which the climbers could hear the groaning cracks and creaks of the glacier below and the thunder-like rumblings on the slopes above. Avalanches were a regular occurrence after dark as much as during the day.

Though they knew they were encamped well away from the funnels through which slabs of snow and debris plunged down the mountainside, the gunshot-like explosions in the dead of night were enough to perturb even the most experienced climbers. During the day, the murmurings of K2's flanks could be heard and seen as mushroom cloud-like plumes of snow rose from the foot of the mountain where the avalanches came to a shuddering halt.

To Pemba, the ominous sounds were part and parcel of the wider Himalaya region, but the frequency and volume of avalanche activity were unprecedented in his experience on the mountains:

> Especially from the south side of K2, all along our route on the left hand side, there was a massive hanging glacier about 7,300 metres and also from the north-east face of Broad Peak, every day several times, avalanches kept falling down from both K2 and Broad Peak. I saw avalanches about 22 times during my 65 days at Base Camp. The biggest avalanche came from the south face of K2; that is the biggest avalanche that I have ever seen.

While Wilco hunched over his laptop to monitor the daily weather forecasts that were sent to Base Camp from Ab Maas in the Netherlands, Pemba preferred to rely on instinct and experience:

> I can analyse the snow conditions – what is the weather, what is the time, what is the route? What is the avalanche risk at the moment? I can understand this. And then I would say today is not very good because of the weather, the temperature. We would get a weather chart and could see

the weather. But, from my experience, I did not depend on the forecast alone. I had to analyse both – what does the forecast say and what is the reality in the local weather conditions. I have to tally both and try to analyse it as best as possible. Because the mountain weather is too complicated; you can't depend on the forecast 100 per cent.

Whatever reservations Pemba had about the multi-coloured and fancy graphics-laden forecasts being emailed daily to Base Camp, towards the end of June the Norit expedition received news that is music to the ears of every climber on a mountain like K2 – a weather window was in the offing; a series of consecutive days of calm and clear weather during which a serious summit bid could be launched. Wilco could hardly believe his luck.

If the predicted period of settled weather materialised, as it was scheduled to do in the first week of July, the team could be to and from the summit within about six weeks, an exceptionally short time frame. The highest camp, Camp Four, had not yet been established but that could be done en route. Everything was set out to about 200 metres above Camp Three, the team having been unable to get further than that point due to bad weather, but now the forecast was very good; they would be able to fix the final ropes on the way to the top.

A frisson of excitement went through the team; the summit could be on. It was too early for the other expeditions who were not yet acclimatised and had not finished roping the Abruzzi to make a bid. Even if their summit attempt failed, the Norit team would still have plenty of time to launch another push.

5 July – the middle day of the predicted weather window – was set as the summit day, and the eight team members prepared to ascend from Base Camp on the second of the month. Pemba felt good about their prospects, confident in the weather forecast and his own instincts. It was calm and warm and a few more days of the same could allow their objective to be realised.

The climb proceeded well initially. By 3 July, the team had reached an altitude of 7,700 metres, between Camps Three and Four, but the weather took yet another of its legendary and unpredictable turns. At times, the team were knee-deep in snow, the terrain varying from steep gullies to slippery ridges which made for challenging climbing.

It was an eventful ascent. On his blog, Ger noted that, from the earliest days of the summit attempt, 'it was evident that things weren't going to go according to plan'.[38] At Camp Two, Roeland van Oss had a lucky escape when he almost poisoned himself with carbon monoxide while using a gas stove in his partially -ventilated tent. He passed out and was unresponsive for several minutes. Roeland returned to Base Camp with Court Haegens and Mark Sheen where he recovered quickly. However, the incident was enough to convince Roeland not to take part in any other summit attempt and he decided to stay at Base Camp for the remainder of the expedition.

The remaining five – Wilco, Cas, Ger, Pemba and Jelle – struggled to pitch a tent in the deep snow at Camp Three where they found they were one sleeping bag short. But Wilco remained characteristically optimistic; they could still prevail.

As they tried to settle in for the night, Hoselito Bite appeared from below – as if out of nowhere – having climbed from Camp Two over the course of 10 hours. He wanted to set up his tent on the steep incline beside the Norit team. Wilco was furious, telling him to descend and reminding the Serb once again that he would not take responsibility for him. Eventually a compromise was reached; Hoselito could stay the night only if he agreed to climb back down in the morning.

Above Camp Three on 4 July, the men were enveloped in strong winds and heavy snow and they were also becoming short of rope. Pemba was surprised by the depth and volume of snow, the realisation quickly dawning that the summit bid was now in serious jeopardy. They were forced to spend another long night at 7,100 metres and the morning of 5 July brought little change – the weather had turned for the worse, with little relief in prospect. So close but yet so far; Ger described the conditions:

> Pockets of deep snow (chest-deep at times), packs laden with fix line equipment, Camp 4 provisions and increasing altitude were all taking their toll. Eventually the grim reaper of "progress for the day" raised its ugly head once more – we ran out of fixed line again. There was nothing for it only to abort the summit bid.

There was nothing unusual about the failure of a first summit push. It was early in the season and, if nothing else, the exercise had proved beneficial for fitness and acclimatisation levels, as well as providing a chance for the climbers to scout the route, familiarising themselves with the spur: 'We were not disappointed," Pemba said, "we still had a lot of time."

A latecomer to Base Camp, who arrived while the Norit team's first summit bid was in train in early July, brought an infusion of good humour and friendly banter to a camp which was becoming solemnly engrossed in fixing ropes and planning for the summit attempts. Coming from the same Italian valley as Achille Compagnoni, one of two climbers who successfully scaled K2 in 1954, Marco Confortola felt he was born to follow in his climbing hero's footsteps.

His father and uncle had introduced him to climbing and, as a teenager, Marco loved to disappear on his own on his motorbike, travelling as far as possible up a mountain before proceeding on foot to climb as high as he could. Rarely mixing socially with his peers, the mountains became his friends and soon became his life.[39]

The affable adventurer was on his second expedition to K2. At Camp Three in 2004, his tent and equipment had been blown away in a storm, putting an end to his ascent. With his fellow countryman, Roberto Manni, he arrived at Base Camp on 2 July. Marco's right arm bore tattoos to represent each of the 8,000ers he had bagged – six to date – and K2 was now firmly in his sights.

Sponsored on his 2008 trip by the Credito Valtellinese bank, Marco was an experienced mountain guide and had developed something of a reputation as an audacious daredevil and a lover of high-speed biking and other extreme sports. He became a popular and recognisable character in the bustling Base Camp, not allowing his admittedly 'Tarzan' English to deter him from jocose conversations with others.

Also a competent alpine guide, Roberto Manni had first stepped onto the ski slopes at the age of three, encouraged by his skiing-loving father. A successful summiting of Colque Cruz in the Andes in 1987 had whetted his appetite for more high-altitude adventure and in Confortola he found a like-minded spirit. Marco embraced life at Base Camp with open arms:

> We got on well, all of us. At first it was a bit harder but Italians are very happy and we smile and after a couple of weeks I was friends with everyone, with Karim, the Serbs, people from the land. We were all getting on very well ... And when I saw Ger I thought this guy is very sympathetic and happy. And he was a very good friend of mine.

For some climbers, getting to Base Camp was a significant achievement in itself and, in many cases, life there was their favourite part of any expedition. Lars Nessa of the Norwegian expedition was a part-time mountaineer who had never been higher than 6,200 metres. He had come to K2 to see if he could improve his personal best.

Summiting was secondary in his mind; if he succeeded he would be thrilled but if Base Camp was to be the extent of his expedition, he would be more than satisfied. Because, for Lars, the cosmopolitan life present in a camp full of different nationalities and cultures was reward in itself:

One of the reasons I'm going on expeditions like that is the daily life in Base Camp. It's somewhere I really relax. You are isolated from the rest of the world and we had one usable satellite phone which we only could call home with, which no one could reach us on. I get really relaxed when I'm somewhere like that. So the daily life, reading books, listening to music, discussing climbing and other stuff, just taking a walk with other climbers from other countries, that's one of the things I remember most from that trip. And also, of course, discussing the climbing of K2, which route, what kind of tactic, what can we do to make it safe and discussing previous attempts.

Lars was part of a four-member team with Oystein Stangeland and newlyweds Rolf Bae and Cecilie Skog, all from Norway. Inspired by the fjords and peaks around her where she grew up on the west coast, Cecilie had embraced the outdoor life from a young age. In Rolf, she found a fellow adventurer who shared her passion for exploration and living on the edge.

The pair had met through mountaineering, on separate expeditions to Russia's Mount Elbrus in 2003, and they soon forged a personal and professional partnership:

I knew right away when I saw him ... when I met Rolf in 2003, I felt that I met a soulmate and suddenly I had a partner that I shared dreams with and I was very, very fortunate to share these dreams and to share these moments together. And when you have people around you in the outdoors that you share these special moments with, it's like they grow and you appreciate it even more.

While Cecilie had spent years scaling the highest summits on each of the seven continents, Rolf had pursued his passion for polar exploration and ran his Norwegian-based adventure company, Fram. Cecilie had joined him for expeditions to the North and South Poles, her achievements bringing her considerable celebrity in her native country.

Rolf proposed on the ice of Antarctica and they married in 2007. In 2008, Rolf had gone to climb the 6,286 metres Great Trango Tower at the western end of the Baltoro glacier with three other Norwegian friends before joining his wife, Lars and Oystein at K2 Base Camp in mid-July.

The dynamic Norwegian couple had already experienced life on K2 during an expedition together in 2005. They spent 93 days on the mountain without reaching the summit but, like Lars Nessa, and in stark contrast to many others, summiting was always considered a bonus rather than a singular objective.

Adopting what some might dismiss as a more conservative approach, there was unanimity in the team that if anyone felt unwell or anything went seriously wrong at any point on the ascent, they would all turn back. Oxygen would be used and safety would be paramount at all times. In Cecilie's eyes, the most important thing wasn't to get to the summit: 'The most important thing for us was to come home with good health and then second most important was to come home as better friends ... and number three was to try to get as far up on the mountain as possible.'

The quartet were also deferential to the mountains, not least K2. It captivated Cecilie from the moment she first laid eyes on it:

> It is a diamond. It's a very, very beautiful mountain and it's located in a very, very special place. It's not like the Himalaya where it's soft and you have flowers and you have tea houses. Everything is raw; it's glaciers, it's black mountains and it's very hard and K2 is absolutely the king ... even from a day away, from a big distance ... it fills you with respect. You know it's going to be very difficult to climb it ... You slowly try to get to know this big mountain and you know you have to be very careful the whole way and just not think about the summit. It's so far away, you're not even at Base Camp when you're at Concordia ... I've heard people say that you try not to look at the summit because it draws you in.

By mid-July, Base Camp had become a global village, home to some 120 climbers and their support staff; it bustled with a cacophony of languages, sounds and personalities. Music wafted out of many tents, some from stereo speakers, other notes coming from the dulcet tones of Rolf Bae playing Bob Dylan tunes on his harmonica alongside Cecilie who knitted her way through many hours of waiting. The Norwegian couple's inflatable IKEA couch became a popular attraction for other expeditions, especially whenever *Borat* or *Brokeback Mountain* were screened on a laptop in their high-altitude cinema.

Climbers invited each other to their tents for evening meals where climbing strategies were debated, previous experiences were shared and tales of old injuries were aired. The merits of climbing with and without oxygen were mulled over, the best way to ascend K2 often top of the teatime agenda. Evening meals meant relaxation and engagement with others, a break from their tents, and some much-needed nourishment, as Ger McDonnell advised his blog readers:

For the most part then, we retire in the early evening to the solitary confines of our tents for some "a lonely-own-some" time. That is until the kitchen lads bang a metal plate with a spoon and we all come running like hungry calves in midwinter, running to their latest incarnation of dahl and such like.[40]

Parties were a fairly common occurrence at camp, acting as an antidote to the tedium of daily chores. These events were usually instigated by the high-altitude workers from Nepal and Pakistan; for one of the celebrations – the Aga Khan's birthday on 11 July – a sumptuous buffet was served on green tarpaulin-covered tables. Qudrat Ali, one of Hugues D'Aubarède's high-altitude workers, sang from the *Quran*, and his performance was followed by general singing and dancing and much appreciated by Mike Farris:

There had been a party a few days before (with beer!) that we hadn't heard about. I made it clear to Deedar [a porter] that we were to be informed about any further parties. Well, there was one last night so Deedar made certain that I was there. About 9pm I got out of my tent and walked down to the party. These parties consist of the Pakistani staff and team members (all male). There is much singing and drumming, and then dancing. I've been to these things before and knew as a team leader that I'd have to dance. You can imagine me doing a solo dance in front of about 40 (mostly sober) guys. No beer last night![41]

Contact with the outside world was a daily occurence at Base Camp though some climbers preferred to detach themselves completely from such engagement. Many of the climbers kept in touch online with news from their home countries on a daily basis. Phone calls and emails with loved ones and climbing friends were commonplace. There was also a steady trail of visitors to camp. Wilco was thrilled when a group of Dutch trekkers visited Base Camp and offered to take his video-laden external hard drive back to the Netherlands in return for a clean one.

Porters were known to scuttle down to Askole for beer or other treats, often returning in half the time it took to get there in the first place. A human version of the Pony Express brought mail to camp, Ger receiving holy water from his mother, Wilco ordering a delivery of Mars bars to boost his energy.

The Serb, Dren Mandic, a shy but friendly climber, preferred to mix with his own team or pursue his zoological interests, photographing the limited flora and fauna in the vicinity. Chhiring Dorje busied himself building a chorten, an altar-like rocky mound to honour the mountain. Chris Klinke dined on Coca Cola and

Pringles and monitored the US presidential election race between Barack Obama and John McCain.[42]

Ger fashioned a bodhrán tipper for the chefs who were prone to drumming on pots and pans. Wilco monitored the forecasts. Pemba Gyalje walked the glacier. Mike Farris enjoyed some of the simpler pleasures in life:

> Base Camp life is pretty nice, if you don't mind living on a glacier covered with a thin layer of rocks ... once you're laying down there's almost no reason to get up all night. So I turned on the iPod, had some M&Ms, sipped some Scotch, and listened to music for several hours. We all have pee bottles, so it's not even necessary to sit up to deal with that issue (for guys, anyway).[43]

Like Lars Nessa, Ger McDonnell also revelled in the cultural, ethnic, linguistic and sociological melting pot that was K2 Base Camp. While expedition leaders like Mr Kim and Wilco remained aloof, Ger saw life at Base Camp as an opportunity to interact with other nationalities, to share ideas, learn new languages and make new friends.

He developed a reputation for reaching out to other climbers, especially those from the smaller teams; his friendly manner proving popular with everyone. Marco Confortola nicknamed him 'Jesus', not least because of his conciliatory persona and shaggy beard, and the two enjoyed much cordial banter.

But Ger also provided another ingredient which brought a cohesion and friendly atmosphere to Base Camp, something which was widely recognised and universally appreciated; he provided a counterweight to Wilco's occasional fiery outbursts, something that even the Dutchman acknowledged.

Whenever Wilco had a difference of opinion with a climber or another team, Ger, his expedition leader recalled, 'was the first guy who went the next morning to the guys, to this American or to the French guy to drink a cup of coffee and to discuss the whole situation ... Gerard was always this mediator, he was in between and he would listen to both sides'. His actions often helped to defuse difficult situations in the sometimes tense and jittery Base Camp.

Pemba looked on, intrigued and concerned in equal measure as the various expeditions prepared for the summit. Experience on Everest and some of the world's other highest peaks had taught him that, beyond a shared love of climbing, people come to a mountain with a diversity of approaches and multifarious reasons for being there. For some, the mountain is an escape from the banality of daily life and work, for others it is the latest attempt to secure another trophy in their quest to join a climbing elite; others come purely for the love of the unspoiled terrain and to enjoy the rugged beauty of nature.

For the South Koreans it was summiting at all costs, for the Norwegians, the summit was a bonus on an expedition which would be deemed a success even without reaching the top; for several smaller expeditions the goal lay somewhere in between – a serious attempt at the summit would be launched but only if it did not jeopardise lives and safety.

For Pemba, reaching the summit was always secondary to returning home safely. He was always prepared to accept and acknowledge his own personal limits and to realise when to stop and turn around. From the early weeks at Base Camp, however, he realised that he was in a minority:

> I found that the majority of people wanted to summit. That is the big problem because many people, they came two, three times to that mountain and they wanted to summit because they don't like to come again to that mountain. And that is the main cause [of] summit fever for the majority. When I was talking to other people in Base Camp during the rest days, many people were saying, "Ah, I don't want to come again to this mountain because already I came here three times" or "This is my second time, I spent a lot of money already and I spend too much time on this mountain". They want to summit.

Summit fever is a powerful emotion which climbers find hard to resist when the summit of any peak is within close reach. It is so potent that every other consideration which is supposed to influence a climber's decision whether or not to continue – the prevailing weather conditions, personal fitness, the safety of other team members or the difficulty of the terrain underfoot – is suppressed in the subconscious, allowing nothing to distract from the goal ahead. The magnetism of the summit can also cause climbers to ignore others in distress, the injured, even the dying.

Summit fever has had such an impact on climbers that it prompted Sir Edmund Hillary to complain that 'the whole attitude towards climbing Mount Everest has become rather horrifying. People just want to get to the top. They don't give a damn for anybody else who may be in distress'.[44] His comments came in the wake of claims that a Briton, who was dying below the summit on Everest in 2006, had been passed by up to 40 other climbers in the grip of summit fever, unwilling to come to his aid.

The incident, in the mind of one commentator, highlighted 'a seemingly callous disregard among mountaineers for other lives, exposing a horrifying secret that, with the achievement of a lifetime's ambition in sight, and gripped by the selfishness of summit fever, it is every man for himself'.[45]

It was a frenzied delirium Pemba had seen time and time again, sometimes with fatal consequences. It was inevitable, he thought, that of the dozens of climbers now eyeing the upper reaches of K2 through the clouds, some would succumb to the same powerful preoccupation with reaching the top. The American team leader was also perceptive of the ambitions of the various other expeditions at Base Camp. Mike Farris had instilled in his team members an approach to the mountain which demanded respect for its reputation, ensuring that climbers were not blinded by the pull of the summit:

> Why should anyone climb K2? It's a hard, scary mountain. Frankly, you should climb K2 for only one reason: for yourself. There are many people at K2 BC who are climbing for other reasons: for fame, for their sponsors, for self-importance, and so on. You can get away with that on easy peaks like Cho Oyu, Everest, etc. But here, these external motivators can colour your perceptions and judgments and lead you astray.[46]

As the month of July wore on, the mood at Base Camp became subdued. Bad weather prevented climbing for weeks on end. K2 was bringing its hostile climate to bear on the region; the conditions that forced the abandonment of the Norit team's first summit attempt persisted for almost three weeks. It was 'snow, snow, snow – it was unbelievable', Wilco said. Weather forecasts indicated that it would be at least the end of July before any realistic opportunity to return to higher altitudes presented itself.

Amid the blizzard-like conditions, Pemba occupied himself with regular treks on the glacier, joining team members to visit the nearby Broad Peak Base Camp or the depot below Camp One. Occasional breaks in the cloud allowed forays to higher camps with supplementary supplies. But, as the days passed, the Norit team began to realise that if they were to get another shot at the summit, it could depend on a break in the weather at the beginning of a month in which most accidents occur on K2.

The prospect did not endear itself to Pemba: 'I was not confident ... because August is almost the monsoon season and I was not confident about the weather.' Statistically, more climbers die on K2 in August than in any other month.[47]

Interpersonal animosities continued to reverberate across Base Camp as the gloom of endless days of bad weather lowered the mood, exacerbating stresses and strains. Nick Rice and the other members of Hugues D'Aubarède's expedition were also planning to use the Cesen, with Wilco demanding that, in return for using the Norit expedition ropes, their high-altitude workers fix the remainder of the route from Camp Three to the Shoulder.

Wilco, Nick alleged, had charged the French team $500 a man for using their ropes while simultaneously complaining to him about ill-equipped and ill-prepared expeditions. Nick was not slow to share his impressions of Wilco with his website readership:

> He (Wilco) became quite abrasive ... accusing us of being lazy, and sitting in base camp while they fixed all the way to the summit. We insisted that it wasn't our fault that they had decided to arrive at base camp a month before us and that they couldn't expect any of us to be properly acclimatized ... Wilco wouldn't have it. He accused us of being irresponsible, took no responsibility for "sitting back and allowing others to fix the route" in 2006, and finally stormed out. The four of us chatted about how to proceed; whether to change routes and take the Abruzzi, as who knows what Wilco might do to the fixed ropes after his team is finished with them now that he is so bitter.[48]

Wilco also found himself embroiled in an unpleasant squabble with team-mate Ger McDonnell. Towards the end of July, the Norit team's cook became seriously ill. Dr Eric Meyer, from the American team, diagnosed acute appendicitis; the cook needed a speedy evacuation for surgical intervention. Wilco spoke to Jasmine Tours, the expedition's travel agency, about an emergency rescue and how best to get the cook down from Base Camp. They could send a helicopter but the team did not have insurance cover for such an eventuality.

Wilco suggested that the cost would be prohibitive so the cook would have to walk to Askole. Ger and others suggested a whip-round – maybe the money for the helicopter trip could be raised between the other expeditions at Base Camp, but Wilco was having none of it.

Pemba looked on as a heated row erupted between the two men. On the morning of 28 July, the cook, agonised with stomach pain, hiked from Base Camp with two Pakistani porters, reaching medical aid a week later. Ger and Wilco didn't speak again for 24 hours.

In the emotional pressure cooker that was Base Camp, disputes were nothing new; the pair were later reconciled but Pemba felt uneasy and impatient. He longed for some better weather to relieve the pressure valve that was building among the disgruntled and irritable occupants of Base Camp.

Only an ascent of the mountain above them would shift the focus from the frustrations of what was becoming a claustrophobic Base Camp. And so Pemba Gyalje prayed for a weather window in which K2 might yield to the waiting climbers' advances.

Chapter
two

Weather Window

20 July – 31 July

After breakfasting in his tent on 20 July, the French expedition leader, Hugues D'Aubarède, decided it was time to go home. For several weeks, K2 Base Camp had been blanketed in heavy snow and battered by high winds. The mountain's notoriously unpredictable weather patterns were living up to their reputation and, as the summer slipped by amid the cloud, wind and snow, so, too, did the prospect of reaching the summit.

Morning after morning for nearly three weeks, the climbers woke to the repeatedly negative weather forecasts in their inboxes. Many of them were growing weary of trying to keep their minds occupied and maintaining their fitness levels at Base Camp. They knew that the later in the summer a summit attempt was launched, the greater the hazards. Time was running out.

Hugues had invested a lot in getting to K2. This was his third trip to the mountain and he had been optimistic that he would finally prevail. But the outlook was grim; he had postponed the inevitable for long enough. There was no foreseeable weather window in which the summit could be attempted; it was time for Hugues to face reality. That morning, his expedition team-mate, Nick Rice, posted a gloomy update on his blog:

> Today, after a late breakfast, Hugues made the final decision to go home. The weather continues to worsen today. Last night there was heavy snow with wind, and today, the snow is blowing horizontally. Hugues and I took refuge in the mess tent, as I worked on transferring data from my website off his computer … He will depart from K2 Base Camp on the 22nd and hopefully should arrive back in Skardu on the 25th. K2 is looking like it might not allow any climbers to reach the summit this year … Morale at Base Camp gets worse by the day.[49]

Hugues was not the only one contemplating a return home. Several climbers, especially those on the Norit team, had spent up to two months at an increasingly mundane and frustrating Base Camp, and were becoming impatient.

The waiting game was nothing new to experienced expedition members who were used to sitting patiently in their tents for weeks on end waiting for the storms and snow to abate on the world's highest peaks. But even those with the highest levels of forbearance were now beginning to wonder if the mountain would accede to their encroachments at all this season. Weather conditions were hindering acclimatisation and forcing long stays in tents, making it difficult to remain focussed and physically ready for an opportunity that might present itself all of a sudden.

Like Hugues, Ger McDonnell was thinking of leaving, as his partner, Annie Starkey, noted: 'I think towards the end he was ready to come home ... he said to me, "I can't wait to have a good meal and glass of red wine". He was kind of ready. It was 60 something days by that point.' The soles of Ger's walking shoes were worn, the prayer flags around his tent tattered from the winds. The bottoms of seven food barrels had started to show.[50]

A much-dreaded boredom had set in for many; there were only so many forays over to the Gilkey Memorial or Broad Peak that any climber could endure. Mike Farris watched as the seconds ticked agonisingly slowly by:

> Today is certainly less exciting (though I've spent 30 minutes typing this). It's partly sunny, slightly windy, and we had a bit of snow earlier this morning. Lunch will be ready in about 30 minutes and will take 15 minutes to eat. After that, the afternoon will stretch ahead. I'll look for more reasonable photos/video, read a bit, talk some, and try to avoid looking at my watch. We are likely to have another 5-6 days before we can go up. The higher we get, the fewer weather openings there are.[51]

As much as K2 was renowned for its often unforgiving weather conditions, so, too, was it liable to experience unexpected and sudden periods of climatic calm. On the morning of 22 July, just as Hugues had begun to pack his things before departing, Base Camp began to buzz with news of a new forecast of a weather window opening up in the final days of July and the early days of August – a number of consecutive days of good weather that would provide just enough time to get to the summit and back.

Four separate forecasts from different sources presented the same information; it was manna from heaven. The revelation electrified Base Camp, as the prospect of a real crack at the summit emerged. Hugues was incredulous and revitalised in equal measure. He ran to the other tents to check that the news was true. All the forecasts tallied; four or five days centred around 31 July or 1 August would be clear, calm and snowless.

Hugues weighed up his options; one of his high-altitude workers, Qudrat Ali, had to leave camp to join another expedition he had made commitments to, but he still had Karim Meherban and Jehan Baig. He was prepared to roll the dice one more time. Immediately, he phoned his agent to postpone his plans for travelling home; Nick Rice had already long-fingered his departure so he could attempt Broad Peak instead of K2, but now the latter looked a real possibility.

The American team's Mike Farris posted their ambitions on the team's blog: '... we are heading up the hill in two waves ... we intend to go as high as possible'.[52] Inter-expedition chatter reached fever pitch: could this be the opportunity they had all been waiting for? Wilco realised that the routine of Base Camp during the incessant snow was becoming too much for his team; the new weather forecasts provided a vital and much-needed morale boost for his climbers:

> If we didn't have this weather forecast, we would have quit the mountain before because you get crazy. There is no food anymore. Normally, we had this coffee hour in the morning but, finally, the coffee was finished. So you are just hanging around. Gerard was just listening to his music. Some other guys, like Cas and Jelle, were playing chess but, through three weeks, it's very, very hard. And then finally we got this weather forecast; there would be this really nice weather window for four, five, maybe six, seven days. We couldn't believe it ... We were convinced, everything was there. We had a strong team, we were not at our end; we had energy still for this last summit attempt ...

The advancing weather window brought the swift realisation that a few dozen climbers would now be advancing simultaneously on the summit of K2 to avail of the short time frame available; this could be the last time the summit could be attempted in the 2008 season and everyone at Base Camp would want to use the opportunity. For Wilco van Rooijen, now on his third and possibly final trip to the mountain, the move towards co-operation with other teams, all intent on summiting on the same day, was inevitable.

Of course, he would have loved to lead his team to the summit unhindered by, and without the distractions of, other expeditions on the ascent. But, in reality, if the mountaineers at Base Camp were to make a serious assault on the summit in such a narrow time frame, co-ordination of their respective efforts made sense.

It appeared logical to pool resources, especially in areas like the installation of fixed ropes on parts of the route immediately below the summit and breaking a path across the more treacherous sections of the upper slopes. A shared approach could be beneficial if the various elements of an agreed plan worked well.

But Wilco was not so inexperienced or naive as to think that such a united effort did not have inherent problems and dangers. A joint summit push involving multiple climbing styles, different languages and cultures and, most importantly, varying levels of technical skill and experience, was not without its risks:

> In the beginning, I was thinking, listen, we don't need those guys because we are much ahead of everybody ... We are making our own plan, we are bringing up the rope, we had a wonderful team ... [but] everybody wants to use this window so you have two options. You say, listen, we will do it our own way or, and I think it's logical for human beings, we are going to work together because we are with a lot of people, we share all the work loads and 80 per cent chance we will get to the summit without any problem. But the mistake maybe we made was, the bigger the chain, the bigger the chance that there is somebody in this chain who is making a mistake or ... is too slow.

Wilco and Mr Kim decided to take the initiative. Teams interested in discussing a joint summit attempt were called to a meeting to explore the options. Along with Wilco and Kim, Pemba observed, the leaders of the American, Serb and French expeditions led the talks and 'defined the agendas'. Everything - from manpower to ropes, the trail-breaking process and the route to the summit - was up for discussion.

On 22 July, just hours after receiving the news of the meteorological marvel, representatives from each of the major expeditions gathered in the Serb mess tent, the largest meeting space available. Included among those attending were expedition leaders Wilco van Rooijen (Dutch/Norit), Mike Farris (Americans), Robert Goh (Singaporeans), Hugues D'Aubarède (French) and Milivoj Erdeljan (Serbs), as well as several high-altitude workers and Sherpas, one or more from each team.

Key to arranging the meetings were the Pakistani ministry liaison officers present at Base Camp. The military personnel facilitated the expeditions and had a largely supervisory role, usually accompanying teams to Base Camp to assist with logistics and to ensure that climbers cleared all of their belongings on departure.

While some of the officers opted to remain in Askole or Skardu, a handful were present at Base Camp. Although not everyone there had entirely positive opinions of them,[53] Pemba was reassured, not just by their presence, but by their involvement in the pre-summit discussions. In contrast to his native Nepal, where such officials had less experience and limited involvement, the Pakistani liaison officers adopted a more hands-on and supportive role:

> The Pakistani liaison officers are very good, much better because they are from military backgrounds – they are military colonels and have good experience of glaciers and altitude. They are very good and very strict with good reporting. I was very happy with them.

The first item to be discussed was when the climbers would head for the summit – the forecast indicated that 1 August was the most propitious date so departure from Base Camp would take place a few days before. But that was still 10 days away and a lot could change by then. Not everyone was convinced; perhaps it would be better to wait a little longer to settle on a date, as Nick Rice's blog from that evening suggested:

> While all the expeditions were trying to secure [a] definitive date to depart for the high camps, Hugues made the very rational suggestion that they should simply wait till around at least the 25th before they made any decisions as the weather forecast for the beginning of August was in no way definite, and without knowing specifics about wind speed on the summit and in high camps, it would be difficult to make an informed decision as to when to leave. The teams agreed to adjourn for the moment, aside from some resistance from the Koreans who had an arbitrary date in mind for their departure, and resume discussions on the 25th, as Hugues had suggested.[54]

Between meetings, teams using the same routes to Camp Four, the highest camp on the Shoulder, had their own bilateral exchanges. Only the Norit team, as well as Hugues' group and the Serb, Hoselito Bite, would climb the Cesen route, which had been roped to within about 200 metres of Camp Four by the Norit team. All of the other teams, including the Serb expedition, the Italians, Singaporeans, Norwegians and Americans, were planning to use the Abruzzi.

Over the course of the following week, a handful of planning sessions were convened, usually chaired by the Serb team's liaison officer, Captain Sabir Ali Changazi. Sitting around a large fold-up table, the climbers fiddled with notebooks and pens and sipped strong, sweet tea. Fredrik Sträng from the American team and Norit's Ger McDonnell switched on their video cameras and zoomed in on each speaker. This was crunch time and the climbers were nervous but excited.

A key decision would be the composition of a party of advance climbers who would break the trail from Camp Four through the treacherous Bottleneck gulley and across the Traverse. The notorious Bottleneck – an appropriate name given its shape – was the steep and narrow passageway or couloir through which climbers had to advance from the Shoulder. From there, they would move across the Traverse beneath a gigantic, looming ice face known as the Serac.

Ropes needed to be fixed through the Bottleneck and all the way to the end of the Traverse, from where the climbers would progress onto the snow plains below the summit and onwards towards the summit ridge itself. The task of roping that most dangerous part of the route would require attention to detail and carefully worked-out procedures. Installing secure ropes here before the bulk of the climbers began their ascent would make for safer climbing as they edged higher and higher.

Mr Kim asserted the strength and experience of his team, insisting that his deputy expedition leader, Hwang Dong-jin, take charge of the trail-breaking party. Nobody made a counter proposal. The trail-breaking party would leave Camp Four at least an hour before the other climbers to get a head start on fixing the lines. Each team was asked to nominate strong and competent climbers for the rope-fixing task.

From the South Koreans, Hwang would be joined by team-mate, Park Kyeong-hyo, who was also given responsibility for the collection and allocation of ropes and other equipment required by the trail breakers once they gathered at Camp Four. Two of the Flying Jump Sherpas, Jumik Bhote and Pasang Lama, were assigned to the trail-breaking team. From the Italian team, the high-altitude worker, Mohammad Ali, was nominated, along with Pemba Gyalje from Norit and Chhiring Dorje from the American expedition.

The selection of three other trail breakers, each of whom came from the Serb team, was not a difficult choice: Shaheen Baig and Mohammad Hussein were the only two climbers present who had previously set foot on the summit of K2 and their experience and knowledge would be invaluable. They were joined by Hussein's friend, Mohammad Khan, who had also been to K2 before.

For many of those present, the English-speaking and multilingual Shaheen seemed the most authoritative and knowledgeable about the logistical requirements for the climb ahead. He and Mohammad Hussein found themselves on the receiving end of many questions from the K2 novices. Shaheen might not have been the nominated leader of the trail-breaking party but he seemed to be leader in all but name – vocal, engaging and informative, in stark contrast to Hwang, the actual leader of the group, who said little and had limited English.

Chris Klinke from the American expedition noted afterwards that 'Mr Hwang was nominally the leader, but that was because the Koreans seemed big into official titles. Shaheen was the one we all trusted to really be in charge [of the trail-breaking party]'.[55] Though he did not attend the meetings, Alberto Zerain later identified Shaheen as 'a leader because he did things simply, with great ease ... he was a key person for everybody'. It was agreed that the trail breakers would depart from Camp Four at midnight on the day of the summit push.

Discussions about rope occupied much time at the Base Camp meetings. Who would supply the rope to fix lines in the Bottleneck? Where would the ropes be fixed and how much was needed? The debate was dominated by Wilco, Mr Kim and Shaheen Baig, the Pakistani summiteer suggesting that, in his experience, 300 metres of rope were needed to fix a line through the steep Bottleneck couloir. Wilco argued for 400 metres for the Bottleneck with a further 200 metres to cover the Traverse. He offered 400 metres from his team's supplies while the Italian team would provide the additional 200 metres. 'Maybe we need more,' a voice said. 'We don't need more,' the Dutchman insisted.[56]

The tension was broken when Chhiring Dorje said that over 2,000 metres of rope would be required, a suggestion greeted with much laughter from his fellow climbers and much embarrassment on his part: 'I tell the people 2,200 metre rope in the Shoulder [would be] better and everybody [was] not listening. Everybody was laughing at me. I am thinking, very crazy these people.'

Pemba made a personal handwritten list of the equipment to be made available to the trail breakers at Camp Four. Apart from rope, his team would supply a dozen ice screws and three rock pitons as well as some spare carabiners. The Italians were bringing 200 metres of static rope. The South Koreans were donating eight ice screws, four snow pickets and another 100 metres of eight millimetre rope.

The Americans would supply some bamboo wands to be used to mark the trail across the Shoulder. They also offered a light fishing line which would be fixed from approximately 100 metres above Camp Four to act as a guide for climbers who might be returning from the summit after dark. The Norit expedition's much stronger spectra rope, made of the synthetic toughened substance, polyethylene, would be used in the Bottleneck, with the Italians' contribution of rope to be fixed on the Traverse.

In his own mind, Pemba was concerned that the micro-management and overly-detailed discussions about the roping of the route – though hugely important – did not allow for discretion on the part of trail breakers or for unforeseen circumstances on the ascent. But he was happy that there would be enough rope to fulfil the obligations placed on him and his fellow trail breakers and that there was at least some consensus about where it should be placed:

> They said we would take 600 or 700 metres of rope if possible so that we could fix the lower Bottleneck section. Then the Pakistanis and the other Sherpas said that last year another Sherpa fell down in this section because there was no fixed line and he did not self-arrest and he died. This was halfway between High Camp and the Bottleneck. And that's why people said if we have enough rope we have to fix [rope from] there.

A key element of the summit bid was not discussed by the team leaders at Base Camp - what time they would turn around or abandon the climb if they were running behind schedule, or in what circumstances they would retreat if a serious incident or tragedy occurred. Only the Norit team had published a timetable for the climb, which listed a target summit time of 2pm[57] but such schedules were often notional; once climbers were on the mountain, time often took second place to the prevailing circumstances and the ambition to succeed.

Despite the prolonged and intricate discussions about ropes and equipment, all Pemba could observe in the eyes of his fellow climbers was the burning desire to summit:

> The majority of people were thinking with K2, it is always a late summit, a late afternoon summit which is not normal for an 8,000-metre peak – it's only good for lucky people but not for the majority of people. In history, K2's summit is always reached in the late afternoon; there are only a few people who were on the summit at the right time but the majority of K2 summiteers were on the summit in the late afternoon and this is what people had in mind – some people climbed at 3pm, some people at 6pm. They were thinking this is normal for K2 but this is wrong. The best time is noon to get back to High Camp before dark.

Not everyone at Base Camp was fully engaged in the preparatory talks. Almost all of the expeditions were represented but the Norwegians claimed they were not invited to partake. This did not concern them unduly. Lars Nessa realised that they 'were four Norwegians and, as a small expedition, I don't think they counted us into the summit push'. As a team with limited resources and only enough rope and equipment for themselves, they understood that they were of little interest or benefit to the others.

Lars and Rolf Bae were present only for the final meeting before the summit push. They thought they needed to familiarise themselves with the agreements being made but felt uneasy about the detail of the minutiae agreed; it seemed almost too perfect. Immediately apparent to Lars, too, were the communication difficulties inherent in a gathering of people with no common language.

Though English was used to hammer out the details of the joint plan, some of the climbers struggled to find the words for the various climbing devices; Lars wasn't confident that everyone was fully attuned to the discussion and he believed that the potential for confusion was very real. The high-altitude workers, guides and Sherpas were less inclined than the leaders of the larger teams to voice their opinions, Lars remarked, perhaps because of the language barriers but also, perhaps, due to deference on their part to the power and expectations of the big, commercial expeditions who dominated the meetings:

> When I say commercial that means the big expeditions, like the Norit expedition was a big commercial expedition, the American in my opinion was a big expedition but, of course, the Koreans were the main old-style big expedition which you can relate to the 1950s and 1960s. The Norit expedition was as commercial as the Koreans in my opinion ... The Serb expedition was also a national expedition, with the president of the Alpine Club as a formal leader ... The Norwegian expedition was only four friends on a trip trying to climb K2 so we had a different approach to the climbing.

Though they finally accepted they had little choice but to ascend with the others, Lars and his friends toyed with the idea of climbing by themselves, shrewdly identifying the difficulties inherent in working with others that they had only just met and on whose nous and abilities they were now reliant:

> It's quite a paradox because you have to depend on climbers who you probably would not take climbing at your home climbing cliff. We had to co-operate a lot with the Koreans on the Abruzzi ridge which means they put up most of the ropes and we did as much as we could and gave them a lot of our ropes. But then you have to depend on their ability to put up safe ropes and find a safe way to the summit and ... sometimes you would like to do it yourself and climb individually by yourself.

Pemba Gyalje knew from experience that all the logistical planning in the world could never account for the unpredictable or the unexpected at high altitude. His career on the mountains had taught him that good preparation and an analysis of the various strategic formulations for a summit attempt were critical to the success of any expedition, but every climber also needed to bring his or her own ingenuity and improvisational abilities to the task.

What concerned him most about the plans for a co-ordinated summit bid, however, was the wide variation in the climbing skills, technical abilities and experience of the many individual climbers who would now form part of a vast assault on the summit several kilometres above Base Camp.

From the moment other teams had arrived on the mountain, he had considered the strengths and weaknesses of their members. He had carefully assessed the capabilities of other climbers, simply by looking at them in action:

> Even in an airport or somewhere, even if they don't say I am an alpinist or a climber, I know he is a climber, he is a good alpinist, he is a beginner, he is advanced. I can recognise easily ... just from their behaviour and my experience. When I go to the airport to pick up some climbers from different countries, I can easily recognise who is the good climber.

Any concerns Pemba may have had about the know-how or aptitude of other would-be summiteers he discreetly kept to himself. It was not his place to tell others whether or not they were up to climbing the world's most dangerous mountain. But everything discussed in the Serb mess tent depended on how climbers would perform at high altitude and how they would cope with the harrowing impact of the Death Zone above 8,000 metres.

Though he was content to co-operate with the other expeditions and the arrangements made at Base Camp, Pemba knew that they could quickly unravel when confronted by the objective dangers and climbing hazards for which K2 is renowned:

> ... meeting is meeting but climbing is different. Even at our meetings in Base Camp, I was not 100 per cent confident about what people said because climbing is different – the situation on the mountain is totally different. According to my experience, those kinds of meetings are just for tentative guidance to bring people together with as much cohesion as possible. But meeting is meeting ... When people start to climb above the

High Camp for the final summit bid, I then find that, automatically, the majority of people forget what they said and what they committed to at Base Camp.

Pemba's concerns were echoed by Mike Farris who, though he had attended and participated in the preparatory meetings, was tired of the 'usual political bullshit that leaders have to deal with when co-ordinating with other teams'.[58] Mike was a purist when it came to climbing, and bemoaned the fact that many modern climbers were so reliant on using oxygen; hadn't K2 been ascended successfully without oxygen three decades before?[59]

Now, several expeditions were stocking up on cylinders, a climbing crutch he considered part of an archaic climbing style. The American team leader had no great confidence in overly-elaborate summit plans:

> We've had two big meetings among most of the teams to co-ordinate our "summit strategies". While these meetings are overall quite positive, it's very clear that some teams are living in, shall we say, an alternate universe where summit attempts can be planned ten days in advance. Rather than planning an attempt like you would book an airplane flight, you have to be a guerrilla fighter and be ready to strike at a moment's notice, whenever the mountain weather shows a weakness.[60]

On the morning of 26 July, and for the first time in weeks, the upper reaches of K2 became clearly visible from Base Camp. The weather was settling and the weather window was opening like a divinely-inspired shaft of light from the heavens above. With a summit date of 1 August finally agreed, most of the teams planned to leave Base Camp on 28 July while a second wave of climbers – including the expedition from Singapore and another led by the Romanian-born George Dijmarescu – would depart from Base Camp a day later if the weather held. Those expeditions were also prepared to spend the month of August at Base Camp for another attempt if necessary, having come to the mountain much later in the season.

Among the second summit group were the other team from the South Korean Flying Jump expedition, including their Sherpas, 'Big' Pasang Bhote and his cousin, Tsering Bhote; they would set out from Base Camp a day later than the first team, on 29 July. Tsering saw a clear delineation in the South Korean team:

In team one the climbers were strong, experienced, enthusiastic climbers. In the first team the main thing was this girl [Ms Go] who was doing the 14 peaks; they probably had an aim of climbing to the summit. So there were strong and experienced Korean climbers in the team. In the second team they were like good climbers, but they were like not crazy to reach the summit, they had to climb but it was not like they had to ace it, maybe because the team leader asked them to stay in group B, not determined to do the summit; they were to just climb. That was how the groups were divided.

Mark Sheen from Wilco's team would aim to summit on 2 August; Roeland van Oss had decided to remain at Base Camp and Court Haegens had quit the expedition entirely with a knee problem. Not everyone was summit-bound, however. For reasons ranging from altitude sickness to inexperience, or the need to remain behind and co-ordinate efforts from below, many climbers would stay at Base Camp during the summit attempt. Expedition leader Milivoj Erdeljan, from the Serb team, for example, would help to direct operations from the top of the Godwin-Austen glacier.

Last-minute preparations now began in earnest; crampons were sharpened, gas stoves checked, batteries re-charged, ice axes and nose guards readied, energy bars and drinks prepared. Radio frequencies were agreed between team leaders to allow communication by walkie-talkie if and when the climbers separated. Those using oxygen deliberated over how many cylinders to bring.

Careful consideration was also required about what to bring to the summit and, critically, what to leave behind; every item meant more weight in rucksacks, a weight that seemed heavier as climbers became tired. For some, a good luck charm, a prayer beads or picture of a loved one was brought on the ascent as a talisman.

The Sherpa climbers again worshipped the mountain, praying for a safe passage to the top. Before laptops were stored away, the final blog entries set out what lay ahead. 'The die is cast,' reported Hugues D'Aubarède, 'we'll see, but it is not easy at age 61!'[61] Nick Rice told his readers about the timetable for the top. Leaving at 5.30am on 28 July, the French expedition would gradually edge their way up the Cesen route:

28th July: Base Camp (5,000 meters) to Camp II (6,300 meters) on the Cesen route; 29th July, Camp II (6,300 meters) to Camp III (7,000 meters); 30th July: Camp III (7,000 meters) to Camp IV (8,000 meters) (Shoulder of K2), meet up with climbers on the Abruzzi; 31st July: 2.00am, depart Camp IV (8,000 meters) for the summit (8,611 meters), return to Camp

III if feeling fit, otherwise spend the night in Camp IV; 1st August: High Camp to Base Camp. Hopefully, the next dispatch I will write will detail our summit day. Wish us luck!'[62]

As Ger McDonnell packed his rucksack, including the holy water his mother had sent to Base Camp, he wrote a characteristically optimistic pre-summit message for those at home:

All weather forecasts jived. The weather on the 1st of August is, for the most part, equally as good. That'll give the lead party a buffer if there are any delays. The following days appear to be more than adequate for a safe descent. Initially the Koreans were keen to use the 31st to gain camp 4 and the 1st as a summit day. But they very honourably and gracefully [acceded] to the logic of not wasting the first possible summit day. More especially because the weather conditions to gain camp 4 on the 30th should be more than sufficient. The [last] meeting had primarily a humorous tone. Spirits were high. Hopes are high. It was joked that the next meeting would take place at camp 4. Cesen and Abruzzi teams meet there on the 30th. Insha'Allah [If God wills it]. The Norit International Team will leave base camp on the 28th. Let luck and good fortune prevail!!! Fingers crossed.[63]

The final lines were in his native tongue: 'Sin é anois a cháirde. Tá an t-ám ag teacht' ('That's it for now, my friends. The time is coming').

Pemba's jumar ascender slammed shut, its grooves gripping the rope as it slid smoothly upwards. He affixed a crab to the line. The other end was tied to his harness and he closed its spring-loaded gate, making him doubly protected in the event of a fall; if his crampon lost its grip on the ice or his ice axe failed to hold, he would slide no more than half a metre.

Tugging at his harness and tightening the strap on his helmet, he was ready to go. He kicked his insulated knee-high boot into the snow and took the first step on the three-kilometre, near-vertical ascent to Camp Four. Perhaps, on his second summit attempt in the space of three weeks, there would a better outcome.

As he glanced up along the serrated ridge, plotting the route ahead in his mind, Pemba was confident about the weather conditions for the days ahead and the preparedness of his team. The forecasts weaving their way to Base

Camp in recent weeks had proven remarkably accurate, although consistently disappointing, but Pemba's instinctive weather vane now pointed to favourable conditions for the ascent.

The much-anticipated weather window had materialised as predicted. He was taking nothing for granted – K2 was always volatile, liable to spew the very worst of wind and snow with little or no warning despite all of the high-tech prognostications that modern climatology could provide. Stomach pains and abdominal cramps in the previous days had almost put paid to Pemba's summit attempt but the medical intervention of Eric Meyer had proved effective.

Pemba had phoned his wife, Da Jangmu, in Kathmandu to tell her they were leaving for the top. He reassured her that all would be well: 'My family was praying. That is normal in my community. My wife was not really worried. She was very confident about my ability.' He had used Ger McDonnell's blog to send a final message to his family and friends: 'We hope weather and health will good favour us [sic]. See you again!'[64]

Departing Base Camp early on the morning of 28 July, two months to the day they had arrived there, the five members of the Norit team felt that the ultimate prize was now well within their grasp. Wilco, Ger and Pemba, along with Jelle Staleman and Cas van de Gevel, planned to make their way, over the course of two days, to the exposed snow plain on K2's Shoulder just below the top of the mountain and at an altitude of 7,900 metres. From there, they would climb the final distance to the second highest point on the globe, an ascent and descent they estimated would take less than 24 hours.

Not all of the Norit team were en route. At Base Camp Roeland van Oss would act as a point of contact and co-ordination for his colleagues on the mountain. Mark Sheen, meanwhile, would set off a day later than the others. The Australian had tried to join the first summit party but Wilco argued that the strongest climbers should lead off and Mark had willingly accepted the expedition leader's decision and advice. Pemba had been impressed by Mark's realism and honesty from the time they first met in Islamabad:

> He was not focussed on the summit; he was just trying to see how high he could climb and he was always telling the truth because he was saying: "I don't know about summit, I am happy where I am but I try to climb. I have minimal experience and still I am learning. I have not enough experience for altitude and still my technical experience is improving, I am not like you." He was really, really honest and he can analyse his limitations. He had a really good understanding.

Beside Pemba at the foot of the Cesen route, the quiet but steely Cas van de Gevel began to ascend with little difficulty. He had never before been higher than 8,000 metres; this would be his first climb into the infamous Death Zone. He and Wilco had shared so many highs and lows on the mountains; this could be the icing on the cake of their career to date. They had come a long way together and Cas was thrilled to be undertaking this latest mountaineering odyssey with his friend. He became enchanted by the prospect of success as he scaled the southern flank of K2:

> Now we are going to be closer and now it is going to be the moment, the night which is coming, where everybody is going for the summit ... It's like there is some kind of electricity in the air. Everybody is very fixed. That's what we could notice already when we were leaving the Base Camp on the road to Camp Four.

Pemba and his climbing comrades performed so efficiently on their first day that they were able to reach Camp Two well ahead of nightfall after a 1,300-metre ascent. The climb had gone well, the fixed ropes holding steady on their anchors and the surface underfoot navigable for the most part. Ascenders glided with a familiar whoosh up the ropes, engaging reassuringly to prevent slippage backwards. Each step was carefully chosen before a crampon was kicked into place and each climber pushed their body upwards again.

Ice axes were used where the terrain became tricky. It was a rhythm into which the experienced mountaineers settled easily. The prospect of stormy weather and avalanches, which increased at the beginning of August each year, niggled in Wilco's mind, but the conditions were perfect, the sun was warm on their backs, team morale was high and his climbing friends looked competent and assured.

Also using the Cesen route were Hugues D'Aubarède's team, who followed the Norit expedition along the spur. Nick Rice found that the crows had helped themselves to the cache of foodstuffs he had stashed in his tent at Camp One weeks before.[65] As he climbed, he passed Ger McDonnell, who was still peeved by the row he had earlier that morning with Wilco over the evacuation of their team cook. Ger seemed hesitant about following his expedition leader; he was contemplating hanging back and waiting to join the second wave of climbers, including Mark Sheen.[66]

Nick proceeded to Camp Two where Hugues had hot drinks waiting which were relished by the American and their high-altitude workers, Jehan Baig and Karim Meherban. The Frenchman breathed in the spectacular and unspoiled scenery. The Godwin-Austen glacier, funnelling southwards, receded further and further out of view.

The Abruzzi route, spanning almost 3,000 uneven and testing metres from the foot of the mountain to Camp Four, was the preferred path for the majority of the climbers on K2 in 2008, including the expeditions from South Korea, the US, Serbia, Italy, Norway and Singapore. Most of the Abruzzi climbers had set out a day earlier than those on the Cesen to take account of the longer hike to the base of the spur, which was much further along the glacier from Base Camp than the bottom of the Cesen.

Leading the way were Shaheen Baig from the Serb team, Chhiring Dorje from the American group and Pasang Lama, the South Koreans' Sherpa, each charting the way for their respective expeditions. The trio made steady progress along the fixed ropes to the first of the camps on the path to the top. At various points on the ascent, steps were hacked out of the snow and ice in a simple arcing motion with the small adzes on the end of their axes. The makeshift steps helped those who followed to get a foothold and avoid any particularly slippery terrain.

Small coloured flags were pushed into the snow anywhere the moraine was loose or unstable underfoot, acting as a valuable warning to those below. The climbers were instinctively attuned to the sound the points of their crampons made as they scratched the surface, a subtle difference in tone telling them whether hard blue ice or a more granular névé snow lay beneath.

Finding a foothold or a grip for an ice axe often took half a minute. Being the first up the lines meant not just confronting the danger of skidding on glassy surfaces, it also meant the added responsibility of verifying the stability of anchor points and ropes. It was painstaking work, requiring total concentration.

The four members of the Singaporean expedition were pleased with their progress along the Abruzzi despite the demanding terrain. They were led by Robert Goh, the holder of a doctorate in aerodynamics, who had been the leader of several Singaporean national expeditions to Everest and Antarctica. Climbing from the base of the mountain to Camp Two was, he said, 'like going up Lhotse face all the way. There are no flat sections to relieve the climb. It was an uphill right from the bottom – 60 to 70 degree gradient with no plateau. It was hard going'.[67]

Elsewhere on the now-crowded spur, a trio of Serbs – Dren Mandic, Iso Planic and Predrag Zagorac – pushed upwards. Together with the South Koreans, they had helped to install the ropes on the Abruzzi ridge with some of the 1,700 metres of rope they had brought to the mountain. They planned to kit out Camp Four only when they arrived there; hardly any expeditions prepared the highest camp in advance; the place was too exposed and open to the elements to leave vacant tents untended for weeks on end.

With their leader opting to remain at Base Camp, the Serbs progressed to Camp One only to discover a tent they had placed there earlier had been rendered unusable because of broken poles which had become bent and twisted in snowstorms over the preceding three weeks. Fortunately, an undamaged tent nearby gave them somewhere to spend the night. The melting of snow was their first task; rehydration, as ever, critical in aiding advancement.

Close behind the trail breakers on the Abruzzi were the Italians, Marco Confortola and Roberto Manni, along with their Pakistani high-altitude workers, Mohammad Ali and Mohammad Amin. Camp One scared Marco – it looked avalanche-prone, he thought, exposed and godforsaken, no place to spend more than one night. New tents had to be pitched by those hoping to overnight, the old ones having fallen victim to the high winds.

Roberto wanted to stay at Camp One for a night to improve acclimatisation and allow the team to pace themselves, but the weather was calm, there was no wind, and soon the Italians and some of the American climbers were stepping nimbly behind the South Koreans along the slopes towards Camp Two.

Taking a brief rest every few dozen metres, they used those moments to glance behind them at the hypnotising vista of Broad Peak and its neighbours across the valley. A seemingly unending mountainscape stretched as far as the eye could see. Their acclimatisation levels were being sorely tested; this was their first serious encounter with the mountain in weeks. Breathing became more difficult and headaches often nagged as the climbers tried to make progress. The proximity of the Death Zone was becoming increasingly apparent.

By the second day of their ascent up the southern fringes of the mountain, unexpectedly strong winds had begun to impede the climbers' progress, making the ascent to Camp Three too dangerous for the expeditions on both spurs. K2 was being its capricious self yet again, unleashing the localised weather events which even the most proficient meteorological analysts seemed unable to predict with any accuracy. High winds began to sweep across the flanks of the mountain, making it too risky for the climbers to ascend on the fixed lines. The aim was to get to Camp Four the following day but that deadline now looked to be in serious jeopardy.

The South Koreans and Serbs conferred on the Abruzzi and radioed Wilco and his team on the Cesen to suggest that everyone wait a day at their respective second camps before advancing simultaneously. At Base Camp, the agreed aim of the various expeditions had been to try to reach the Shoulder at the same time so that the hours spent in the Death Zone could be minimised; they needed to co-ordinate their progression up the slopes. There was no point in having some expeditions spend an unnecessary night on the Shoulder, waiting for others to arrive.

The decision made sense to Pemba but, for Wilco, it was another example of the drawbacks of co-operation with others. He had planned to lead his team onwards to Camp Three despite the increasing wind but, now, he was being forced into a long day and night of inactivity, perched on a lonely, desolate ledge halfway to the summit: '... sitting in front of your tent the whole day, without space to move, is dull, dreary and dispiriting ... You always try to avoid wasting days high on the mountain. It drains strength and reserves, and requires valuable gas to melt snow; in short, it means that you are using up essential reserves that you have built up.'[68] They had little choice, however.

Across the vast south face of K2, snow and cloud made for increasingly testing conditions. Poor visibility, coupled with temperatures of 10 below freezing, made passage to the next camp extremely treacherous. Pemba worried that the weather would not clear: how could all of the forecasts have got it so wrong?

The Norit team took whatever refuge they could find in their tents and drank as much as they could; hydration and sleeping their only possible activities as the tents' fabric began to vibrate like the skin of a snare drum, pounded by the tempest whirling outside.

The sudden storms and unpredictable weather events on K2 have puzzled climbers for generations. Unlike other 8,000-metre peaks, it has always been a challenge to predict with accuracy the climatic patterns on K2's slopes, one of the many reasons that so many climbers have stayed away. Investigations of the mountain's mercurial and erratic weather conditions suggest that the sometimes sudden and usually very localised blizzards and storms can be accounted for by the fact that K2 juts above its nearest neighbours and into the upper layers of the troposphere.

There, like a rock in a river, it can create eddies in the jet stream 'with good weather on one side of the mountain, and life-threatening conditions on the other'.[69] As the jet stream – a fast-moving air current which travels north and south all the time – meanders around the Karakorum region, its manoeuvrings can become difficult to forecast.

The Norit team's weather guru, Ab Maas, said that the problem meteorologists have with a mountain like K2 is its sheer height: 'It's under the direct influence of the jet stream. The month of July [2008] is a good example because the jet stream was in the direct neighbourhood of K2 during that period, causing a lot of wind and precipitation.'[70] The winds which detained the various expeditions at the intermediate camps en route to the summit were most likely caused by what is known as the Venturi effect, whereby the northerly winds over K2 are sucked downwards towards the glaciers below where air pressure is dropping.

The mountain is also well known for a phenomenon known as katabatic winds, usually occurring in late afternoon and caused by denser air being pulled by gravity to lower altitudes at very high speeds. Climbers who are unfortunate enough to find themselves in their path rarely prosper in the face of their ferocity.

Following the unexpected delays at Camp Two, 30 July brought the desired fine weather for advancement, but not everybody was able to progress. The mountain-hardened Pakistani guide with the Serb team, Shaheen Baig, had started to vomit and experience stomach cramps when he reached the Abruzzi's second camp. Fortunately for him, the American team and their doctor, Eric Meyer, were using the same route.

Eric suspected that contaminated drinking water was the culprit and administered an anti-nausea drug, but the impact was minimal as Shaheen continued to retch violently. Predrag Zagorac, the Serb climbing leader, insisted on a speedy descent to Base Camp by his team-mate, but Shaheen would have none of it; he was determined to recover, conscious that he had an important role with the trail breakers and knew the route to the summit.

He pressed them to go on without him, believing he could follow once he had recuperated for a while. After several hours' rest, however, the 39-year-old's symptoms were worsening. Recognising his own deterioration, Shaheen decided to sit it out for the rest of the day before descending to Base Camp the following morning. His expedition was over:

> 'I talked to the others. My condition was not good, I could not go to Camp
> Three and I would go back to Base Camp and stay one day and then leave.
> I thought my problem was [a lack of] acclimatisation.'[71]

Alberto Zerain had also arrived at Camp Two and looked on in horror as convulsions racked Shaheen's body. The pair had become friendly at Base Camp; Alberto had been impressed by Shaheen's easy-going demeanour and natural leadership abilities. The Pakistani was about to pass some of his responsibilities onto the Spaniard:

> Shaheen came to me and said, "Alberto, why don't you leave your tent and instead of taking the tent, take these things that I was supposed to take for my expedition with the Serbs because that way you can help me, because I am going to have to go down. I am ill". Behind that gesture of giving me the ice screws, from what I can tell, from what happened later, he was passing on to me some of the responsibility, but I didn't realise that at the time.

As Alberto proceeded from Camp Two, it seemed as if the mountain was communicating with him and he felt that, at that altitude, 'the mountain really shows you what options it's got and what options you are going to have. It's something that one has to feel, [the] sensations that you have from Camp Two to Camp Three, when you go past the 7,000-metre barrier'.

Though the Basque climber was happy with his progress, he remained perturbed by the numbers now ascending the various routes to the Shoulder, concerned about some climbers' apparently excessive reliance on others for progress. The chain would only be as strong as its weakest link and that could seriously undermine the endeavour:

> ... it makes me think when so many people from different teams are joining their forces together to attack the mountain. I think the best arms, the best weapon, the best is really hidden within the person, himself. I think the answers for the mountain have to come from within a person so if you start sharing responsibilities with other people, I think, in the end, as we are human, we relax. K2 really demands knowing how to do things, giving the right answer, giving an answer for everything.

Moving ahead of the South Koreans, Serbs, Americans and the others, Alberto was the first to reach Camp Three at 7,350 metres, clambering around the imposing ridge, known as the Black Pyramid, to a small ledge from where the last lap of the ascent to the Shoulder would be launched. The space for climbers was limited; spending the night on the tiny plateau would be uncomfortable and cramped.

One of the South Koreans was next to arrive and Alberto was surprised to see him using oxygen so early in the ascent even though much of their supply would be required for the summit climb. Clearly the rigours and privations of the ascent to higher altitudes were having a pronounced impact on some.

Alberto observed how fixated the high-altitude workers and Sherpas were on checking the lines and carving out a route for their clients, noting a worried responsibility on their faces. He was also conscious of the pressure now evident among the men hauling gear to the highest camp; they seemed driven to proceed without adequate rest, their taskmasters' ambitions for the summit appearing to leave them little time for rest and sustenance:

> It worried me especially because the Sherpas were coming [to Camp Three] and they weren't getting into the tent to eat or to rest. They were having a drink of water or orange or something and then automatically they emptied their backpacks with all their loads, with all the equipment they were carrying for their clients, and they started filling up again. They were leaving Camp Three without having spent longer than a half hour there, heading off for Camp Four, loaded ... carrying that kind of weight at that height; that surprised me a lot. And that's when I thought poor guys, poor Sherpas, what kind of work they have got.

Gradually, the other climbers trickled into Camp Three, tiredness etched on their faces, their limbs throbbing inside their down suits. The demands of the ascent now stood in stark contrast to the many days they spent at Base Camp waiting for the weather to clear, denied exercise and acclimatisation. In a fatigued stupor, tents were fixed, water was boiled and snacks were digested. Despite the physically demanding climb along steep ridges, few were hungry. For many climbers, feelings of hunger dissipated at higher altitudes; they longed only to sleep and rest their aching bodies.

Shaheen Baig lay in his sleeping bag, alone at Camp Two on the Abruzzi spur. For several hours he had tried to will himself better. His team had gone ahead but he hoped he could find the strength to descend of his own accord to Base Camp when the nausea and empty retching passed. But, rather than improving, Shaheen continued to weaken. He crouched on all fours as his stomach tried to empty itself. He was too weak to drag himself outside.

As well as the stabbing cramps in his stomach, a croaky wheeze had begun to develop which he worried might be the early stages of pulmonary oedema, a debilitating flooding of the lungs at high altitude which can lead to respiratory failure. His suspicions were confirmed when he began to cough up a pinkish, frothy sputum.

By nightfall, the Pakistani guide realised he was not physically able to descend alone; he doubled over in pain, sweat oozing through his clothes. Reluctantly, he picked up his radio and called his friend, Nadir Ali Shah, a cook for the Serb team, at Base Camp. Nadir was just about to go to his tent for the night. Shaheen told him he could not make it down alone; it was now dark and the rest of the team were on the way to the summit. Nadir showed no hesitation and grabbed what he could from his tent, yanking on his boots and locating an ice axe. 'I am on my way,' he told his stricken friend.

At midnight, Nadir, who had no experience at high altitude but was training to be a guide, left Base Camp in an audacious bid to reach Shaheen 1,700 metres above. After a few hours' hike across the glacier to the foot of the Abruzzi, he moved up the fixed lines as fast as he could, with only the light from his head torch to guide his ascent. The frozen ice face was harder and more navigable than it would be during the heat of day, but Nadir had never climbed the Abruzzi spur before and his pace slowed as he climbed higher on rocks and ridges that were foreign to him.

At Camp One, at about 5am, Nadir radioed Shaheen but there was no reply; was he asleep or had he passed out? He continued upwards, pausing often to regulate his breathing. As dawn approached, the rising sun over Broad Peak warmed his aching muscles but he was still hours from Shaheen. Nadir, however, had come too far now to turn back.

Noon finally brought the cook to Camp Two, a full 12 hours after his solo ascent began along one of the most dangerous flanks of K2. There was no sign of life on the silent ridge. He checked each of the tents. Eventually, a lifeless Shaheen was discovered under a sleeping bag in a pool of vomit. He groaned; he was barely alive. Nadir quickly realised he would be unable to marshal Shaheen back to Base Camp alone; he could hardly stand, never mind walk.

An hour later, one of Marco Confortola's high-altitude workers, Mohammad Amin, descended from Camp Four. He was on his way to Base Camp; substandard quality clothing had brought his expedition to an end, and now he offered to help. Shaheen, despite his incoherence and incapacity, would have to climb down the mountain with the help of Nadir and Mohammad.

A barely responsive Shaheen managed to clip onto the fixed line with Nadir's guidance. The cook wondered how he was going to get his friend down the kilometre and a half to the safety and medical intervention of Base Camp. If he passed out, he would be too heavy to lower down the ropes. Shaheen was in a dangerously weak state: 'It took all the day to get down because I was not in good condition, I was vomiting. Three of us came down together – me, Nadir and Mohammad. If I had gone to Camp Three, maybe we would have had a serious problem. I continued vomiting, sometimes black.'

The pace was frustratingly slow and Shaheen passed out several times; Mohammad and Nadir battled to revive him with hot drinks and energy bars but he could keep nothing down. The descent took over six hours. When they finally made it to Base Camp before nightfall, the Serb expedition leader, Milivoj Erdeljan, was already on his satellite phone, seeking the advice of their team doctor back in Serbia.

The medic urged that Shaheen be taken to hospital as soon as possible, but there was no insurance cover for an airlift from K2's Base Camp. Shaheen swallowed pills and collapsed into his tent. The following morning, he was put on the back of a mule and accompanied by two porters on a harrowing four-day trek to Askole from where he was finally taken to the military hospital in Skardu.

The final night before their departure for High Camp represented a key opportunity for the climbers to rest well and prepare for the physical and psychological demands and challenges of the summit bid. Each of the five Norit team members reached Camp Three in good time, taking over an hour to dig out a foundation for their camp on a steep slope.

Finally, they settled into their tents – Wilco and Cas in one and Ger, Jelle and Pemba in the other. Ger and Wilco had put their argument of a few days earlier behind them; they made hot drinks and checked their supplies and personal items for the following day.

Hugues, Nick and their high-altitude workers had already proceeded up the ridge, aiming to encamp somewhere between Camp Three and the Shoulder to get a good head start for the top camp. Wilco warned them that such a plan was dubious and foolhardy; there were few, if any, natural ledges or shelves on which to set up tents below the Shoulder. But Hugues was resolute.

By the time they managed to locate a camping position, his group had begun to suffer from hypothermia as a result of the freezing squalls that blasted downwards along the Cesen. Hugues, Nick, Karim and Jehan huddled together, crammed into one tent, precariously positioned at 7,500 metres. Below, at Camp Three, just after 9pm, Pemba detected the first murmurings of strong winds.

Within an hour, they were in the grip of a full-blown storm, the gales reaching at least 100km/h and blowing spindrift across the mountain face and against their tents. Pemba was on high alert as the currents became increasingly fierce in the seemingly endless night:

> I could understand there was something wrong during the day. It was unnaturally calm and I thought there was something wrong. It was very sudden with high winds and snow. I was worried about the tent – it was quite extreme. We couldn't sleep.

In the neighbouring tent, Wilco and Cas were stupefied by the return of the hostile weather conditions, angered and dismayed at a second successive night of bruising winds which had the potential to derail their entire expedition. They decided to prepare for the worst; such violent gusts were enough to blow their tent and its occupants off the mountain. They donned their boots and down suits and huddled under their sleeping bags while the ferocity of the winds intensified. If the tent was to be ripped open by the gales, they needed to be ready to get out of there very quickly and salvage what essentials they could.

Wilco felt wretched, unable to sleep amid the thunderous flapping of the tent. K2 was beginning to exasperate him; he had hired highly qualified and experienced meteorology experts to supply weather data, but now, at a critical phase of the ascent, such expertise was being rendered irrelevant and useless. If these storms continued, who was to say such a tempest would not suddenly blow up as they climbed along the Bottleneck and the Traverse?

Wilco flicked on his small Canon camcorder and spoke into the lens as he lay huddled against the canvas, enveloped in his suit and sleeping bag, his voice barely audible above the turbulence: 'I think this is the moment when our expedition ends. It was all or nothing. We ended up in this storm and we'll have to see if no other expedition members are in trouble.'[72]

There was more than just the howling wind to keep Pemba awake that night. Close to midnight, a shriek nearby startled him and his tent companions. Was it the wind or the screams of another climber? Had somebody fallen from above? Pemba knew that Hugues and his companions were already above Camp Three, perched somewhere just below the Shoulder; in this storm they would be mercilessly exposed to K2's terrible gales.

Ger heard someone call his name; it was a voice he quickly recognised. Hoselito Bite, the bane of Wilco's expedition, had returned to torment his team yet again, but now he was genuinely in very serious trouble. Having left his own tent which he had perched near the Norit tents for the night, he was being blasted by 100km/h winds and was struggling to cope:

> ... the problem was the place where I built the tent. The wind took too much snow from my left side ... and slowly that snow started to push my tent down ... All the time I needed to sit in it and keep the tent in place. I couldn't leave. I couldn't start to boil the water... my tent in that moment was going up and me with the tent. I was very afraid and I dropped my legs to the left side, there was a wall [of snow]. I figured out that the wind was blowing under my tent and that there was a big possibility that my anchor would [be] crushed and I would fall down 2,000 metres; I would fly down.

A huge surge of wind and snow sent his flimsy one-man tent cascading down the mountain into the abyss. Hoselito had tried everything to keep it grounded but the gales ripped through the canvas, lifting it into the darkness just moments after he abandoned it to the storm. Left with nothing but his sleeping bag and down suit, he crawled around in the blizzard. His teeth chattered in the bitter wind. Five metres away, he managed to find the snow-covered dome in which Pemba, Jelle and Ger were huddled, sleepless and apprehensive. His cries barely registered above the freezing gusts.

Pemba feared that opening the door flap to let him in would force the tent to peel away from the ledge. Ger roared at Hoselito to use the rear entrance as it was more sheltered than the front one. A shaking outstretched hand reached towards them. Ger and Pemba hauled the freezing body inside, battling to shut out the spindrift piling high against the tent. Hoselito was panting and shivering, hardly able to talk:

> When I got inside I was totally white because of the wind and snow on my chest ... They put me on the sleeping bag and I started to shake ... and Pemba gave me water immediately to drink and Ger made me a place so that I can lie down, so I feel comfortable as possible ...

A tent which was already barely large enough to accommodate the three Norit team members now had another occupant. Getting any rest, on the night before the summit push would begin, would be almost impossible. There was only one option; Wilco and Cas in the adjacent tent had enough room to take Hoselito in.

Ger radioed Wilco, shouting as he was hardly able to hear himself against the wailing gusts pummelling the fabric around him: 'Wilco, this is Ger here. We have a situation. We have Hose here. He is hypothermic. We are going to bring him inside your tent because you have more space.'[73] Wilco was uncompromising, giving the Irishman's request short shrift. He had repeatedly warned Hoselito not to interfere with his expedition's progress; there was no way he was going to admit him to his tent; he had enough of the Serb who, he felt, now threatened the viability of the Norit expedition.

There was no doubt in Wilco's mind - Hoselito had to go down: 'If he had knocked on my tent, I would have said, "Go down immediately because I can't have you in my tent now. I have to rest because I have to go to the summit".' Nobody in Pemba's tent slept that night; accommodating the tent-less Serb in such a confined space forced them to sit up, unable to lie flat or get comfortable in the small, congested dome.

Alberto lay squeezed into a tent at Camp Three alongside three high-altitude workers. He had left his own tent at Camp Two having agreed to share theirs in return for helping them to lug gear up to the highest camp. They listened as the winds began to buffet the canvas and the guy ropes which were the tent's only anchor to the mountain. Some of the other tents on the ledge, which belonged to the South Korean and Serb teams, were broken when they arrived in the afternoon and Alberto feared their own cramped lodgings would also succumb to the winds.

About 10pm, a high-altitude worker reached Camp Three as the blizzard took hold. The weight of his gear and the equipment he was hauling from Base Camp for his team had hindered his ascent from the camp beneath, the final metres being scaled in the dark. A sense of obligation to his clients meant he continued, unable to leave anything behind. The stranded climber was forced to seek out lodgings from those already resident at Camp Three. Alberto heard his cries:

> He was asking us to open the tent door. He was almost crying. You could hardly hear him because of the fury of the wind. It was tremendous. We thought "Who is it?" He was completely covered in snow, completely white from the blizzard. He couldn't feel his hands. He was totally frozen. He came into our tent and there we were wrapping him up for three hours and five of us slept in that tent together. It was a long night.

By dawn on 31 July, the winds had finally eased. At Camp Three in the Norit tents, there was silence. Hoselito lay exhausted following his overnight ordeal. In an act of audacity for which he was becoming renowned, he took out his camera to film his tent companions. The silent, grainy footage portrayed a sombre Norit trio, after yet another sleepless night, wondering where the energy would be found to mount a serious summit push.

Pemba and Jelle looked ashen-faced, sleep-deprived and shell-shocked following the relentless battering of the night gone by. Ger sat by the door of the tent, motionless and mute, his head bowed. Hoselito perceived anger on the Irishman's face, although the Serb was unsure if it was directed towards him or towards Wilco for refusing to accommodate him just hours before.

Pemba and Jelle didn't speak, appearing pensive and reluctant to leave the warmth of their sleeping bags. Pemba realised that the summit bid now looked to be in serious jeopardy; the weather conditions were worsening and more unpredictable than ever. In the tent next door, Wilco was extremely worried about the unforeseen storms and was furious with the climatologists and meteorologists who had miscalculated the conditions. How could they have got it so wrong? Were there more storms in the offing?

The normally unflappable Dutch team leader thought the game was up and his Netherlands-based advisers were on the receiving end of his disgruntlement:

> We were phoning in over the weather forecast in Holland saying, listen, this can't be possible. You said there would be good weather and there is such a big storm ... the weather forecast man said, "I can't see any disturbance in a radius of 300 kilometres around us ... Trust me, tomorrow it will be clear and there will be no wind, there will be no wind anymore". So we were shouting through the radio, "Listen, this is not the kind of weather [in which] you climb K2. So let's abandon this expedition". We did everything, we gave everything. There's 4,000 metres of rope, we have invested a lot of money but we have to quit.

Wilco feared that the localised weather incidents were not being picked up by his meteorologist, Ab Maas; what if there was a similar storm at Camp Four? It was much more exposed and the climbers could be blown off the narrow ridge that would have to accommodate their tents. Wilco thought about his wife and son. K2 was such a focal point in his life, a raison d'être, but there were more important things to consider. For the first time since they had arrived on the mountain, Wilco contemplated failure. The eventual goal of the team temporarily exited his mind in an uncharacteristic and rare moment of doubt:

> We were not thinking of the summit actually because we were still not trusting this weather pattern because of this local thing, we were thinking maybe it will happen again and when it will happen we could be at Camp Four. We will go back because we don't want to take the risk that you are blown off the mountain above Camp Four. And that's very easy because you are such a tiny spot on such a huge mountain, with more than 100 -kilometre winds, with your big down suit, you are just flying through the air ... So we were saying it's not worth that. You know, K2 was important but it was not the only thing in life. We were really happy in life at home; it was just a passion so we should not be taking that big risk. I have a little son at home, so why should I go [on]?

He was not alone. Pemba expressed grave concerns about continuing. He was convinced the mountain was resisting their attempts to reach the summit by unleashing the worst of its weather:

> Now we had to make sure about the weather forecast. I was not comfortable for the summit. I said we have to make sure about the forecast because it is very unpredictable. Because otherwise we have to go back, we have to quit ... Jelle agreed with me that we should go back down.

For two hours, the team discussed their dilemma. Bailing out now would put paid to their last real prospect of summiting that season, but continuing upwards could put their lives at serious risk. By 8am, the wind had eased completely and Wilco made one more phone call on which would hang their decision to proceed or return to Base Camp.

Maarten van Eck insisted that the information he and Ab Maas had to hand pointed unmistakably to clear weather – no wind, no snow, perfect conditions: 'A case of beer for the team if I am wrong and a case of beer for me if I am right,' Maarten told Wilco.[74]

The Norit expedition was using a sophisticated computer model from the ECMWF (European Centre for Medium-Range Weather Forecast) to forecast climatic conditions on K2. Fed with the relevant data from a range of sources, it calculated the various extrapolations up to 50 times, resulting in complicated graphs with multicoloured fluctuating lines which showed the most likely outcomes. The closer a set of green lines converged on the charts, the more reliable the prediction. The result was a graph with a 'plume' of green lines, predicting wind speeds at the altitudes of seven, eight and nine kilometres.[75]

On the morning of 31 July, the lines converged and were tightly bunched together, pointing to perfect conditions in the days ahead. Wilco was reluctantly – but eventually – convinced. He trusted in the advice he was receiving and decided to roll the dice; the weather had settled, there was a stillness on the mountain as if no storm had occurred overnight. Conditions had stabilised again; the climbers were weary but focussed. Pemba and the others were reassured. They would continue to Camp Four.

Hoselito was still not countenancing defeat. He decided to brave Wilco's tent. His jacket, which he assumed had blown away in the blizzard, was wrapped around the guy rope of the tent where Wilco and Cas were now preparing their gear and he deftly retrieved it. The Norit team leader scowled when he learned that Hoselito was still intent on trying for the summit; he was planning to wait for the second wave of climbers and join in their attempt. Wilco told him he was crazy, that he must descend to Base Camp, that it was too dangerous.

The Serb used Wilco's stove to melt some water for tea and moved out of their way as the team packed their gear for the push to Camp Four. For Hoselito, Wilco's advice was 'not totally honest. I think somehow he liked for me to go down, because that's supposed to be best for him, not for me'. However, he eventually accepted his fate and bade farewell to the others as they clipped onto the fixed ropes once more:

> I just wished good luck to Ger and "bye" and see you after the expedition, and we will see each other in three or four days again in Base Camp ... I knew it was a dangerous trip and everything, but somehow I thought we [had] crossed the hardest part to Camp Three. Up over there will be rope on the Bottleneck, a good team will put the rope, the good team, not western climbers, that rope would be put by the Sherpa people and high-altitude workers ... That was the last moment.

Pasang Lama was the first of the climbers to reach what was about to become Camp Four, at an altitude of 7,900 metres, on the afternoon of 31 July. Despite climbing alien terrain on his first visit to K2, he had led the South Korean climbers along the ropes from Camp Three on the Abruzzi route where the same ferocious winds that hindered the Norit team's ascent had also delayed their departure.

On some parts of the spur, the ropes, fixed weeks before by the Flying Jump expedition, had disappeared, buried under heavy snowfall. Newer ropes were needed from time to time and, in fixing them, Pasang, despite his lack of experience of K2, was left to spearhead his team's ascent from Camp Three:

> We started our journey from Camp Three, we climbed as we had rope fixed through half the way, so it was not a big deal to come half the way, but after that we had to fix the rope and carry along the equipment. I was leading my entire team and placing the rope. As I was not well acquainted with the way to High Camp, I had to place the rope finding the way on my own. While I was placing rope, I saw a huge crevasse, I almost fell down ... but, as I had already placed the rope, I only slipped down a bit. After that, I climbed through the steep portion and with great difficulty reached the ridge of the High Camp.

Pasang glanced skywards to behold the view. He was alone, higher on the mountain than anyone else. Six weeks earlier, he had sat in a luxurious hotel in Kathmandu being served chilled drinks in opulent surroundings; now he was within reach of the second highest point on the planet.

The early afternoon sun was above and behind the summit, making it difficult to detect the outline of the gigantic ice Serac looming below and to the right of the summit ridge. It glimmered like a diamond in the afternoon light and its size and position on the ridge troubled Pasang; it seemed tenuously affixed to the mountain, liable to break away and plough downwards at any moment.

Pasang could just about make out the contours of the narrow funnel that led up the Bottleneck, which looked steep and treacherous even from where he stood. From the top of the Bottleneck, the route veered left across the Traverse, away from the perils of the Serac. Turning to look behind him, Pasang gasped at the peaks stretching in all directions as far as the eye could see, like a rocky bed of nails jutting out of the glaciers beneath. It was spellbinding and Pasang paused, soaking up the panorama as he awaited the arrival of Mr Kim and his team. He dropped his gear onto the hard snow; pitching tents at this altitude and in this exposure would not be easy.

One by one, Kim and the other South Koreans emerged over the ridge of the Shoulder – Ms Go, Hwang, Park and 'Little' Kim with their lead Sherpa and Pasang's cousin, Jumik Bhote. Mr Kim wasted little time in mobilising his team at Camp Four but soon realised that they had left oxygen behind at Camp Three: Pasang and Jumik would have to climb back down and ascend again before dark.

'Good job. Let's get the tents up, the stoves going,' a breathless Fredrik Sträng told his team-mates as they arrived at 7,900 metres.[76] He had reached Camp Four with another American team member, Chhiring Dorje. The Swede made sure to capture his first moments at High Camp for his documentary film, panning from the summit towards Broad Peak and its neighbours at the other side of the glacial valley. A gentle breeze could be heard on the microphone but the bright sun and warmth signalled that the best of the weather window was yet to come.

Fredrik looked up at the summit. 'The Bottleneck looks scary. Shit,' he said. The Serac glistened like royal icing on a Christmas cake; it looked intimidating. Fredrik turned his camera to Mr Kim, resplendent in his black and turquoise down suit, the lapel of which bore a miniature South Korean flag. 'How do you feel Mr Kim?' The rarely expressive leader allowed himself a smile: 'Yeah, good.'

A green-suited climber wandered over, exhilarated. Looking into the camera, Marco offered a 'Ciao' as he pointed to a handful of small orange-coloured flags he had placed in the snow a few metres above in the direction of the Bottleneck. The bright flags would help the trail-breaking party to find their route through the darkness in the early hours of the following morning.

Marco headed off to organise his tent. The Serac looked like a skyscraper to him and he felt insignificant beneath it. From below the ridge, Fredrik's camera captured Eric Meyer as he took the final steps along the route from Camp Three. He was immediately mesmerised by what he saw:

> The sun was out, the winds were calm. The views over the Karakorum range were absolutely stunning. There was just this amazing feeling of anticipation and elation having reached Camp Four. I think we all felt so fortunate to be in such an amazingly beautiful place, in such an incredible austere environment at that time.[77]

Below the Shoulder on the Cesen, Pemba edged higher; jumar up, ice axe in, crampon out, step by step. It was early afternoon and they were behind schedule but there would still be enough time to set up camp and get some rest before the summit push. Halfway to Camp Four, Pemba noticed the remains of the camp in which the French expedition had stayed overnight. He was astonished that

Hugues, Nick and their high-altitude workers could have survived on such an unstable and hazardous perch:

> I was 100 per cent sure they wouldn't reach Camp Four that day. They had
> to stay somewhere and I was thinking about that. And then next day I saw
> their campsite and it was quite an exposed area. We didn't sleep that night
> and they must not have slept either.

Pemba reached the Shoulder just before 5pm, the first of his team do so. It had taken almost nine hours to ascend from Camp Three, the journey delayed by the early morning deliberations over whether or not to continue with the expedition. The weather had improved, which augured well, but the depth of the snow on the ridge and the loose moraine below Camp Four on the Cesen route had taken Pemba by surprise.

He was forced to fix some additional rope along the route where the snow reached waist height. The Norit team had not previously been able to fix lines as high as Camp Four which meant the work had to be done on the way from Camp Three. They took it in turns to lead the way along the steep incline.

It was an arduous ascent but the conditions at 7,900 metres were impeccable. Pemba could see the Bottleneck and the Serac high above, but was not perturbed: 'I was trying to suss out if there was any Serac avalanche but there was no sign of that. I thought it was stable, quite stable.' He nibbled on a chocolate bar as he enjoyed the vista. The location for Camp Four was a gentle slope which would need some levelling to allow tents to be pitched.

Hugues and Nick were already setting up theirs, with Karim and Jehan sorting through their equipment. They had survived a horrendous night of bad weather a few hundred metres below the Shoulder and had been first to Camp Four from the Cesen route. Nick tried to warm himself in the sunshine. Most of the items in his backpack were still partially frozen following the subzero winds of the night before.[78]

On reaching Camp Four, Wilco's eyes were drawn immediately to the summit ridge above – a mountain on top of a mountain, he thought. The panorama featured many of the world's highest peaks, with a dome-like curvature on the horizon perceptible at such an altitude. Wilco felt so energised he could hardly wait for the next step of the journey. This was the highest he had ever reached on K2, a milestone in itself, and it was magical:

> I look around ... What a fabulous view, what overwhelming beauty. It is
> unrealistic to be so close to the Bottleneck. We feel like ants crawling

across a white bed sheet, so tiny on this huge mountain. We arrive at the Shoulder and it feels like a victory.[79]

Ger clambered towards Wilco, trudging through the snow, their argument of the previous days forgotten as they shared a celebratory moment together. Gasping for air and with tears in his eyes, this was an emotional moment for the Irishman who had failed to get this far up the mountain just two years before. Wilco turned his small camcorder towards his friend who was wearing climbing goggles and his Norit-logoed helmet.

Despite an increasing breeze buffeting the microphone, Ger's words were recorded: 'Ah, so happy to be here, I could almost cry. In 2006, we failed to get here but here we are now, and, ah, it's wonderful.'[80] From behind him, Cas entered the shot and thumped his team-mate on the shoulder; they'd made it.

The Norit team's snow shovels made slow progress on the surface as they sought out a level dais. They set up two tents, one for Ger and Pemba, and the other for Cas and Wilco. Jelle stayed with Marco and Roberto in their larger tent; one of Marco's high-altitude workers, Mohammad Amin, had descended and was now with Shaheen Baig at Base Camp. Only Mohammad Ali from Pakistan remained with the Italians at High Camp. The hiss of gas stoves soon became discernible from the dozen or so tents now in situ. Hydration was critical and the climbers took in as much liquid as they could.

Marco retched, nauseous from drinking so much sugar-laden tea but he knew that the long-term benefits outweighed the short-term drawbacks. There was little interaction between the expedition teams as they set about putting their tents up and getting comfortable inside. The trail breakers were due out at midnight, just hours away, with the bulk of the other climbers scheduled to leave from 1am onwards. There was a narrow window in which to rest and prepare for the climax of the expedition.

By nightfall on 31 July, there were 33 people at Camp Four with over a dozen other climbers bedding down for the night at lower camps. Mark Sheen was at Camp Three on the Cesen waiting to attempt the summit on 2 August. The second Flying Jump team, including Jumik Bhote's cousins, 'Big' Pasang and Tsering Bhote, and the Singaporeans were at the third camp on the Abruzzi, from where Robert Goh reported a temperature of minus 11 degrees and concerns about the acclimatisation levels of his team.[81]

Also on that route were Alberto Zerain and the Americans Paul Walters (Camp Three) and Mike Farris (Camp Two). In his final blog entry before departing for the summit, Mike Farris signed off until he would return to Base Camp in a few days:

> We will be carrying satellite phones on the mountain, so each member can contact his relatives if desired. That is a personal choice of each member. Even so, we have limited battery power so don't be surprised if you don't hear from us for many days. No news is good news! We may not post on the web again until August 5 or so. Maybe earlier, but don't count on it. All members are in good health and good spirits. We'll talk to you soon.'[82]

As the sun set over the Karakorum mountains, the atmosphere and mood at Camp Four were far removed from those at Base Camp just days before. The exhilaration and expectation of going to the summit had been replaced by the sombre realisation that the key moment of the expedition had arrived. As the climbers zipped up their tent doors for what they hoped would be their only night at Camp Four, they were alone with their thoughts. The silent, final hours before leaving for the summit tested the mettle of even the most experienced and competent climbers.

For some, especially the K2 novices, the adrenalin which had sustained them at Base Camp for the past two months was now replaced by nervous tension and apprehension about the objective dangers that lay above. The main source of concern was the forbidding and unstable Serac, with the climbers preparing themselves mentally for a high-altitude version of Russian roulette, testing the odds against what Cecilie Skog called 'the little monster' which was liable to send ice and rock hurtling towards the climbers at a deadly speed.

A few climbers phoned loved ones, others choosing not to for fear it might distract them from their psychological preparations. The tug at the heartstrings from the end of the phone line could be enough to convince some climbers to turn around. Others, though they might not admit it, privately hoped that the weather might worsen, providing an excuse to descend and leave the desolate and godforsaken place behind them.

Inwardly, thoughts and emotions jostled with each other – the obligations to sponsors, the longing to be with loved ones, the expense of having reached this point, the fear of injury or worse. But, for most, the pre-summit push time at Camp Four was the culmination of years of training and fundraising, extensive preparation and logistical planning; it was the zenith of their careers and a once-in-a-lifetime opportunity which they were not about to forego.

The plummeting temperatures and the adrenalin pulsing through his veins prevented Cas van de Gevel from sleeping. He couldn't warm his feet despite trying to do so with a flask of hot water.[83] Notwithstanding his discomfort, Cas' mind kept returning to the day ahead and the prospect of claiming his first 8,000er. He noticed how introverted other climbers had become, with the elation and relief of having reached Camp Four being replaced by a contemplative silence, each climber focussing on their own mental composure.

The team now seemed secondary to the individual, with everyone needing to dig deep into their own reserves and competencies. Nothing could prepare you for the mental toll of those final hours, Cas thought: 'The ... difference above 8,000 metres is that everybody is taking their own decision. Do I go on or do I return?'

Pemba made a deliberate decision not to sleep, focussing on the task that lay ahead just a few hours later. Though they were joyous that they had reached the threshold of their common goal, he and Ger conversed little as they tried to settle into what comfort they could derive from their cramped tent. Like Cas, Pemba was perceptive to the subtle shift in mood among his fellow climbers and the other expeditions. Base Camp seemed a world away:

> I found most of the climbers quiet inside the tent and trying to take a short nap. There was not too much conversation. In my experience, when I compare people in Base Camp and High Camp, they are totally the opposite – it is totally different. When those people are talking in Base Camp about safety, about equipment, about the schedule, they are talking too much in Base Camp about everything. And when they are in High Camp, they are almost quiet; they don't want to speak and become quiet.

Despite his vexations and discomfort in his tiny, freezing tent, Wilco was philosophical as the time ticked by:

> ... everything is freezing because it's only one layer of the tent. So outside it's minus 30 and inside, it's maybe plus 10 so you have a lot of condensation so we were complaining. Ah, shit, little tents and this and that, but the most important thing was we were drinking, drinking, and melting, melting snow ... We were just waiting and we were happy because everything was just in time and on schedule.

A kilometre away, in the bleak darkness, the summit stood sentinel above the sleeping visitors, awaiting their incursion.

A Deadly Ascent

31 July – 1 August

Pemba Gyalje poked his head through the door of his tent into the crystal clear night. Camp Four was silent; many of the almost three dozen climbers had only just settled down for a few hours' sleep before setting off for the summit in the early hours of the following morning. Although he hadn't slept, Pemba felt primed for the work ahead. He knew that the trail-breaking party had to begin their preparations and get moving quickly so they could capitalise on the good weather that had been predicted for days and which had arrived right on cue.

Beside him in the tent, swaddled in his sleeping bag, lay his Norit team-mate, Ger McDonnell. Nearby, Wilco and Cas lay sleeping in their tent. They and the other climbers wouldn't wake for several more hours when they could enjoy the security and guidance which the ropes set by the trail breakers would provide.

Pemba yanked on his boots and crampons; stepping onto the frost-encrusted snow, he felt a sharp blast of cold air and noticed immediately that the weather was near perfect; it was calm and dry and there was no sign of the high winds that had besieged the various expeditions as they climbed to Camp Four. Once outside the tent, Pemba detected a lack of activity around him. Where were the other trail breakers and why weren't they getting ready, he wondered. In the stillness of the Shoulder, no sounds emanated from the other tents which were pitched close together.

Pemba noticed that Hwang Dong-jin, the South Korean expedition deputy leader, who had been nominated as the leader of the trail breakers at the Base Camp meetings, had not yet emerged from his tent. The otherwise mild-mannered Nepali was exasperated by Hwang's inactivity and failure to organise his team:

> I went to the Korean tent and knocked there. Jumik Bhote was inside and I asked where the climbing leader, the chief of the trail breakers, was. It was now time to get ready ... Jumik said he is here, he is inside here smoking. And he didn't came out, no response, no talking. And then I told Jumik,

Chhiring (Dorje) and the Pakistanis we should get ready because we have to sort out all the equipment. But everybody was inside the tents; they didn't want to come outside ... I was shouting outside the tents, "Wake up", calling for equipment, but everyone was asleep, like they had taken a drug.

The behaviour of those at Camp Four seemed bizarre to Pemba. This was D-Day, in which climbers had invested passion, money and years of their lives; it was time to move, but lethargy seemed to have taken hold. Perhaps, he thought, some of the climbers were succumbing to the travails of life in the outer regions of the Death Zone, their movements more sluggish, their thought processes slowed.

In his experience, at this stage of a summit bid, everyone involved in breaking trail would be preparing for the climb ahead, cross-checking gear and supplies and preparing to depart on time. Pemba approached Wilco's tent and asked him what to do. Roused from his slumber, the Norit team leader replied, 'I don't know. Ask Mr Kim'.

Pemba confronted the South Korean leader, who was pottering around outside his tent, and asked him why Hwang had not taken charge. Mr Kim shrugged, saying he had already told his deputy to get going; Pemba fumed. Eventually, he heard the long-awaited rustling of sleeping bags in other tents, the zipping up of down suits and the hacking coughs – known to many as the Khumbu cough[84] – that pierced the deafening stillness at 7,900 metres above sea level. Camp Four was slowly coming to life but nobody was co-ordinating, organising or taking control.

Hwang eventually roused himself but Pemba thought that he seemed morose and sullen, little interested in fulfilling the role for which he had been chosen:

> Then finally the climbing leader also came outside the tent and he joined us, but he was not enthusiastic, he was not like a co-ordinator, he was very quiet, not speaking. He was carrying some equipment and then he just followed the group. He was not acting like a co-ordinator; he was absolutely very, very quiet.

Mohammad Hussein, a high-altitude worker with the Serb expedition and a member of the trail-breaking group, approached Pemba. He told him that a key member of the leading party, Shaheen Baig, had taken ill at Camp Two the previous day and had been forced to descend to Base Camp due to vomiting and cramps.

Pemba realised that Mohammad was now the only climber at Camp Four who had previously summited K2 and also the only one with experience of the route ahead. The absence of Shaheen created a dearth of leadership at this critical stage of the summit push.

There was another problem; the South Korean climber chosen to quartermaster and co-ordinate the equipment and rope for the trail breakers, Park Kyeong-hyo, had failed to do so. He had been expected to do an inventory of the gear required before the trail breakers embarked on their ascent, an essential task on any expedition in which ropes and other climbing gear are checked and distributed to key personnel. But Park was nowhere to be seen and Pemba was not impressed.

Out of the darkness, Pemba saw a figure emerging from the shadows – it was a man whom he had only laid eyes on a few times before at Base Camp. Alberto Zerain approached, his head torch dazzling Pemba momentarily in the black darkness. 'I am Alberto from the Basque Country. I am ready for the summit. I am ready to help the trail-breaking team,' he told Pemba.

Alberto detected an aura of safety, confidence and security in Pemba; the Spaniard would do whatever he could to assist him and those placing the ropes. Fresh in his mind was the request made of him by Shaheen Baig to take his place on the trail-breaking party and smooth the passage to the summit. Alberto had brought a few items of gear which the Pakistani guide had given him; he planned to put them to good use.

It had taken him just two hours to scale the Abruzzi route between the third and final camp. He did so without using the fixed ropes and despite the darkness and jagged topography. He now intended to head straight for the summit as soon as the trail breakers were ready. The 37-year-old was surprised to see so little movement around him apart from a few shadows moving about in the dim light inside a couple of tents. He put his head into Marco's tent; the Italian told him that the trail breakers would leave at midnight. Alberto stepped away and waited:

> I was there an hour waiting ... because I was thinking they are going to break this trail and I'm going to help. I'm not in a hurry. Why should I head off up front when there are Sherpas going up when I can go up with them and between us all, maybe we can do it. I also thought I'd wait because the night was really dark. It wasn't a good idea to go up so early ... To try and go alone, to go solo, I thought it was too dark, too deep in the night. So I thought I'll go slowly, go with the Sherpas and that's what I did.

Having gathered what equipment he could find, Pemba, along with Jumik Bhote and Pasang Lama, began to pile the coils of rope, five non-lock carabiners,

11 ice screws, three rock pitons, four snow pickets, and a few bamboos on the snow in the centre of Camp Four. There were 780 metres of rope in total – 480 metres of five millimetre spectra rope from the Norit team and 200 metres of eight millimetre static rope from the Italians, as well as another 100 metres from the South Koreans.

During the Base Camp meetings there had been a lot of talk about how best to ensure the safety of climbers returning from the summit to Camp Four; this was an issue of concern because most climbers would be returning in the dark in an exhausted condition, and it was agreed that having a well-marked route would aid a safe arrival at High Camp.

The American team said they had fishing line which they would bring to Camp Four to fix the route towards the bottom of the Bottleneck, but Pemba could see no sign of it when he was checking the equipment. He wasn't unduly perturbed, however, thinking that the fishing line might be placed later, and began to distribute the rope among those waiting to break trail, each climber taking lengths of between 50 and 100 metres.

Chhiring Dorje, from the American team, joined the trail breakers at the centre of the encampment. He had hesitated about participating in the path-finding process over the previous weeks, but now he was well and truly on board. In the leadership vacuum at High Camp, Chhiring immediately recognised Pemba's innovation:

> As the Korean leader was not responsible enough to distribute the rope, Pemba had initiated the job and he and Jumik were responsible enough to carry on the job. I joined them and ... we decided to start at 12.30, so we rested in our tent and had a cup of tea.

After midnight, the 10 trail breakers checked their head torches and adjusted their down suits, each placing a coil of rope and other equipment in their rucksacks. Along with Pemba and Alberto, the team included Mohammad Hussein and Mohammad Khan from the Serb expedition, Mohammad Ali of Marco's team, Chhiring Dorje from the American expedition, along with Hwang Dong-jin, Park Kyeong-hyo, Jumik Bhote and Pasang Lama from the Flying Jump expedition.

One of the biggest challenges in making the advance party work efficiently and effectively was not immediately apparent to anyone. The most obvious test for the diverse group of climbers – many of whom had only met each other for the first time in the previous weeks – was communication. The language barrier which presented itself among the trail breakers was largely overlooked when they were nominated for the role at Base Camp, but it soon became clear that communicating the most basic instructions to the team members was going to be a problem.

It was something which Lars Nessa and others had detected at the Base Camp meetings. The group spoke a diverse range of languages and dialects – Korean, Balti, Urdu, Nepali, and Spanish, among others. There was no common language which allowed instructions, questions and commands to be conveyed with certainty and clarity.

And the one climber who had sufficient linguistic knowledge and ability to understand and exchange commands and responses with all of those setting the ropes was Shaheen Baig, now recovering from gastric problems three kilometres below at Base Camp. He had a sufficient grasp of each of the varied vernaculars among the trail breakers to ensure that instructions would be clearly understood and acted upon.

The group's nominal leader, Hwang, did not have any English, the language that was the common denominator between the numerous teams on the mountain. Park Kyeong-hyo had a little more English but seemed reluctant to use it. Were there to be any doubts among the trail breakers about what they were doing, any requests for clarification, any discussions about where and when ropes would be placed, such interactions would be extremely difficult.

Camp Four was located at approximately 7,900 metres above sea level and, just after 12.30am on Friday, 1 August 2008, the advance party who were entrusted with laying out a guiding line for the other climbers who would follow later, were about to cross the boundary that leads into what mountaineers call the Death Zone, those far reaches of the planet above an altitude of 8,000 metres in which human life is unsustainable for longer than a few days and, in some cases, for much less. Life at Camp Four was barely tenable – now the human body was about to be further suffocated by the depletion of oxygen and forced to confront the likelihood of hypoxia and oedema.

The terms 'Fatal Zone' and 'Lethal Zone' had been coined by a Swiss doctor, Edouard Wyss-Dunant, in a research paper as far back as 1953, in which he vividly described the conditions for climbers above 8,000 metres:

Survival is the only term suitable for describing the behaviour of a man in that mortal zone which begins at about 25,500ft. Life there is impossible and it requires the whole of a man's will to maintain himself there for a few days. Life hangs by a thread, to such a point that the organism, exhausted by the ascent, can pass in a few hours from a somnolent state to a white death. This depends first on the age of the subject, and then on his reserves of energy. It is now no longer a question of adaptation, but only of the number of days or hours allotted to the strongest persons.[85]

Chillingly, Wyss-Dunant added that, above 8,000 metres, climbers are obedient only 'to that euphoria which is nothing but an anaesthesia of the organs of control'. From the moment they left Camp Four, how the trail breakers and the climbers behind them would cope with the privations and punishing demands of this 'mortal zone' would colour every decision, influence every step and impact on every thought as they battled to push their bodies and minds to the limits of endurance.

With only his head torch to pierce the blackness of the night, Mohammad Hussein led the trail breakers away from where they had gathered to spearhead the setting of the first section of rope. His fellow climbers had told him that he should lead as he was a previous summiteer. It was four years since he had walked the route to the summit, with an expedition from China.

His experience and that of the now-absent Shaheen Baig made the pair two of the most knowledgeable climbers on the mountain in the summer of 2008, but they had made little public play of their experience. The American, Chris Klinke, for example, was under the impression that, of all those on the mountain that year, only Shaheen Baig had summited K2 previously.[86] The humble Mohammad's track record was largely overlooked.

At Base Camp, Shaheen and Mohammad had privately agreed that if either of them fell ill, or could not make it to the higher reaches of the mountain, one would take up the other's role and the associated responsibilities.[87] Now Shaheen's friend found himself leading the trail breakers out of Camp Four. The South Korean deputy leader showed little or no interest in taking the initiative, so Mohammad began his advance onto the Shoulder's snowy ridge. Every so often, a different climber would take his place in the lead as the trail-breaking party rotated their positions. They scanned the ground ahead of them, the glow from their head torches lighting their way.

For the first hour or so, the trail breakers' pace was fast and steady. The small, orange flags which had been placed by Marco Confortola the previous evening helped them to find their way. After that, the conditions underfoot became more difficult, with unexpectedly deep snow in some places, at times up to knee level. It made for slow progress as the trail breakers were forced to shove snow aside and away from their path.

About 350 metres from the camp and after trudging across the snow for almost an hour and a half, Mohammad Hussein plunged the first silver-coloured stake into the snow. It crunched deep into the freezing surface; a rope was tethered to it and uncoiled along the ground.

Mohammad didn't consult anybody about where to install the first anchor point for the fixing of the ropes and nobody questioned his decision; he was in front, he knew the route and the dangers of its terrain. Further back on the trail-breaking team, Alberto was surprised at the early placement of ropes on a plateau that he considered reasonably safe and navigable:

> I was surprised that they should put fixed ropes at areas which really didn't need it. At least I thought that it was easy. Even if someone has a higher [skill] level, a lower level, ropes weren't necessary. They shouldn't have been fixed there. [I was] thinking because they wanted to take the weight off the Sherpas. If they left the fixed rope maybe they could get rid of some of the weight, maybe that could be the explanation.

Whatever Alberto's opinion, he didn't make any comment. Where to set the ropes had been the subject of much discussion at Base Camp and Mohammad and several others were under the clear impression that ropes needed to be fixed along the Shoulder to ensure safety, especially following the death of a Sherpa who slipped and fell from the ridge the previous year.

On 20 July 2007, 33-year-old father of two, Nima Nurbu Sherpa, from Nepal, the sirdar of the South Korean Dynamic Busan K2 expedition, had fallen from the lower part of the Bottleneck while ropes were being placed for the rest of the team. He had unclipped from a fixed line and slid rapidly downwards until he disappeared over the south-east ridge of the Shoulder, making no attempt to self-arrest.[88] Pemba had seen pictures of where the experienced climber had died. His understanding was that the Sherpa had fallen from the Shoulder about halfway between Camp Four and the Bottleneck: 'We had a lot of information about that Sherpa, how he fell down, where he fell down.'

The trail breakers may also have felt a need to cater for the varying degrees of technical proficiency and abilities among the climbers still resting at Camp Four; though the terrain may have been relatively manageable for the lead party, others may not have found it so. Perhaps the trail breakers had also been subconsciously influenced by Mr Kim's suggestions, though rejected by other teams at the preparatory meetings, that more rope should be placed both above the top of the Traverse and below the bottom of the Bottleneck to maximise the safety of the would-be summiteers.

Pasang Lama seemed to have been so influenced. He was second in line behind Mohammad and declined to discourage him from placing the first snow stake where he did. Whatever about the 2007 accident or the individual concerns of the trail breakers, Pemba, despite thinking that the ropes were not needed for someone of his capacity, was under no illusions about the agreement from the Base Camp meetings about where the ropes ought to be set down:

> We had decided already in Base Camp that when we find hard and icy snow surfaces, even if it's not very steep, if we find that type of slope then we immediately start to fix ... the majority of people decided at Base Camp that when we find that type of difficult slope, icy and hard, we will fix it immediately. When exhausted people slip it is impossible to self-break, then they continue to fall and it is quite dangerous. That's why we started to fix ... For me it was a waste of time, but for other people it was necessary because everyone has a different capacity.

As he did on all the mountains which he climbed, Pemba regularly looked back along the trail to assess the terrain and his position so that he could pick out reference points and recognise the topography on his descent, especially if it was dark. A point of reference, be it a rocky outcrop, an icy incline or a flat ledge, could act as a life-saver if he deviated from the right path.

There was little conversation between the trail breakers, apart from some talk in their own languages among the Nepalese and Pakistani members. Hwang, from the South Korean team, said little or nothing, taking no commanding role, giving no instructions, and Pemba despaired at his lack of leadership.

The snow became deeper and increasingly difficult to navigate as the climbers zigzagged their way towards the Bottleneck. The varying climbing abilities of the trail-breaking party became apparent to Pemba, with some of the climbers struggling more than others in the challenging subzero conditions. Notwithstanding the deep snow, the men were encouraged by the near-perfect weather conditions that greeted them on the slopes above Camp Four. It was bitingly cold but there was no wind and a calm had settled over the mountainside, the trail breakers' peace of mind compounded by the fact that the summit and the domineering and deadly Serac were not yet visible in the darkness.

Inside his tent at Camp Four, something told Wilco that there was a surprising lack of movement in the tents around him, as if climbers were somehow reluctant to begin their preparations for the summit push. Why weren't more people out of their tents, he wondered. Beside him, Cas was still struggling to get his feet warmed up. Shortly after midnight, the Dutch pair began to melt snow for their drinking water flasks.

Wilco did a quick inventory of his equipment, opting to leave some safety gear behind, including a GPS tracking device and a lamp. He didn't need them; the conditions were ideal. And, anyway, every item left behind reduced the weight he had to carry and allowed for an easier and faster ascent. Anything which lightened the load, no matter how small, was a plus.

By 2.30am, Wilco and Cas were setting out from Camp Four with their teammates, Jelle Staleman and Ger McDonnell. Cas' feet had warmed enough to allow him to get moving without discomfort. A sense of anticipation rose within him:

> ... the feeling that we could do it was there because otherwise we would not have gone up. That feeling had always been there. There never was any doubt that we couldn't do it because ... when I was looking around I saw that we were a very strong team compared to other expeditions.

Standing outside his tent, Marco peered towards the summit and, despite the absence of any moonlight, he was able to make out the shape and contours of the towering Serac above the Bottleneck. On waking earlier, he had felt extremely well, physically and mentally, but his friend, Roberto, was cold, urging Marco to proceed without him; he would catch up with him later. Marco turned on his head torch and departed Camp Four on his own, reassured when he found the coloured flags he had placed the previous evening jutting out of the snow.

Lars Nessa tried to put his concerns about the meetings at Base Camp in the previous weeks behind him as he folded up his sleeping bag. From the outset, he and Rolf Bae had been troubled about the excessive detail which had gone into co-ordinating the joint summit attempt by the various teams at Camp Four, minutiae which he believed left little room for improvisation. For a time, the Norwegian team had considered bringing their own ropes, ice screws and anchors for the Bottleneck and the steeper snow in case they had to fix the route to their own satisfaction.

Lars was worried about the absence of Shaheen Baig and noticed how the other Pakistani guides were so dependent on him. Maybe the Norwegians would have to be self-reliant if the trail breakers did not succeed in their task? Lars realised, however, that carrying so much equipment was not realistic; it would only weigh them down.

The focus now had to be on the day ahead. The narrow weather window meant that they would likely have just one serious shot at the summit. For Lars, it was beyond his wildest dreams – he had never before been above 6,200 metres and now he had a chance to get to the top of the second highest peak in the world, 8,611 metres above sea level. Lars, Rolf and Cecilie melted snow at 2am and the team drank tea, setting out just before 3am. Several others had yet to depart. Despite abandoning plans to bring enough rope so that they could fix the Bottleneck and Traverse independently, Lars stashed 50 metres of spare rope in his rucksack in case of emergency.

Jehan Baig, the Pakistani high-altitude worker with the French expedition, was noticeably sluggish and disoriented as he prepared to set out for the summit, and his climbing abilities were being sorely tested. His journey to the highest camp had not been without incident following his sacking by the Singaporean team for what they perceived to be inadequate skills and expertise on Jehan's part. He was also adjudged to have been insufficiently acclimatised. Those same problems were now re-emerging at a critical juncture in the expedition. As he prepared to leave Camp Four, Jehan complained of a headache and was given medicine by Hugues, who was impatient to get moving.

The Frenchman had postponed his departure from the mountain to avail of this long-sought weather window. He could do without any problems on this crucial morning and reprimanded Jehan for his tardiness. It had taken Jehan over half an hour to get his crampons on and he struggled with his head torch.[89] As a result, it was 2.30am before the three French team members left camp. His team-mates should have recognised the seriousness of Jehan's symptoms but, in their collective urgency to leave camp, the obvious signs of altitude sickness in their climbing partner were discounted.

Nick Rice intended to set out from Camp Four just behind Hugues and their two high-altitude workers. But a simple accident delayed him; while preparing to make tea, Rice tipped a pan of hot water over the socks he was about to pull on. He waited until they had dried and got going at about 3.30am but, a short distance from camp, Nick was cold. His feet and hands had failed to thaw: 'I realised that my hands weren't about to warm up, and I wasn't ready to lose my fingers for the summit of K2.'[90] He turned around, realising he was too late to catch up with his team and unlikely to reach the summit that day. He got back into his sleeping bag at Camp Four and fell asleep within minutes.

Eric Meyer, Fredrik Sträng and Chris Klinke were out of their sleeping bags by 2am. Fredrik checked his video camera equipment and hoped that he would finally get some momentous footage for the documentary he was making. The travails of the Abruzzi were behind them: it was time to focus on the summit. Everybody on the team felt physically strong, it was a perfect night; it was a great opportunity. A couple of hours earlier, Chhiring Dorje had left their tent to join the trail breakers. Fredrik and the others felt reassured that the Sherpa would play a productive role with them and plot a way forward to the summit.

An orange dawn broke over K2 at about 4.45am as the trail breakers made their way towards the bottom of the Bottleneck. Above them was the steep and narrow passageway through which climbers needed to ascend to reach the diagonal Traverse which led to the snowy incline beneath the summit. There were alternatives to using the Bottleneck – also known as the gulley or the couloir – but they involved perilous climbs over treacherous, snowless rocks further across the south face which left little or no room for error, and required a longer, circuitous climb to the summit snowfields. The ExplorersWeb website left those following the expeditions online in little doubt about what now lay ahead of the climbers:

> The crux of the route – the Serac-threatened Bottleneck and the horribly exposed and icy Traverse to the summit slopes – is a classic of mountaineering literature. Add bottomless snow, icy rock pitches, and terrifying exposure, this is the place for K2's greatest history of triumph and tragedy. A 100-meter narrow 80-90 degrees couloir at 8,300 meters, the section is windswept and cold, and the ice in this couloir can create extremely challenging, sustained climbing.

Fixing the tricky and frequently unstable ice on the Bottleneck was always a challenge. The trail-breaking team were encouraged by the warm sunlight that bathed the slopes. But the rising sun also brought an ominous lurking hazard into sharp focus – the menacing and glistening overhanging ice above the Bottleneck, known to everyone as the Serac. The Serac had been dubbed the 'Motivator' by the eminent mountain climber, Ed Viesturs, and it was easy to see why.[91] It is one of the most prominent features of K2, like a huge tidal wave of ice that has swept over the summit and which is suspended in time a few hundred metres above the Traverse.

At over 60 metres in height and a kilometre across, it is the most significant of what mountaineers refer to as objective dangers on K2, like a ticking time-bomb that could blow at any minute, sending shards of ice at high speed onto the plateau below. And though Viesturs noted that the Serac has been remarkably stable in recent years, it is always susceptible and responsive to the warmth of the sun during the daytime.[92]

When it freezes hard in the depths of nighttime, any water which has flowed between the cracks and crevasses during the day, freezes and expands. This expansion is akin to pouring nitroglycerine into the ice, and the continued expansion and contraction of water between its crevasses causes blocks of ice – from the size of ice cubes to sections weighing half a ton – to break away from the Serac and submit to the inevitability of gravity. If a climber happens to be in the way, survival is unlikely.

But, because the Bottleneck - an integral part of the most accessible route to the summit of K2 - lies directly beneath this overhanging menace, spending time under it is inevitable and unavoidable. Speed is of the essence. "We had a lot of respect for the Serac. We knew it was a little monster up there," Cecilie Skog said. The trail breakers tried not to think about the Motivator and its ominous presence.

As 5am approached, Pemba and Alberto were the first of the trail breakers to reach the foot of the Bottleneck. The team had left Camp Four over four hours earlier and progress had been slow in places owing to the depth of the snow. Now the trail-breaking conditions began to deteriorate further. From about 200 metres below the Bottleneck, the situation underfoot startled Pemba:

> The snow conditions were very bad. We were almost swimming, me and
> Alberto. We were the two in front. The snow was very deep and we were
> both swimming up to chest level. For other people behind it was not like
> that because, for them, there was a proper trail. We were waiting a long
> time for the others at the bottom of the Bottleneck ... they were not very
> fast, they fell behind.

Alberto and Pemba took time to examine the Bottleneck up close, craning their
necks to assess where ropes might be placed and to identify the best locations for
the anchor points. Tired of waiting for the rest of the team, Alberto decided to
take the lead and began to ascend the steep incline with a coil of rope and several
ice screws. He noticed that many sections of the couloir were covered in deep
snow which made it difficult to gain purchase for his ice screws. He was already
concerned that too many people would end up dependent on too few anchor
points. Spreading the anchors too far apart presented its own dangers but they
needed a firm hold in the ice – that was more important.

Standing at the bottom of the Bottleneck in the brilliant light of the new day,
Pemba got his first close-up view of the Serac, looming above him and Alberto:

> I observed it clearly from the bottom of the Bottleneck and I saw that
> the Serac was completely dangerous, completely dangerous, but I believed
> that we were lucky. God bless us, that's all. But I was not thinking too
> much about the danger because I was thinking this was a good day for
> me, a good day for everybody. I believed that even though we were under
> the Serac and it was extremely dangerous, any time ready to fall, it would
> not be today.

Alberto made his way up the couloir, showing no signs of fatigue despite
having risen at Camp Three nine hours earlier. The heat of the sun warmed him
and he felt more energised than ever. His decision to abandon the nearby Broad
Peak and his re-location to K2 seemed to have been vindicated.

Pemba followed in his footsteps just metres behind. Due to the difficult
snow conditions, it took the two men one hour to fix lines on the Bottleneck,
somewhat longer than Pemba would have expected. By the time the line fixing
was complete, the remainder of the trail breakers and some of the other climbers
had arrived at the bottom of the Bottleneck.

From there, Pasang Lama watched as the domed horizon slowly changed
colour, the rising glow in the east signalling a warm day. Far below, a blanket
of low-lying cloud covered most of the neighbouring peaks, only a few jutting
above the plumes. But, despite the increasing warmth from the rising sun, Pasang

felt apprehensive. Hours earlier at Camp Four, he had been worried that the trail breakers did not have enough rope to secure lines all the way to the top of the Traverse; he believed that they were at least 100 metres short.

But Pasang Lama, now on his first summit push on K2, was willing to trust Mohammad Hussein – after all, he was the only trail breaker who had summited before. His South Korean clients knew what they were doing. And Pemba Gyalje had exuded nothing but composure and competence. Pasang could see Alberto powering ahead through the Bottleneck and he tried not to allow his eyes drift even higher to the enormous slabs of the Serac which were now shimmering brilliantly in the sunlight.

Pemba soon joined Alberto at the top of the Bottleneck; they both remained fixed by their harnesses to the gulley's highest anchor point. The 200-metre ascent had been tricky in parts although it had troubled the seasoned pair little. Pemba anticipated that it would be some time before all the climbers would get through the Bottleneck and he sought out the safest place to wait, out of the path of K2's notorious objective dangers; he made his calculations and found a spot that he considered the least likely to be in the line of fire should the Serac disgorge a lethal load of ice:

> There was a small ledge, enough for only two people. Where I fixed the anchor for my personal safety is quite steep with very hard ice and I made a step with my axe and a bucket seat. It was very difficult for other people [further down the Bottleneck] because the ice condition was very hard; even crampons didn't work here.

Some of the trail breakers were still making their way to the foot of the couloir; others seemed hesitant to go any further until the ropes were placed at the beginning of the Traverse. Alberto had fixed a secure line to the top of the gulley and another 200 metres of rope were needed for the Traverse. It was time to use the supplies which the other trail breakers had brought. Pemba shouted to his colleagues below: 'Who has rope? We need more rope for the Traverse.'

The members of the lead party began to check in their rucksacks. Asked if he had rope, Mohammad Ali, one of the Italian team's high-altitude workers, replied 'No.' But hadn't he brought his allocation of rope from Camp Four? Whether the guide, apparently experiencing high-altitude sickness, had left the rope behind or forgot that it was in his bag remained unclear. None of the others searched his backpack.

Jumik Bhote was carrying 100 metres of rope which was part of the allocation agreed at Base Camp, but they were still 100 metres short. Jumik and Chhiring Dorje wanted to ensure they had the full complement required for the Traverse before the consignment was relayed up the line to Pemba. There was one viable option: some of the lines used to set the trail below the Bottleneck would have to be removed and taken higher for the fixing of the Traverse. It would delay the placing of ropes for a period but it seemed like the only solution.

By 8am, the final climbers had arrived from Camp Four and a human bottleneck had begun to form below the Bottleneck itself. The various expedition members were incredulous; by this stage of the ascent, all of the ropes to the top of the Traverse should have been in place to facilitate a steady and uninterrupted climb towards the summit.

On arriving at the bottom of the couloir, Cecilie and the rest of the Norwegian team noticed that many of the South Korean climbers were sitting on the snow with their head torches still on despite full daylight. She heard the shouting from above: 'We don't have any more ropes.' Wilco van Rooijen's patience was wearing thin:

> We just saw that they were complaining there was no rope anymore. So we were thinking how in God's sake is this possible? We discussed it many, many, many times. So we said listen, the only thing you can do is go back, cut the rope and bring it up and then that's what we did.

Chhiring Dorje moved down the line and sliced a knife through the rope which lay resting on the snow. A number of climbers doubled back to collect the cut ropes and bring them back up the Bottleneck. With her team-mates, as well as Wilco, Cas and Ger, Cecilie moved down the Shoulder, gathering the ropes that had been severed. The South Koreans still hadn't advanced as the other climbers took up their positions in the Bottleneck again and clipped onto the ropes, waiting to ascend. The sun beat down on them, its rays bouncing brilliantly off the glimmering ice.

By the time Cecilie and Rolf reached the upper parts of the Bottleneck, doubts about the entire enterprise began to cross Rolf's mind: he was uneasy about the pace of the ascent – it was already mid-morning and an early afternoon summit time was now looking unattainable. The later in the day the summit was reached, the later the return to Camp Four.

Ascending in the dark was rarely too difficult, but a descent in the dark was a completely different matter. If any of the other climbers on the mountain felt similarly, they kept their thoughts to themselves, but Cecilie and Rolf voiced their concerns to each other about how slow the ascent had become and the possibility that they might have to turn around:

> We stopped at the top of the Bottleneck because we were talking about this – that it was taking so long. We stopped many times ... we thought okay if this is going to continue slow and not organised like this, we always wanted to stop and see if we wanted to turn around.

Equipped with the additional rope which had been sent up from below, Pemba began to belay Alberto across the Traverse. Still affixed to the anchor, Pemba fed rope using an Italian hitch through his crab to the Spaniard as he made his way slowly forward; if Alberto slipped he was tied to Pemba who, in turn, was tied to the top anchor. Once Alberto had inserted a new anchor and tied a rope to it, he could use the new anchor point for safety.

Halfway across the Traverse, Alberto made an unexpected but welcome discovery; there was old rope from an earlier expedition still tied to previously installed anchor points on the ice. Perhaps it was there from the year before? To Alberto it looked undamaged and secure. Pemba was reassured that it was in sufficiently good condition to act as a fixed line for the climbers below:

> I was on an anchor. [Alberto] set the new fixed line and then met the old fixed line and I was still belaying him. This is about halfway across the Traverse, and then he told me, "Okay, now, belay off because I have rope here", and he told me it was good rope. We used the old fixed line.

The discovery of the old line, which ran all the way to the top end of the Traverse, meant that the 100 metres of rope that Jumik Bhote still carried were not required. On reaching Pemba, he asked him what he would do with his rope:

'Maybe I should leave it here or will I bring it to the summit?' If the old line Alberto had found was not strong enough, they would need Jumik's allocation; even if the old rope was sufficient, Jumik should bring it anyway. 'Bring it with you,' Pemba told him, 'we might need it for an emergency later.'

From his position at the top of the Bottleneck, Pemba could hear the Serac creaking above him. He tried not to dwell on its overwhelming size and its Sword of Damocles position over the Bottleneck. He had now spent an hour at the head of the couloir. He glanced downwards and could see a long line of climbers stalled below. They were anxious to move on and the Traverse had not yet been fully fixed with ropes.

The South Koreans, the Norwegians, the Norit team and the Americans wanted to make it through the Bottleneck as quickly as possible. They did not want to spend a moment more than necessary underneath the Serac. Even when ice or rock comes loose several metres on either side of the Bottleneck, the debris is often funnelled towards and down the gulley, usually obliterating everything in its path.

Pemba was disappointed to see that his team-mates had not ascended before the South Koreans. At Base Camp, he had repeatedly urged Wilco, Ger and the others to get ahead of Mr Kim and his comrades. His experience had taught him that the South Koreans were traditionally slower ascending mountains, more laboured and methodical in their approach:

> I told them, try to avoid the Koreans because I know them and they are
> very slow, poor technique, you guys must be in front of the Koreans ... if
> you are behind them and other people then you are stuck somewhere, that
> means you have to wait behind.

Instead, Pemba's team-mates and the members of the other expeditions were now interspersed along a line of climbers which had become stationary and increasingly agitated.

Below him, Pemba could see climbers unclipping from the fixed lines. They seemed to be losing patience; some were overtaking their fellow climbers to try to get out in front. The trail breakers at the base of the Bottleneck implored the climbers to wait their turn and maintain a safe distance from the climber above them. The calls fell largely on deaf ears. The trail breakers had overcome the problem of the shortage of rope but now the presence of so many climbers, so tightly knit together, all of whom would be reliant on so few anchors, presented a potentially lethal hazard.

Pemba could count about a dozen climbers reliant solely on the top anchor alone, each of them apparently oblivious to the danger:

> Because we had a long distance between the anchors in the gulley the majority of climbers kept climbing very fast and they came tightly on the fixed line which was secured to the top anchor. There were almost 10 or 12 climbers on the line and that made me quite afraid because if 10 people are hanging on the one single anchor it is sometimes really dangerous because the anchor could break.

The point where the Traverse ended and the more navigable snow plains that led to the summit began could not be far away, Alberto thought, as he inched his way along, looking for a suitable berth for the final ice screw. This would be the last anchor point before the climbers would heave themselves onto the steep slopes beneath the summit and leave the fixed lines behind. Alberto found the last phase of the climb through the Traverse – on a gradient of 80 degrees – to be the most technically demanding. He reached a very steep and narrow passageway which he was forced to lie down on and crawl through:

> The Traverse, at first it's hard snow and ice until you get to an area where it's all ice and where you are using your pick. It's an area between rock, ice and snow and you're using your ice axe. It's a delicate area, difficult. I used two ice screws for that Traverse and then there's a passage where you get to the left hand side. That's the most complicated ... It's easier if you lay down on it and in that way you can crawl across and use your feet to support you, it's really difficult.

When he had placed the final anchor at the top of the Traverse, Alberto hoisted himself over the ridge and onto the long, crevassed snowfield which led towards the summit of K2. The soaring apex of the mountain was finally visible; it had remained hidden to the climber as he had edged his way through the Bottleneck and across the Traverse. The summit was closer now, yet it still seemed so far away.

Alberto moved away from the top of the Traverse, out of sight of the climbers still making their way along the ice beneath him. The old rope had fitted the bill; the others could not be far behind, he thought. He sat on the snow and waited. Across the vista, the top of Broad Peak was below him at 8,046 metres, looking almost insignificant beside the colossal summit of K2.

Eric Meyer and Fredrik Sträng from the American team and the Italian, Roberto Manni, were the last climbers to leave Camp Four at about 5.30am. A stomach upset had delayed Fredrik's departure but he and Eric felt buoyed and encouraged by the settled weather conditions. Like the others, they were surprised to see how close to High Camp the fixed ropes started. Fredrik had brought the agreed fishing line for fixing along the Shoulder but didn't place it: 'The bamboo sticks were not put out so I could not fix my fish line to mark the Shoulder.'

They made their way several hundred metres out onto the Shoulder from where they could see a chain of stalled climbers in what looked like a human traffic jam just below the Bottleneck. Fredrik and Eric knew that something was amiss. They still had some way to go to get to the couloir; if the queue hadn't moved by the time they got there, it would be far too late to ascend further. They stopped to consider their options.

Fredrik took out his camera to film the stationary queue beneath the most hazardous danger on the mountain – the tonnes of crystallised ice of the Serac lurching over them. He was puzzled and infuriated by what he saw:

> They should be at the Traverse by now and I was so devastated, I was so disappointed. We are not going to make it. We are too late. And that's when I realised for the first time that it's over. You put in so much effort, so much energy fighting and struggling to making this happen and you have this perfect day. And then you just realise that there is no way that we are going to be able to summit and come back down in daylight and I was not prepared to take that risk. Not a chance in the world.

Eric slumped onto the snow and fidgeted with his gloves: 'Words cannot convey how crushed we were. You have put so much into the climb at that point, you have so much invested.'[93] The two men confronted the inevitable. They felt no compulsion to radio those ascending the Bottleneck to urge them to turn around; they were experienced climbers and would make their own choices. Checking their watches, they knew they had a momentous decision to make. It was a difficult judgment call but it came quickly: they would turn back.

At this rate, the climbers might not reach the summit until late afternoon and Eric and Fredrik did not relish the prospect of descending in the dark. The mountain would still be there next year; it wasn't worth going any further. They might even get an opportunity a day later if the weather held good, but another night in the Death Zone would further deplete their energy and stamina. Dejected and annoyed, they turned around and were back at Camp Four within two hours.

'It is exhausting to wait, to be in a queue – you can't climb at your own pace,' said Lars Nessa, who was dismayed at the delays now unfolding in the Bottleneck. Self-sufficiency and individual responsibility were core to the Norwegian team's mountaineering ethos, and Lars was already beginning to regret that they had not gone it alone, but co-operation with others could not now be avoided. Above him and below him, other climbers stalled:

> When we finally got to the Bottleneck there was a great queue there, the Korean team in front and there were other climbers there following ... I didn't feel very safe to be on the fixed rope that I [hadn't] put up myself and also [being] together with so many other climbers. So me and Oystein we decided to climb on our own by the side of the fixed ropes.

Pasang Lama found himself waiting near the top of the Bottleneck. He unclipped from the fixed line to rest, his breathing hastened by a reduced oxygen intake. Mr Kim appeared; his Flying Jump team were making their way through the Bottleneck but they had ground to a halt, as had the long line of ascenders behind. Pasang looked down at the stationary chain. Seconds seemed like minutes. Some climbers clipped off the fixed ropes, searching for somewhere to rest. Others fiddled with their oxygen bottles. Some unzipped their down suits in response to the unexpected heat.

Stalling on a steep gradient for any length of time put pressure on all the limbs as the climbers tried to beat their crampons into the ice to get a grip on any available natural or man-made step, always difficult on a sharp incline. Instead of using the fixed line for its designated purpose – as an anchored handrail to be used as a safety device in the event of a fall – the climbers were now placing hundreds of kilogrammes of weight on the rope, using the anchors above to ease the pressure on their limbs.

Wilco looked for a perch on which to rest. He unclipped from the rope, moving to one side. He decided to leave his rucksack behind. It contained a thermos flask, ski poles, a balaclava, spare gloves, goggles, sun cream and a small first aid kit.[94] Such was the delay, he wanted nothing to hinder his ascent from this point; he would collect the supplies on the way down. He drank from his flask and tucked his camera into his down suit, still eager to capture the elusive photograph of his team at the summit.

The wait had become too much for some climbers who were struggling to adapt to the demands of being in the Death Zone; Jelle Staleman from the Norit team and Chris Klinke from the American expedition were both battling headaches and recognised the need to stop. Reluctantly, they turned and began their descent to Camp Four. Soon after, Mohammad Khan of the Serb team and Mohammad Ali from the Italian expedition departed, their rope-fixing duties having been completed.

Chhiring Dorje waited in line. Marco and Wilco were just above him, trying to rehydrate and opening their suits to cool down. Chhiring spotted the potential for a serious accident if one or more climbers slipped or fell from the fixed lines, which were now dependent on just over half a dozen anchors inserted in the warming snow, not to mention the perils for those temporarily untethered from the lines.

Experience had taught Chhiring to bring spare ice screws with him on expeditions and this situation called for their use. From his rucksack, he retrieved a screw and inserted it in the ice beside him, tying his harness to the independent anchor: 'There was a traffic jam and if they got carried away, everyone would get flushed so I made my own anchor.'

Moments later he heard a grunt and a scratching noise. Wilco had re-clipped himself to the rope but had slipped from where he stood, crashing into Chhirring and the Serb, Iso Planic. The Norit team leader had been trying to traverse to the right of the Bottleneck to find a ledge where he could wait but his crampon hadn't gripped. He slid no more than two metres, the rope holding him upright, but the teeth of his crampon ripped Iso's suit. The tumble reminded those around Wilco of the inherent dangers of their situation. Chhiring watched as the feather lining from Iso's clothing floated down the mountainside.

The climbers crammed into the Bottleneck tried not to look directly above at the wall of glistening ice that is K2's iconic and sinister-looking Serac. Instead, they looked left to the Traverse, the incredibly steep section which they would have to cross from the top of the Bottleneck to reach the path towards the summit. As Pemba observed the others, he noticed that they seemed transfixed and entranced by the Traverse, anxious to cross it as quickly as possible.

The climbers were hoping to pick up the pace, ensuring that Pemba's warnings about overcrowding on the ropes and the treacherous blue ice beneath the thin crust of the Traverse were largely ignored:

> When those people who had already reached the top anchor saw that the Traverse section was fixed, I was trying to convince them that from here they must climb one by one on that section. There was a short anchor on the Traverse section, not like on the gulley ... I was telling them from here to climb one by one, but then the people wanted to keep climbing. I said no, first some strong people ... the others must wait below and then after they should climb one by one, don't make a rush for it, but nobody understood that. Everybody wanted to go in front and then that makes a lot of traffic on that technical terrain ... Crampons don't work on that ice. It is like glass, so you have to be on the fixed rope at all times.

Roberto Manni had not felt well from the moment he left Camp Four hours earlier. He had a pounding headache and was sweating; his body was buckling under the severity of conditions in the Death Zone and pushing himself any further would be counterproductive and dangerous. He returned to his tent to rest and recover from the nausea he was experiencing and, by 10am, he managed to rise and move out of his tent.

As his eyes squinted in the mid-morning sun, Roberto tried to make out the line of climbers beneath the Serac – they looked like tiny ants on an anthill from that distance; ants that were not moving very fast. Within minutes something caught his eye on the mountain above; it was moving, rocketing down the slope beneath the Bottleneck. He cried out.

Hearing Roberto shout, Fredrik Sträng and Eric Meyer jumped from their sleeping mats and clambered out to the space between the tents. They cast their eyes upwards. 'Look! Look!' Roberto shouted. What looked like a human form could be seen clearly on the snow hundreds of metres away. Somebody had fallen.

At 8,300 metres, Cecilie Skog was trying to manoeuvre her way to the top of the Bottleneck and onto the Traverse. It was approaching 10.30am. As the fixed lines were secured, the climbers had begun to pick their way along the ropes from the top of the couloir. Finally it seemed that the logjam of people below was about to be freed. The ice was blue underfoot on parts of the Traverse, requiring the climbers to use the front points of their crampons and ice axes to secure purchase on the crystalline, rock-hard surface while remaining tethered to the fixed ropes at all times.

Cecilie tried not to look up at the gargantuan Serac. Face to face with it, the climbers could see little else in their line of sight but the multi-storey blocks of ice and the deep crevasses of which it is comprised. Ahead of Cecilie were several South Korean team members and she could also see some of the trail breakers further along the line. Not long now, she thought. The heat of the sun warmed her as she stalled briefly so that others could pass her and move forward; several climbers were becoming frustrated by the pace of the ascent and, in their impatience, were trying to overtake the slower climbers.

Dren Mandic of the Serb team was a short distance ahead of Cecilie near the beginning of the Traverse, and he seemed agitated. The 31-year-old carpenter and amateur zoologist from Subotica in Serbia needed to replace his oxygen cylinder. The only safe place to do so was a small, flat outcrop of rock further back along the line near the top of the Bottleneck where his team-mate, Iso Planic, had already stopped to replenish his supply.

Dren needed to double back; trying to change his oxygen bottle while hanging from a rope and relying only on his crampons for grip on a near-vertical wall of ice would be absurd. Out of the corner of her eye, Cecilie saw Dren approach from just above her to the left. He wanted to pass by her to get back to Iso, and she pressed herself close to the frigid ice to allow him climb around her.

Moving adjacent to Cecilie, Dren unclipped his carabiner from the rope and was in the process of stepping around her in what should have been a relatively uncomplicated procedure. He tried to get a grip on the ice with his right leg as he manoeuvred. But, for a fleeting moment, Dren lost contact with the fixed ropes, his left boot skidding from under him. He had unclipped on one side of Cecilie, but he hadn't clipped on the other side. Then he slipped and took her with him. Cecilie was suddenly falling downwards and she shrieked in horror.

Within seconds, her jumar had pulled tight, holding her on the ropes. She spun round and came to a shuddering halt, her back now to the mountain, hanging there like a puppet on a string. In desperation, and with nothing connecting him to the ropes above, Dren reached out to try to bear-hug her, but he slid away at high speed and, without his ice axe, which had fallen, all attempts at self-arrest failed abysmally. There was nothing to hold onto on the slick-like ice. From the Bottleneck, Rolf Bae looked up and roared his wife's name, 'Cecilie! Cecilie!'.

Several metres away, Pemba heard a woman scream. He looked down just in time to see Dren slip from the line and pull Cecilie off her position on the fixed ropes; he saw her stop suddenly as her jumar engaged. The Serb continued to freefall like a stone, and Pemba thought he saw Cecilie trying to grab Dren as he plunged. 'Oh my God!' somebody shouted. Emitting a guttural wail, Dren plummeted further and further, passing right by those climbers still in the Bottleneck. Their heads turned like dominoes as they watched him rocket downwards.

Suddenly, Dren came to a halt a short distance below them and, within seconds, he bounced to his feet, like an unloading spring. Lars Nessa noticed him stand up. He waved, as if to say, 'I am okay, I am okay', and Lars felt relieved that Dren had survived the fall. But, immediately, the disoriented Serb flipped backwards in an awkward cartwheel motion and began to slide again at speed. He plunged a further 300 metres across the ice, his body hitting some rocks and coming to a halt several hundred metres below the Bottleneck. This time, he didn't stand up.

Dren's team-mates had seen him fall. Iso Planic and Predrag Zagorac, with Mohammad Hussein, their only remaining high-altitude worker, had been waiting to move across the Traverse. Predrag and Mohammad roared Dren's name as he hurtled past them and, within minutes, all three Serb team members were rappelling downwards, the other climbers moving aside to allow them descend: they had to rescue their friend.

Zooming in with the lens of his camcorder to create an improvised telescope, Fredrik Sträng quickly located a body splayed about 300 metres below the Bottleneck. 'How can someone fall on this perfect day?' he thought. 'No wind. It's bright, it's great. How is it possible?' As soon as Eric realised there had been an accident, he radioed the only American team member on the slopes above. 'He is still moving,' the doctor heard Chhiring Dorje say, 'and he needs medical help.'

Turning to his team-mate, Fredrik said, 'We have to do something. I'm going to save this guy'. His companions weren't sure what to do. Chris Klinke had just returned from the foot of the Bottleneck, discommoded by headache, and Roberto Manni was still suffering badly from the effects of high altitude.

Fredrik decided to consult with those at Base Camp; he knew that he and the others at Camp Four could be affected by hypoxia and cognitive problems brought on by being at a high altitude, and consequently handicapped in making a sensible decision. 'We were not as smart as the people down in Base Camp so we wanted their neutral suggestion,' said Fredrik, 'and when we got their approval after explaining our situation we started to arrange all the materials.'

Eric delayed no longer; he knew his expertise would be required and he rushed to grab a medical kit from his tent. Fredrik hurriedly assembled what he would need when he got to Dren – oxygen, water, a sleeping bag, a walkie-talkie. 'I'm going to save this guy. There's no way he's going to die, not this day,' he yelled. Having taken off his suit in the warmth of his tent, he quickly re-dressed and he and Eric set out from camp, the Swede ascending much quicker and some distance ahead of the Colorado medic.

The climbers bunched underneath the Serac who had witnessed it were shocked by Dren Mandic's fall. It was a horrible accident. But he was an inexperienced climber, some of them thought; he had been careless but was probably still alive. Accidents like this happened all the time, they reasoned. The Serbs had gone down to tend to him; they could do no more to help. Their reactions unsettled Pemba who was shocked at what he perceived as the lack of empathy shown by his fellow climbers:

Only a few climbers were talking about how long he fell, whether he was alive or not, a short conversation between a few climbers. But the majority of climbers were quiet for a few minutes, then afterwards they continued to climb. But nobody was asking or saying what do we do now. There was not a big conversation about the accident. Just a few climbers were talking about how far down he fell and whether he was still alive and what happened.

Pemba began to feel deeply uneasy about what was happening around him. Dren's fall was an unfortunate accident but had drawn into sharp focus the dangerous consequences of the delays that were afflicting the ascent and the inability of some of those climbing to deal with the hazards of the most difficult sections of the mountain. Climbers had carelessly unclipped from fixed ropes, some had mindlessly overtaken their peers, and others were panting heavily and floundering on the ice, evidently ill-prepared and inadequately trained for the physical demands of the terrain.

Pemba was exercised about the physical limitations of many of the climbers and concerned about their ability to reach the summit. The further into the Death Zone they climbed the more compromised they would become, he believed. The private conclusions he had drawn about the skills and capacity of some of the mountaineers during their time at Base Camp were being confirmed in the harsh reality of climbing in the Death Zone.

For an hour, he had watched from the top of the Bottleneck as several climbers struggled to climb the fixed ropes and cope with the delays, disregarding basic safety procedures, whether through altitude sickness or inexperience:

> The other climbers did not understand very well about safety, they did not try to maintain the distance and maintain the anchor ... they wanted to climb and they forgot about the traffic and the majority of the safety measures. The majority of climbers were always hanging on the one anchor and it was too close ... There was a lack of oxygen or something. People could not think; they were unable to think.

Even Pemba's own team had failed to get ahead of the South Koreans and other teams despite his repeated advice. Enough had gone wrong to make him believe that the summit attempt was not meant to be; it was time to consider a retreat. Of the Norit team, only Ger was nearby, and Pemba approached him: 'I spoke to Ger. I said to him, "Physiologically, now I am not very well so what do you think? Maybe we should go back down?".' He hoped Ger would convince Cas and Wilco to reconsider the summit bid. 'He [Ger] looked at the other people on the line on the Traverse section,' said Pemba, 'and he looked at the sky, and he said the majority of people are still climbing and we have good weather so we have to keep trying for the summit.'

Pemba considered returning to Camp Four alone; he was disillusioned with what he considered 'dirty climbing' and the failure of other climbers to recognise their own limitations and the toll the mountain was taking on them. But his team were unprepared to entertain his fears. Wilco reassured Pemba: the Serbs had gone down to help and the Norit team could still make the summit. Ger and Wilco had not yet begun to cross the Traverse and didn't want to delay any further.

'The weather was good,' said Wilco, 'there was no wind, nothing was falling down; no avalanches, no rockfall, nothing. So we just moved on.' Unlike the Norwegians and others, descending the Bottleneck in the dark was not an issue for Wilco; there was plenty of time.

Pemba stalled, drifting to the back of the line of climbers and allowing them to ascend ahead of him, partly to reflect and gather his thoughts, and partly because of the dangers along the fixed ropes:

> After that I always stayed behind the team, I did not try to go in front. I was prepared to stay a little bit separate from the others because I did not want to have five or six or 10 people on one anchor, so I prepared a separate anchor to stay away from the traffic, and that's why I stayed behind.

His dilemma was now acute. He felt deeply apprehensive about progressing, but he also felt that he owed his team a loyalty and commitment to assist in any way he could to make their summit push a success. The pressure on him to advance further was palpable, entrapping him in the desire of others to proceed:

> I couldn't say to them we have to go down, I couldn't say that ... or you guys keep climbing, I want to go back. Because Wilco and Ger, both of them, they were expecting 90 per cent summit chance when I was with them. During the trekking and the Base Camp stay on the mountain, they said this time we could summit because we have a good team and you are here. They had a big expectation from me about their summit chances, they said this easily. Ger said this time we could summit ... At Base Camp and at the other camps we didn't talk a lot about what to do if it was too late, about a turnaround time. But we did talk about if something is a problem with you, you must go down; it was left up to each person

to make that decision, the whole team would not turn around. But my solution is always that the party [should] stay together on the mountain.

'The climber is alive,' Pasang Lama had screamed when he saw Dren come to a halt, 'he is moving his leg.' He shuddered when he saw the body flip over again and tumble hundreds of metres backwards and across the ice. Notwithstanding the mind-numbing brunt of the Death Zone which appeared to anaesthetise the climbers' reflexes and responses to what they had seen, Pasang was shocked by the others in the Bottleneck, seemingly inanimate in their reactions to the plummeting climber: 'I questioned my profession at that instance ... not a single climber reacted.' The western mountaineers seemed unmoved by the accident, he thought:

> That is what shocks me there, a human falling down and the climbers have no reaction. I saw the whole incident. I was shivering. Maybe they couldn't visualise the whole accident, they didn't want to see what happened, they, without any comment and reaction, just carried on with what they were doing.

Cecilie, now restored to her position on the fixed rope, tried to think clearly. She had seen Dren stand up after his fall and saw him slide again but had no reason to believe he was dead. She convinced herself that he would be alright. Camp Four was sending help and the Serbs had descended.

Despite her shock, Cecilie had made up her own mind to go on. Weren't accidents and death part of mountaineering anyway, and weren't they synonymous with the 'Killer Mountain'? Should the fall or death of another climber – not even a member of your team – jeopardise your own summit bid or that of dozens of others? She thought not:

> I understand that people think we are mad and that how can you continue if someone died but ... how to explain it to people that don't understand ... You drive a car, you see people crash. You see people die in traffic and you keep on driving because you think it's not going to happen to you ... I've seen dead people on mountains before, on Everest, people that have been there for years ... if you don't think that people die on these mountains then you haven't prepared at all.

Cecilie observed that Pemba was sitting down at the top of the Bottleneck, pensive and agitated. He wanted to descend but Ger wanted to keep going, just a little longer. It sounded familiar to Cecilie: 'Yeah, to go just a little bit more. That's the thing, it's so hard to turn around and it's so easy to continue just a little bit, just a half an hour and see.'

Lars Nessa had seen Dren jerk backwards when he first landed below the Bottleneck. Then Dren disappeared out of sight. Lars' instinct told him it was time to retreat. Apart from the fall of another climber, the amount of time he and his team were being forced to spend beneath the Serac was troubling him:

> We wanted to descend, both to help him down and also because we got scared. All the mess with the ropes, we were delayed because of that and this accident made us want to descend immediately when he fell. The main tactic to avoid the dangers of the Serac is to be fast to minimise the time when you're exposed to it. So it didn't feel good to get exposed to the Serac for that long time. And you want to be fast when you're traversing. And you could be if the fixed rope was there before you arrived. So it was not with a good feeling we were waiting there.

A quick discussion with Rolf and Cecilie changed Lars' mind, however. The Serbs were going down to help Dren; there was little point in sending anyone else to help, they thought. Hemmed in on either side by other climbers, the Bottleneck would not be an easy place to descend from anyway. Moving out of line would force others to be displaced temporarily and cause further hold-ups.

Despite his personal reservations, Rolf suggested that the team would review their position at the end of the fixed ropes, but would continue for now. If they remained on target to have summited and returned to the fixed lines before dark, they should go on. Their team-mate, Oystein Stangeland, decided to call it a day, however. He was tiring fast and didn't think he would make the summit. He bade farewell to his friends, hoping to see them all back at Camp Four soon.

After Dren fell, Chhiring Dorje admitted to himself that he was scared. Such was the volume of climbers in the Bottleneck and the evident risks they were taking in unclipping from the ropes to rest, that he feared others might face the same fate as the Serb: 'If we don't stick or clamp ourselves strongly with the rope, we will be carried away in the same manner. That was bothering me a lot.' Every so often, small chunks of ice and snowy debris fell near him as climbers above him battled to find a foothold for their crampons, displacing shards of ice in the process; it was dangerous in the extreme.

But Chhiring's unease acted as an incentive to move on up and get out of the area as quickly as possible rather than as a spur to turn around. Pemba told him it was too risky, the snow had been too deep, the ice a struggle for many climbers; they should turn back. 'No,' Chhiring told Pemba, 'as we have come a long way without oxygen and it is only [a short] distance more to the summit. Let's go, we are almost there.'

Marco Confortola insisted that the group had enough time to get to the summit. Unperturbed by the Serb's fall – death and accidents were ever-present in mountaineering and couldn't be avoided – for Marco, the decision to advance was a simple one. 'Let's go to the Traverse and let's climb the peak,' he told those near him. He thought that two hours had been lost because of delays with the ropes and the reaction to Dren's fall, but there was still time to reach the summit. In 1954, the first-ever climbers to reach K2's peak had summited at 6pm, he told his fellow climbers; it was still eminently doable.

But was it now two hours to the summit? Was it five hours? How long would it take? Would the climbers have to descend in the dark? Inherent in Marco's argument was a potentially fatal flaw. Unlike Everest, which has become intimately familiar to mountaineers and on which the schedule for a summit attempt can be closely timed and co-ordinated, the pool of knowledge and experience of K2 is much shallower, simply by virtue of the fact that, relatively, so few climbers have been there.

In fact, it is a summit to which few ever return – to date, only three people have summited K2 twice.[95] Nobody on K2, at this point in time, had ever been to its summit before, now that the two previous summiteers, Shaheen Baig and Mohammad Hussein, were no longer on the ascent.

Even with people with such experience on the expedition, Pemba believed that it was not possible to get a full picture of what climbing K2 entailed: 'We cannot get perfect information from them because they are only one-time K2 climbers, they don't have that much clear information. The one-time summit experience is minimal for everybody for every mountain.'

The lack of familiarity made K2 much harder to plan for and, deep in the throes of a summit attempt, climbers were bereft of experience or information to calculate their position and distance from their goal. Lars Nessa observed that some said one hour where others said four or five. Confusion reigned about how long it would actually take to reach the summit:

> If it was one hour it would be perfectly fine for everyone to get to the summit, if it were five it would be dangerous ... I remember Ger said that when you get around here you will see the summit and get summit fever. So he was warning us that if you plan to descend you should probably not continue to where you can see the summit. It's not that easy to make that decision.

Immediately after Dren Mandic's plunge from the Bottleneck, some of the other climbers began to shut out of their minds not just his tragic fall, but also how long the climb was taking and any niggling beliefs that the summit bid was falling behind schedule. Many climbers dismissed thoughts of retreat, ignoring their watches, any advice they had been given, any notions of a turnaround time. Nobody seemed willing or able to critically evaluate their situation. Few were willing to challenge the consensus and suggest what may have been thought but remained unsaid.

One analysis of the sort of groupthink behaviour which can become pronounced in the Death Zone has suggested that it is 'associated with people retaining the status quo by minimising their conflicts without critical assessment, analysis and evaluation. Motives may vary but essentially those involved seek to avoid standing out in the crowd and any risk of embarrassment'.[96] Morality and any understanding of the right and wrong things to do on a mountain become distorted as the oxygen-deprived brain cells thwart independent analysis and thought.

The norms and ethics which operate at sea level can easily change by necessity at high altitude to suit the blurred decision-making processes and confused actions of the climber. Inwardly, the individual justifies their actions by reference to the hostility of their alien surroundings and is more easily influenced by the decisions of the majority. Alberto Zerain recognised that subtle shift during the ascent:

> Experience tells us there are cases where people don't help, where they continue towards their goal and leave behind the other person. We could even say abandoning them. And the difference between this and normal altitudes where people live at 1,000 or 1,500 metres above the sea level [is] those kind of human attitudes get confused a lot.

No universal laws of morality can explain the diversity of reasons climbers use to justify going on when things start to go wrong - advancing further and further when it is too late in the day, or continuing to climb when every muscle and brain cell is ravaged by oxygen depletion. The allure of being the first from one's country to reach the top, the kudos to be had from friends and family, the financial rewards from summiting, are among the drivers that cause some climbers to dispense with ethical norms and excuse themselves from the blame or guilt of breaching those standards.

It took the Serbs approximately 30 minutes to get to their stricken friend, about half the time it took Fredrik Sträng to arrive from Camp Four. The scene that greeted the Swede shocked him: Predrag Zagorac, the Serb team climbing leader, was kneeling over the fallen climber, administering mouth-to-mouth, as Iso Planic and Mohammad Hussein looked on in disbelief. Dren Mandic's badly battered face was still warm but there was no pulse. Predrag radioed his team leader at Base Camp. Milivoj Erdeljan told him to terminate the expedition immediately.[97]

K2 had claimed its first victim. 'He hit on the rock. He lost control, kept falling for 200 more metres and stopped,' Predrag told Fredrik as they stood over the crumpled remains. 'He was wrapped in rope and giving no sign of life, already pale and grey with cuts on the head, nose broken, blood from mouth, totally finished.'[98]

Fredrik had brought his video camera and recorded what Predrag told him. In their shock and grief, the Serbs decided they wanted to take Dren's body to Base Camp, a suggestion which struck Fredrik as ludicrous and nearly impossible. Lowering a corpse from a steep mountain was never recommended and, if it had to be done at all, it would take a dozen or more people, not a handful of climbers who were already exhausted, shell-shocked and probably hypoxic after so many hours in the Death Zone.

One of the most important tenets of mountaineering is to never jeopardise one's own life or safety if and when a fellow climber is endangered. Dead bodies should be left where they are. Notions of burial or moving a body to somewhere more appropriate should never be entertained. Fredrik realised that moving Dren's remains from such a precarious position was a near-impossible task:

> Put a straw in your mouth, tape your nose and put 40 kilos on your back and walk up a stairway and you get a feeling of how it is at that altitude. Then picture yourself dragging a body which is 100 kilos with all this gear and everything ... then you get a good sense of what it feels like, after not having slept for five days.

Had he known Dren was dead, Fredrik thought, he would not have come up from Camp Four. But Dren's team-mates were traumatised and grief-stricken; their expedition over, they just wanted to bring their friend's body down. Fredrik felt a certain sympathy for Predrag and Iso. He gave them chocolate and water, trying to take stock of their physical and mental states.

He now had to decide whether to leave the Serbs to their own devices or help them bring the corpse to back to Base Camp. A compromise was finally reached; they would attempt to move the body down to Camp Four where Dren could, at least, be given a proper burial. Despite his reservations, Fredrik agreed to help.

Shortly after Dren fell, Jehan Baig started his descent from the Death Zone. Ever since he had climbed out of his tent at 2am, Jehan had not been feeling well. His expedition leader, Hugues D'Aubarède, had asked him to bring some extra oxygen bottles to the top of the Bottleneck. He had just done so and now he wanted nothing more than to get back to his tent. Jehan's visit to K2 had been a litany of misfortunes and mishaps.

Sacked by the Singaporean team for an alleged failure to comply with instructions and for poor climbing techniques, his friend and mentor, Shaheen Baig, had secured a place for him on Hugues' team. The 32-year-old from the Shimshal Valley had won high acclaim for rescuing a Japanese mountaineer buried in snow on Gasherbrum II the year before, something which was a source of great pride to his two young sons.[99] But that now seemed like a very distant memory.

The impact of several hours in the Death Zone on K2 had taken their toll. Those around him on the Bottleneck sensed Jehan's disorientation and sluggishness. Some recalled his battle with his crampons and his obvious delirium hours earlier as he prepared to leave Camp Four. But Jehan was alert enough to realise he needed to descend. Hugues wished him well; he would continue to the summit with his other high-altitude worker, Karim Meherban. Climbers beneath Jehan on the Bottleneck stepped aside to allow him to get down, and his clumsiness on the descent irked many of them.

Cas van de Gevel saw a figure climbing down straight into his path. He noticed that the Pakistani was using his jumar to come down the rope although the device was only to be used for ascending. Cas warned him that what he was doing was extremely dangerous but Jehan seemed not to care, telling Cas he always descended like that.[100] Wilco looked on in disbelief; Jehan was evidently incoherent and dangerously unsteady. He was the fifth climber to have retreated from K2's upper slopes since dawn.

The Serb flag, which had been brought for what was anticipated would be the team's victorious pictures at the summit, was used to wrap Dren's bruised and bloodied head. His legs were tied together at the ankles and his body swaddled in the sleeping bag Fredrik had brought from Camp Four. As the rescue party wrapped up the remains in as dignified a way as possible, they noticed another climber approaching from above. It wasn't Eric – he was still making his way towards them from below.

Jehan Baig, now descending quickly and becoming increasingly debilitated by altitude sickness, had stumbled upon them and offered to help. It didn't take long for Fredrik and the Serbs to realise that Jehan was clearly unwell and confused. But he was another pair of hands, which was welcome in the attempt to move a 90-kilogramme body down the slippery surface across the Shoulder. Mohammad Hussein handed Jehan some rope and he took up his position beside the remains of Dren Mandic.

The treacherous descent began. On one side were Predrag Zagorac and Iso Planic, while Fredrik led on the other side of the body with Jehan Baig at the rear. Each of the climbers held a rope which had been tied around the remains. Mohammad Hussein walked behind the group, carrying the gear that needed to be brought down. The impromptu pallbearers allowed slack on the line to ensure that the body, sledding a few metres ahead of them, did not drag them down.

Fredrik, now the effective leader of the operation, shouted instructions to the others and they moved at what he considered a safe and steady pace, stopping every few minutes to catch their breath and make sure everyone was okay. They were dependent on the same ropes and on each other. An error by one could prove fatal for all. 'You have to stay in line. Please focus,' Fredrik yelled at Jehan. 'Yeah, yeah,' the Pakistani mumbled. 'If you do fall,' he warned, 'you release, okay. It's our lives too, okay, remember.'[101] Fredrik could see Eric in the distance. At least, when he arrived, he would be able to replace the semi-coherent climber now traipsing behind Fredrik.

As the pace quickened slightly, Fredrik sensed that Jehan was not coping well with the task at hand, regularly bumping off or stumbling into him as they moved downwards. He was out of step with the others. 'Stop, stop, stop,' he shouted, but it didn't seem to register with the now punch-drunk mountaineer. Seconds later, Jehan stumbled badly and lost his step, crashing into Fredrik.

The Pakistani spun around, fell onto his back and began to slide rapidly downwards. He was still tied to the rope which was being used to lower the remains. The rope became entangled around Fredrik's leg and he was yanked, face first, onto the ice, but managed to get himself upright immediately. If Jehan did not release the rope he was now holding, and quickly, he would pull Fredrik and the others to an almost-certain death.

Predrag and Iso felt the weight of not one, but two, bodies on the rope. 'Release the rope! Release the rope,' Fredrik yelled. For what seemed like an eternity, Jehan kept tugging the rest of the men towards him as the other climbers pressed their heels into the snow, struggling to get a foothold. Fredrik prepared to fall, trying to plan how he might self-arrest with his ice axe. But he was tied up in a complex web of ropes; if he fell, Jehan would drag him down.

Showing no effort to use his ice axe to arrest his slide, Jehan continued to plunge, accelerating like a rocket, the ice rink conditions beneath his body providing no grip. 'Release the rope, release the rope!' Fredrik roared, his plea echoing across the Shoulder. Within seconds, the rope went slack as Jehan finally let go, his crampons catching the shiny surface and causing him to flip over and continue his downward slide. He made not a single decipherable sound as he continued to hurtle lower and lower, passing within 10 metres of Eric Meyer, who was still ascending and who yelled at him to stop. The call went unanswered.

'He did not make one single move to stop his fall,' Fredrik said, 'instead, he just let go and he shoots off like a rocket straight out to the open air and just disappears.' Jehan had gone out of sight, vanishing over the Shoulder ridge, leaving a stunned silence in his wake. 'What the hell is this?' Fredrik cried out to the others. 'One guy died. I came up here to help you guys ...' as he fell to his knees in tears. Shock numbed the group. This was just too dangerous; they could not risk another accident. The burial plans at Camp Four would have to be aborted.

Eric Meyer soon reached the others but they were too stupefied to talk. His team-mates used Dren's ice axe and some snow stakes to pin his body to the mountain. Fredrik tapped the ice axe into place under Dren's armpit, the 'ding, ding, ding' of metal clashing with metal reverberating across the impassive mountain face. 'This is enough,' he said, 'we are doing no more. I don't want to be part of this.'

Dren's remains would be left forever on K2's merciless and unsparing slopes. Predrag and Iso said what prayers they could muster over the body before turning towards Camp Four. 'There on the height of about 7,900m is the permanent home of Dren Mandic,' said the Serbs' post-expedition report, 'citizen of Subotica, alpinist, a friend and a brave, good man.'[102]

Fredrik's camcorder, stowed in his pocket, had unknowingly been left switched on. In a searing and chilling, but pictureless, audio, the recording device had captured the full real-time horror of the tragic fall and death of Jehan Baig.

K2 as seen from the Godwin-Austen glacier
courtesy of Wilco van Rooijen/www.teamwilco.nl)

Supplies and rations being prepared in Askole

Laying out the Norit expedition gear in Askole

Porters on one of the jeeps on the road to Askole

Porters wait in line in Askole

Porters on the trek to Base Camp

Expedition porters break to eat en route to Base Camp

Pausing for rest on the hike towards Concordia

The Norit team organise their supplies on arrival at Base Camp

Porters deposit the climbing gear and supplies on the Godwin-Austen glacier

Some of the tents at Base Camp with K2 in the background

Stocking up on chocolate

Climbers edging along the top of the glacier

Base Camp as seen from Chris Klinke's tent

Alberto Zerain

Dren Mandic

L-r: 'Big' Pasang Bhote and his cousin, Jumik Bhote

Hoselito Bite

Tsering Bhote

Kim Jae-soo (Mr Kim)

Shaheen Baig

L-r: Nick Rice, Hugues D'Aubarède and Qudrat Ali

Rolf Bae

Pasang Lama

Ger McDonnell

Pemba Gyalje

L-r: Oystein Stangeland and Cecilie Skog relax in a tent

Fredrik Sträng

Chris Klinke

A group of climbers pictured at Base Camp in the days before they set out for the summit. It includes Kim Jae-soo , Go Mi-sun, Karim Meherban, Shaheen Baig, Wilco van Rooijen, Jehan Baig, Dren Mandic, Eric Meyer, Chhiring Dorje, Chris Warner, Mike Farris, Milivoj Erdeljan, Miodrag Jovovic, Hugues D'Aubarède, Pemba Gyalje, Marco Confortola, Roberto Manni, Predrag Zagorac, Iso Planic, Rolf Bae, and Lars Nessa.

The Norit expedition members relaxing at Base Camp, l-r: Jelle Staleman, Roeland van Oss, Court Haegens, Mark Sheen, Cas van de Gevel, Pemba Gyalje, Wilco van Rooijen, and Ger McDonnell.

The American International K2 Expedition, l-r: Chris Klinke, Tim Horvath, Eric Meyer, Chris Warner, Paul Walters, Fredrik Sträng, Chhiring Dorje, and Mike Farris

Karim Meherban

L-r: Italian team-mates Roberto Manni and Marco Confortola

L-r: Eric Meyer and Chhiring Dorje

Members of the Norit team enjoy a meal, l-r: Roeland van Oss, Jelle Staleman, Mark Sheen, and Cas van de Gevel

Taking a shower at Base Camp

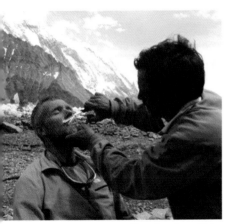

Time for a beard trim

The cooks prepare some fresh meat

L-r: Ger McDonnell, Marco Confortola and Wilco van Rooijen

An avalanche sweeps past Base Camp

A snow-covered Base Camp

Porters in party mood at Base Camp

A new arrival at Base Camp

Meal time at Base Camp

Cooks cleaning up after dinner

The South Korean team banner

Cas van de Gevel slices his Spanish ham

Pemba Gyalje's puja altar at Base Camp

Wilco van Rooijen with oxygen from a
previous expedition to K2

Husband and wife, Cecilie Skog and Rolf Bae

Flags and tents on the rocky moraine

one of the meetings to prepare the joint
summit push, clockwise from left: Mike Farris,
Captain Sabir Ali Changazi, Milivoj Erdeljan,
Hugues D'Aubarède, Miodrag Jovovic, Kim
Je-soo, Go Mi-sun, Hwang Dong-jin, Wilco
van Rooijen, and Rolf Bae.

L-r: Shaheen Baig, Predrag Zagorac and Dren Mandic with Roberto Manni (front) at one of the pre-summit meetings

Wilco van Rooijen makes a point as the climbers discuss their joint summit push, with Ger McDonnell (with camera) and
Marco Confortola (right)

SUMMIT
8,611m

CAMP FOUR
7,900m

CAMP THREE
7,300m

CAMP THREE
7,100m

CAMP TWO
6,700m

CAMP TWO
6,200m

CAMP ONE
6,000m

CAMP ONE
5,800m

ABRUZ
Route

CESEN
Route

The two routes to Camp Four
(Courtesy of Nick Ryan)

SUMMIT

TRAVERSE

SERAC

BOTTLENECK

SHOULDER

A close-up of the Death Zone on K2, above an altitude of 8,000 metres, showing the Shoulder, Bottleneck, Traverse, Serac and summit

(Courtesy of Rick Ryan)

The view from the Abruzzi ridge with the Godwin-Austen glacier running south towards Concordia

Members of the French-led expedition at Camp One on the Cesen ridge

Tents at Camp One on the Cesen route

The Norit team prepares Camp Three at 7,100 metres

The view from Camp Two on the Abruzzi ridge of the Godwin-Austen glacier which runs south from Base Camp towards Concordia before it joins the Baltoro glacier

Tents pitched at Camp Two at 6,200 metres on the Cesen route

Camp One on the Abruzzi spur

Ascending the Cesen

Pemba Gyalje ascends the Cesen ridge with Concordia in the background

Pasang Lama ascending the Black Pyramid on the Abruzzi ridge

Chris Klinke ascending House's Chimney on the Abruzzi ridge

Members of the Norit team place ropes on the Cesen route

A precariously positioned tent at the Cesen's Camp One

Camp Four on the Shoulder of K2 as seen from the Bottleneck on 1 August

Approaching the Bottleneck with Camp Four in the background

Climbers on their ascent across the Shoulder on the morning of 1 August

L-r: Marco Confortola and Ger McDonnell crossing the Traverse beneath the overhanging Serac

Climbers waiting to advance at the Bottleneck, from top to bottom: Marco Confortola, Chhiring Dorje, Pemba Gyalje, Jehan Baig, Ger McDonnell, and Cas van de Gevel (obscured from view)

The climbers make their way across the Traverse and towards the summit

Pasang Lama smiles at the summit

Pemba Gyalje and Karim Meherban reach the top

Lars Nessa waves the Norwegian flag on reaching the summit

Hwang Dong-jin takes the final steps towards 8,611 metres

Park Kyeong-hyo of the South Korean team at th summit of K2

Kim Jae-soo (Mr Kim) and Go Mi-sun (Ms Go) at the summit

Marco Confortola, the last of 18 climbers to reach the summit on 1 August

Ger McDonnell is the first Irishman to reach the summit of K2

The only two women to reach the summit of K2 in 2008, Cecilie Skog and Go Mi-Sun celebrate their achievement

Chhiring Dorje, the only member of the American expedition to make it to the top

The shadow cast by the summit of K2 on the evening of 1 August

Cecilie Skog approaches the summit of K2

Climbers just 50 metres from the top

Wilco van Rooijen back at Base Camp having spent two nights without food or shelter in the Death Zone

Chhiring Dorje and Pemba Gyalje on their return to Base Camp

Roberto Manni greets team-mate Marco Confortola following his return to Base Camp

Marco Confortola collapses before the chorten following his descent

Oystein Stangeland, Cecilie Skog and Lars Nessa at Base Camp after their return from Camp Four

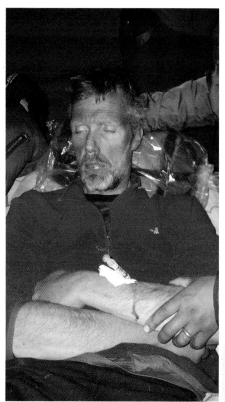

Cas van de Gevel recovers at the improvised hospital at Base Camp

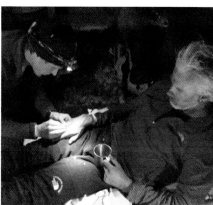

Wilco van Rooijen is treated at Base Camp after his three-day ordeal on the mountain

Marco Confortola is treated following his rescue

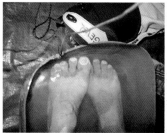

Wilco van Rooijen's frostbitten toes are bathed at Base Camp

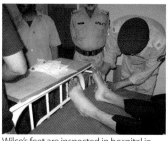

Wilco's feet are inspected in hospital in Skardu

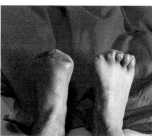

A picture of Wilco's feet from November 2008 following the amputation of his toes

Cas van de Gevel awaits evacuation from Base Camp

Wilco van Rooijen and Cas van de Gevel outside the Combined Military Hospital in Skardu

Wilco van Rooijen is stretchered to the helicopter which would take him to hospital in Skardu

(courtesy of Chris Kinkie)

Climbers help Wilco into the helicopter on 4 August

A picture, taken by Pemba Gyalje just before 10am on 2 August, which shows a number of climbers at the top of the Traverse (A), believed to be Jumik Bhote, Hwang Dong-jin and Park Kyeong-hyo, trapped on the ropes and being tended to by Ger McDonnell and Marco Confortola. A lone figure (B), believed to be Karim Meherban, can be seen above the Serac.

Another picture, taken by Pemba Gyalje at 7.16pm on 2 August, which appears to show bodies or climbing paraphernalia (A) still in place near the top of the Traverse. The other figure, which had been seen in the morning picture at B, has disappeared.

Nameplates put on the Gilkey Memorial following the deaths of 11 climbers
(Courtesy of Chris Klinke and Mike Farris)

Jumik Bhote, 'Big' Pasang Bhote

Ger McDonnell

Rolf Bae

Hugues D'Aubarède

Jehan Baig, Karim Meherban

Hwang Dong-jin, Kim Hyo-gyeong, Park Kyeong-hyo

Dren Mandic

(Courtesy of Chris Klinke)
The Gilkey Memorial

(Courtesy of Chris Klinke)
Some of the memorials and nameplates at the Gilkey Memorial

(Courtesy of Hoselito Bite)
Hoselito Bite and one of the porters fix nameplates on the Gilkey Memorial

K2, standing at 8,611 metres on the China-Pakistan border
(Courtesy of Lars Nessa)

Alberto had waited for long enough; it was almost 11am. The first climber to reach the top of the Traverse, he had secured the final anchor at the end of the ridge that runs beneath the summit snowfields and across the top of the Serac. There was enough fixed rope in place to get everybody up and down safely, he believed. Despite many cracks and crevasses, fixed lines were not required on the snowfields leading to the summit; the gradient was less severe, still dangerous but more navigable. Alberto could not see anybody coming behind him and was surprised the others were taking so long.

Completely unaware of the fall and death of Dren Mandic, which had taken place out of his sightline and earshot, Alberto had assumed the others hadn't yet appeared simply because they were tired or struggling with their climbing techniques on what were increasingly tricky surface conditions.

He had reached the top of the Traverse two hours earlier and sat, waiting on the snow. As the minutes and then hours passed, he reflected on his options: he had a choice to either proceed to the summit or wait for the others. Alberto could hear voices and glanced over the ridge and down the Traverse. A handful of climbers could be seen far below making their way towards the final anchor, but their pace was laboured and slow.

'I was there two hours waiting until I saw that they weren't coming.' So Alberto started to climb on his own; having plotted a secure line for them across the Traverse, he had no further obligation to wait for the others. He turned to face the summit and began to march determinedly across the glistening snow.

Oblivious to the human catastrophe unfolding below them, the climbers continued their ascent deeper and deeper into the Death Zone. Like an irresistible force, the notoriously perilous Traverse now beckoned those who had made it through the Bottleneck. Nineteen climbers were still en route to the summit, leaving the hazard that was the gulley in their wake. The faster they got across the Traverse, the sooner they would be free of the menacing Serac which loomed ominously overhead, but each step had be planned and executed with precision.

It was hard going. Wilco was the first member of the Norit team to begin on the Traverse. As he stepped away from the Bottleneck, he slipped a short distance on some steep rocks but held firm on the ropes. Lars passed Hugues along the way; the latter was changing his oxygen. The Frenchman looked beaten: 'He said he wanted to turn around because he ran out of oxygen. Maybe summit fever made him continue,' Lars thought.

The South Korean climbers were causing new delays. Most of Mr Kim's colleagues had been at the head of the chain of climbers as they stepped and axed their way across the Traverse, their faces pressed to the ice, many of them unaware that Dren Mandic had fallen. They moved industriously, though at a pace considered far too slow by those behind, frequently stopping for what seemed like an eternity to change oxygen bottles. 'It was so, so slow,' said Cecilie Skog.

As they crossed the Traverse, further evidence of the poor physical condition of many of the climbers became clear to Pemba, now at the back of the line. Their behaviour in the Death Zone, rather than just how far behind schedule the climb had become, or whether they should have descended following Dren Mandic's fall from the Bottleneck, was again his principal concern:

> Everybody was very slow, too slow, and physically they did not have enough energy. Normally on the mountain when people are getting ready for the summit they must be strong, but at that time everybody was kind of dazed ... They were unable to analyse the conditions on the mountain. I saw many people there who were not fit for that climate ... there were only five, six people who were efficient on that part. Many could not stand up on the front point crampon system and they were always pulling the fixed line.

It was early afternoon by the time the two Serbs and Mohammad Hussein, along with Eric and Fredrik, made it back to Camp Four. Fredrik was almost inconsolable, choked with tears. He slumped onto the snow, trying to gather his thoughts about what he would report to Base Camp. The second South Korean team had arrived from Camp Three and quickly realised that their summit plans for the following day might be endangered.

Mark Sheen from the Norit team and Paul Walters, an American expedition member, had also reached the Shoulder. They were shocked to learn that two people had lost their lives at such an early point in the ascent. The stunned climbers at Camp Four said little, trying to take in what had happened. It was difficult to absorb. Beside them, Nick Rice, of the French team, had seen enough and was packing his gear to begin the downward climb to Base Camp:

> ... I wasn't willing to climb on a route that wasn't properly fixed and was by nature dangerous, as there was a significant amount of snow weighing down the Serac that hangs over the route, and had already killed someone ... I began packing my things, which at this altitude, took around three hours. I started heading down around 3:00pm.[103]

Dubbed 'a mythic figure' by Lars Nessa because of his pace and prowess, Alberto Zerain sped ahead of all of the other climbers in his personal quest to reach the summit. Despite delays caused by his involvement in fixing ropes, he thought he could still achieve a summit time which would allow a safe return to High Camp before nightfall.

His first sighting of K2 from Broad Peak Base Camp had filled him with reverence and wonder for the world's second highest mountain; now the approach to K2's apex made him even more respectful and grateful:

> Little by little, I could see I was getting closer and closer to the summit and that builds up the excitement in you. In the last moments, you really live it fully. I knew the summit was waiting for me. I had won it. You get there and, you know, it's a fantastic day, a marvellous day. Wonderful.

It was 3pm when Alberto reached the summit, a full 18 hours since the Spaniard had stepped from his tent at Camp Three.

Without his camera, which he had earlier given to Chhiring Dorje, Alberto tried to take a mental picture of what he saw – an undulating panorama of the Karakorum mountains stretching countless kilometres in all directions, the Chinese side of K2 now visible for the first time. The sky seemed to sit down upon and envelope the multitude of jagged peaks. A short distance away, he could see Broad Peak, the mountain he had abandoned to scale K2. The change of plan had been fully vindicated. The decision to leave the others behind and ascend alone was also justified:

> In this case, the idea of going solo on ascent can have its inconveniences, but it also has a lot of advantages and one of the main advantages is being

able to decide in a more serene way, more direct and simple, that's for any situation ... you don't need to ask anybody else.

Alberto lay back for several moments on the snow, almost dozing in the glow of the summit sun. He remained there for half an hour, savouring the view and inhaling the pristine air. There was little space on which to sit; the very top of the mountain was a gentle slope which would not accommodate too many climbers at the same time.

Alberto could just about make out the tiny forms of the other climbers approaching from below. The hours of daylight were now numbered, he thought. What was taking them so long? They were still a long way from the top. The amount of time left to summit and descend to the fixed ropes before dark was shrinking rapidly: 'So I was thinking, wow, I am feeling the danger here. And the ones coming up, they are going to be tired. They are going to have problems so I felt worried.'

Pemba was the last of the 19 summit-bound climbers to reach the end of the fixed lines on the Traverse. He estimated that the summit was about 400 metres away. The snow on the summit flank looked to be quite unsafe and would require careful steps. He thought all of the conditions existed for slab avalanches, a dangerous, naturally-occurring phenomenon in which a large volume of snow can easily be displaced, and often caused by human activity on the slopes.

The pace of the climbers ahead of him seemed to have slowed yet again. Coupled with the difficult terrain, the ordeal of traversing along the fixed lines at such a cripplingly high altitude had fatigued many, their only impetus to continue coming from the sight of the summit, which now appeared within reach. Every four or five steps brought the need to stop, to rest for a moment, to process the lower oxygen intake, willing it to fuel the lungs, the heart and the brain. Concentration became more difficult, like every other bodily and mental function, but it was all the more vital now at yet another critical part of the ascent.

Though free from the hazards of steep ice, the climbers were facing into a crevasse-riddled and increasingly steep plain that brought its own dangers. The ability of the would-be summiteers to notice the distinction between the faint and subtle sounds which their crampons made on the snow could be the difference between life and death, these sounds indicating to a climber whether or not the ground was solid underfoot or if there was a crevasse beneath the covering of snow. The difficult conditions caused the expeditions to break up and scatter across the snow, each climber focussed on ploughing their own furrow towards the top.

Pasang Lama picked his way cautiously across the snowfields. He found Alberto's footsteps in the snow, which was now knee-deep in many places. In a moment of distraction, Pasang put his foot on some yielding snow and sunk into a crevasse. He was shocked but relieved to have sunk no further than his waist, and hauled himself back to the surface where he placed a small wand with a flag on the snow to warn others of the danger.

As he paused to rest, Pasang could see Alberto moving down towards him and to his right on a slightly different path than the route of his ascent. He shouted to warn the Spaniard about the crevasses in the area. Alberto seemed not to understand and tumbled into a crevasse, but it was not deep, and he was on his feet quickly. They kept on moving in opposite directions. Pasang allowed himself occasional glimpses of the summit. The conditions were immaculate, K2's pinnacle set majestically against a pristine and cloudless sky.

Rolf Bae had been having a bad day. He made it to the top of the Traverse with Lars and Cecilie, but his ongoing discomfiture was niggling at the back of his mind. As he moved across the Traverse with Lars, he glanced up and was recorded by Wilco who was filming the climbers with his tiny video camera. Rolf appeared to be in some emotional distress: 'Not a great day today. A hard day for me today. It's not a good day. Also, personal condition.'[104] Beside him on screen, Lars Nessa's oxygen supply whirred mechanically through the plastic tube wrapped around his ears and under his nostrils.

Pemba caught up with Rolf about 100 metres above the Traverse. The Norwegian seemed anxious and unhappy as he trudged through the snow. 'I don't know why everybody keeps climbing,' he told Pemba. He wanted to quit. Though Pemba thought Rolf seemed in a good physical condition, the latter was anxious that his team would not now make it back to the Bottleneck before dark, a descent which didn't endear itself to him: 'Rolf was always talking about the timing. He wanted to descend on the Bottleneck before dark; that was his main thing,' said Pemba, 'Rolf and I talked several times and again when we reached 8,500 metres.'

Pemba shared many of Rolf's concerns but he could now see his team-mates, separated and ahead of him, edging towards the top. Scattered across the plateau but heading in the same direction, Wilco, Cas and Ger showed no interest in, or intention of, turning back. Pemba felt compelled to join them and his own physical condition gave him the confidence to go on. He said goodbye to Rolf as Cecilie and Lars were about to join their team-mate.

Rolf had relied heavily on oxygen to cross the Traverse and Cecilie decided to give him her spare oxygen cylinder to help propel him to the summit. She wanted to share that special moment with her husband but Rolf had already decided he'd had enough. He could see the summit ahead; it was just 300 metres away. But he had reached a personal and psychological summit, a point at which he would not, or could not, go further. Rather than descend, he would sit and wait on the snow for his team-mates to summit and return. 'Okay, you continue, you go,' he told Cecilie. 'You are strong, you feel strong. You go to the top with Lars.'

Rolf's friends knew him as a very conscientious adventurer, not driven by ego or the limelight but, rather, by the love of the outdoors and remote and unspoiled places. He seemed pragmatic about his own limitations and abilities. He had been known to stop short of a summit or a polar landmark if he felt physiologically unwell. It was a characteristic which his wife admired and shared. The ethos of the Norwegian team was built on recognising the limits of one's strengths and capacity, focussing on safety and security, knowing when to yield to the rigours of high altitude.

Lars and Cecilie decided to go on; it would not be the same without Rolf, but they were close to the summit and it was the chance of a lifetime. Lars stepped aside to stow the spare rope he had been carrying since Base Camp near a rocky outcrop, in case of emergency on the descent. As he and Cecilie moved towards the summit, she looked back and could see Rolf urging her on with an occasional thumbs-up. He seemed fine, she thought, just tired, and the oxygen and the rest would help to revive him.

Digging out a temporary seat, Rolf sat on the snow and soaked up the sun-drenched panorama before him, stretching hundreds of kilometres over Pakistan and towards India beyond.

Mr Kim led his train of climbers across the deepening snow. Still using oxygen to fuel their ascent, the South Koreans had picked up speed since leaving the Traverse. Mr Kim paused and surveyed those following him. Pasang Lama had steamed ahead of them towards the summit while Jumik Bhote remained with the main climbing party. In her pink and black down suit and wearing a multi-coloured bandana, Go Mi-sun was en route to the sixth peak on her ambitious high-altitude bucket list of 14 8,000ers.

Close by was 29-year-old Park Kyeong-hyo, who had summited Everest just a year before, Hwang Dong-jin, aged 45, the South Korean climbing leader who had topped three 8,000ers, and 'Little' Kim Hyo-gyeong, aged 33, who had been to K2 in 2000 when he didn't get anywhere near the summit. The team ploughed on, increasingly confident of success.

Meeting Alberto, on his descent from the summit, Mr Kim thanked the solo climber for helping to fix the ropes on the Traverse. They shook hands and wished each other well. Alberto descended further, passing Hugues D'Aubarède and Karim Meherban, as well as each member of the Norit team:

> I remember Hugues was shouting to me when I passed everybody. He turned around and I could recognise him. He said hello, waved to me and said something in French. I didn't understand him well but it was some kind of greeting. I also remember when I was passing through the people, they said thanks. Thanks for having gone through, saying thank you, thank you.

The sight of the day's first summiteer reminded the other climbers of how far they had fallen behind but it also infused them with a renewed energy to go on.

Minutes after leaving Rolf, Lars and Cecilie met Alberto. Lars thought that Alberto looked 'amazingly, amazingly fit' for someone who had just climbed to 8,611 metres alone, without oxygen or the support of another climber. 'He was afraid that the snow on the ice face to the left of the Traverse could avalanche off,' said Lars, 'I think he soloed further to the left from where we were climbing and it's obvious that the snow didn't stick at all on the ice. It was really dangerous.'

Cecilie asked Alberto how long it would take her to reach the top. The Spaniard hesitated; he knew that, at their current pace, the Norwegians and other climbers would not reach the summit in two hours, or maybe even three, but he questioned if telling them otherwise would be helpful; they could not now get back down before dark anyway:

> You have a problem if you tell them at that rhythm, that pace, you've got three to four hours left, you are going to sink her into misery. And if you

lie to them and tell them there's only an hour, well, that's not going to help much either. I told her it was at least two hours, but two hours at that pace, it's difficult, but I didn't want to put her off by saying three or four hours.

Whatever Alberto's concerns, many of the other climbers were now oblivious to the time of day; all notions of an estimated summit time or adhering to a schedule, however provisional, had been firmly dispensed with. Cecilie shouted to Lars, who was just ahead, to wait for her at the summit. 'Of course,' he replied.

The sheer size of K2 can be fully appreciated when its shadow is seen stretching across the horizon in the late evening, putting many of the peaks around it in the shade. It dwarfs its peers, standing like a pyramid and casting a triangle of grey umbra across the landscape. It was the first thing that enthralled Pasang Lama when he set foot on the summit over two hours after Alberto Zerain. He swivelled a full 360 degrees to enjoy the vast horizon. It was 5pm and it would be an hour before the rest of the South Korean team gathered beside him.

The gradient on the summit was not steep and there was a small space on which to rest. Pasang savoured the time he had alone to revel in the experience, surveying the dramatic vista from the second highest point on the planet. He had been to its highest point just two years before, a summiting he shared with his father, the mountaineering guide Phurbu Ridar.

Far below, a scattering of human forms wound their way towards the final ridge that led to the top. Higher up, a group of climbers looked to be bunched together near a short ice face which Pasang had found particularly slippery and dangerous on his ascent. He turned again to view the incredible panorama of snow-capped peaks which were swathed in plumes of cloud. He imbibed the scene, blinking deliberately to ensure it was not all a dream.

Just as Pasang Lama stepped onto the summit of K2, Alberto arrived at Camp Four, having descended at almost breakneck speed from the top of the mountain in just two hours. The descent hadn't troubled him but, as he made his way down, he had been shocked to find several empty and discarded oxygen cylinders hanging from an anchor on the Traverse: 'I was surprised because of the danger that was there with the weight of the bottles. If the screw fell, they would fall, phew, like missiles.'

Camp Four was eerily quiet. Alberto saluted Eric Meyer as he dropped his rucksack onto the snow. Eric seemed troubled, lost in his own thoughts, and he said little to the returning climber, not even to offer a congratulatory greeting: 'I was waiting, thinking that maybe he was going to make me a cup of tea or something. I had just come down from the summit but this guy didn't talk, didn't make any kind of gestures ... he didn't say a word.'

Alberto looked back towards the Bottleneck but could see no sign of life beneath the still-glimmering Serac. The brightness of the sky had dimmed as the sun shifted its position above the Karakorum region. Alberto knew it would be dark within two hours; the other climbers now had no prospect of making it back to Camp Four in daylight. He decided there was little point in waiting on the Shoulder. After a quarter of an hour, he moved on, descending to Camp Three. He could sleep there and recuperate.

Wilco van Rooijen made slow but steady progress towards the top; he had fallen behind many of the others, including each of his team-mates. Where cracks and crevasses above the Serac had not troubled the climbers, the depth of the snow had slowed progress. Now within sight of the summit, a new hazard presented itself. Wilco arrived at a bank of ice that was steeper than any other part of the route towards the top. Several climbers were already there, waiting to ascend.

As he began to haul himself up with his ice axe, he was forced to pause until the route cleared of others. He sipped from his water flask but, as he tried to put it back into his suit, his cold fingers allowed it to slip and tumble down the slope. It was the only water he had.[105] The others, including a group of South Koreans, were ahead of him trying to scramble their way upwards on the short, almost vertical, blue ice face with limited success:

> One of the Koreans in front of me is trying to climb the band with just one ice axe, but is not being very successful. He keeps slipping down. Precious time is being lost. I end up giving him my ice axe so that he can try with two of them. After several attempts he manages to work himself up. He returns my ice axe and I continue. In the meantime everyone is waiting impatiently below. The pace is unbelievably slow.[106]

Cecilie and Lars watched and waited as the South Koreans scaled the difficult ice face. So concerned was Cecilie by the delay that she reduced the flow of her oxygen to just 0.1 litres per minute to conserve her supply. The flow through the tube wrapped around her nose abated and she inhaled deeply.

———

Lars overtook the South Koreans a short distance from the top and set foot on the summit just after 5.30pm. Cecilie joined him minutes later. Rolf had given Lars his woolly hat with rabbit ears and he pulled it over his head in tribute to his friend and team-mate waiting below. They beamed for a photograph. 'It was beautiful,' said Cecilie, 'it was absolutely beautiful with that shadow of K2 into China. And there was no wind.'

The euphoria of summiting was punctured for Lars by a nagging sensation that told him of the lateness of the hour and the urgent need to escape the clutches of the Death Zone:

> I felt like there was really something on my shoulders and I couldn't relax and I couldn't get a really good relief until I was down safe. And I didn't want to stay there for a long time. I wanted to just take some pictures and then go down safe. And stay conscious and stay alert until I got down.

Mr Kim and his team members arrived within minutes of each other. The late summiting time was cast from Kim's thoughts as he celebrated another national success for South Korea. Before she departed, Cecilie joined Ms Go for a photograph, their smiles brimming from ear to ear, the Norwegian and South Korean flags intertwined as they celebrated becoming only the ninth and tenth women ever to have summited the mountain.

Pasang Lama helped the South Koreans take photographs to record this proud moment for their nation and he celebrated their triumph, revelling in the congratulatory atmosphere: 'The ambience was perfect. It was warm and the weather was satisfying, as there was sunlight and the wind was not there. Everything on the summit was suitable and perfect.'

An array of rituals began to play themselves out at 8,611 metres above sea level – the unfurling of flags, the taking of keepsake photographs, capturing pictures for sponsors with strategically placed logos and products, the calls to loved ones, the prayers to higher beings. Climbers who might have become temporarily estranged in the hustle and bustle or the tensions of Base Camp, and in the solitary focus required on their ascent, joined together in celebration at becoming members of K2's climbing elite. The climbers had reached their Mecca, their place of pilgrimage, the altar of the high-altitude cathedral to which they had come to worship.

Forty-five metres from the top, Pemba noticed the small but precipitous ice cliff which had troubled the others on their way up. If it was dark on the descent, this section could be even more hazardous. As he clambered along it using his ice axe, he remembered that Jumik Bhote had spare rope in his rucksack. Pemba met Jumik as the latter was leaving the summit with some of his team members. 'Okay, you have rope,' he told Jumik, 'please fix in that section for the safe descent of everyone.' Jumik nodded and continued. The afternoon sun was beginning to drop towards the west.

Just after 6.30pm, Pemba reached the summit of K2, the first member of the Norit team to do so: 'The weather was very nice, no wind, very clean, clear, blue sky, nice 360 degree view. I felt very well, quite strong. I was not very emotional and I did not feel weak.' Pasang Lama was still sharing the moment with Mr Kim and Ms Go; Hugues and Karim had also arrived. Pemba thought that the other climbers looked completely drained, deliriously happy but physically spent. He took Hugues' camera and photographed the Frenchman on the summit with Karim.

At 61, Hugues had become the second oldest person to successfully scale K2.[107] Hugues spoke to his partner, Mine Dumas, in Lyon, telling her this would be his last climb; he had finally fulfilled his ambition. Hugues and Karim were blissfully unaware of the fate of their climbing partner, Jehan Baig. Pemba declined the offer of Hugues' phone to call home – he was becoming increasingly anxious about how late it was and he was concerned that there was still no sign of his team-mates.

Chhiring Dorje summited soon after Pemba and joined him as the sun continued its descent in the west, projecting the climber's bulky shadow across the summit snow. They embraced and exchanged congratulations; they had both made it to the top on their debut to K2 without recourse to supplementary oxygen. Chhiring was thrilled to have summited but, like Pemba, he was troubled by the encroaching darkness and the other climbers' apparent disregard for the travails that lay ahead of them: 'I always wanted to summit K2, I wanted to do it, it was fulfilled and I was happy. But it was bothering me as the ascent was done around 7pm, and it was getting dark.'

Pemba and Chhiring had, once again, instinctively slipped into the role and mindset of the Sherpa on the mountain. Though neither was a paid climbing guide or high-altitude worker with their respective expeditions, they felt a sense of obligation to the others, a care they had shown to countless paying clients in the past.

So often Sherpas in the region had seen foreign climbers come to the world's highest mountains only to be overcome by hypoxia, a lack of acclimatisation, inadequate preparation, and the overwhelming grip of summit fever. And so often they had sought to warn, to advise and to implore.

But those concerns were, in the main, suppressed by the Sherpas, who, for generations on the mountains, were reticent in the face of the determined focus of their employers, who were often part of ambitious, commercially-driven and heavily-sponsored expeditions. Alberto Zerain noticed that heightened sense of responsibility in the Sherpas to the others around them on K2:

> The Sherpa is a disciplined person, that's a characteristic of them. They are efficient. On 1 August, I know for sure that some Sherpas, among them Pemba and others, stayed there and they knew their work hadn't finished. Because they felt responsible for everything, for everybody, for all those people who were up there.

As they descended, Lars and Cecilie passed Ger and Wilco who were heading upwards. Lars thought they seemed to be in good shape and really focussed on the summit: 'Both Ger and Wilco really had the summit in their eyes. You could see it.' Ger powered on ahead while Wilco fell behind. He was almost spent and there was still an hour's climbing to go. However, adrenalin was laying siege to the exhaustion within the Dutchman's body; he hadn't come this far to turn around at the final hurdle. His knees buckled and he found himself crawling some of the last metres.

Nothing other than getting to the top occupied his thoughts. Wilco had spent years fighting to get here and when he finally reached the summit, it was wonderful. Warm tears flowed down his cheeks as he hauled his aching body onto the rocky pinnacle, almost nine kilometres above sea level:

God, everything hurts. I climb another ten steps, look up to see if I am any closer, and manage another ten steps. I arrive at the last slope, incredibly steep. After five I stand still. I need to stop. No more strength. I watch Cas who is resting above me. Has he made it? I am on my hands and knees. I look up and I am at eye level with the summit – a 50 metre snow ridge. Prayer flags fly at its other end. I crawl the last metres. Tears, I cannot believe it, we have made it! I hug Cas, Gerard and Pemba, we dance around on the highest point. Now here we have this point in common that is even higher than K2's summit. At this highest point, in our minds, there is nothing but absolute joy.[108]

Cas van de Gevel reached the summit of K2 just after 7pm and he allowed himself to bask in the glory with his comrades. This was one for the team as much as for the individual and the humble carpenter from Utrecht embraced it fully as he planted one boot in front of the other in those agonising final steps onto the snowy dais:

One moment you are coming higher. Then one moment you realise that the summit is within your reach. You feel like you are going to make it, it's only a matter of time to keep on going to reach the summit ... The view was really fantastic so we were holding each other. There was a very warm moment because we were reaching the summit. It was the best thing that could happen to us on our expedition.

Wilco pulled out his sat phone and was able to get a signal. He called the number which connected to a house boat in Utrecht. Maarten van Eck, the Norit team webmaster, answered almost immediately. He had been waiting for the call. 'Maarten, we are standing on K2!' Wilco hollered. Surrounded by a bank of telephones, computers and maps, Maarten punched the keys in front of him to update the expedition website.

The expanse of the view almost dizzied Wilco, his light-headedness compounded by the impact of oxygen deprivation and lack of sleep. Near him, Hugues and Karim seemed not to heed the congratulations of others. Their oxygen supply was now exhausted and they would descend without the safety net the life-sustaining gas could provide; a descent they began just behind Mr Kim, Ms Go and Pasang Lama.

The Norit team were alone at the summit. Although it was more than five hours later than their published timetable had envisaged, that would not be allowed to cloud this moment. Four friends and climbing partners hugged each other and held back tears. Ger McDonnell unzipped the front of his down suit and reached inside for his nation's colours. The flag unfurled itself in the breeze and was held aloft for a memorable photograph of the first Irishman to conquer K2.

Thousands of kilometres away in Alaska, his partner, Annie Starkey, answered the phone and the connection held good. It was a conversation she won't ever forget. 'It wasn't a great connection; there was a lot of static and stuff. Oh my God, what a gift ... he felt great, he was elated. He told me everybody was feeling good, that there was no problem ... it was an emotional phone call for both of us.' Ger tried calling his mother's home in the south-west of Ireland but the call didn't connect. He handed his camera, flags, his phone and some other equipment to Pemba, asking him to carry them for him on the descent.

Cas gathered his thoughts and radioed Roeland van Oss in Base Camp to relay the good news that the Norit quartet had reached the summit, his elation momentarily punctured by the sad revelation of Dren Mandic's death, something that was still unknown to the many climbers who thought that the Serb had survived his fall.

Wilco took one last opportunity to pan his camcorder around the darkening horizon. He relished the scene and banished thoughts of descending from his mind:

> The light was exceptionally brilliant. You are the end of the Earth, in heaven almost. You are thinking "This is it, it's over, we have done it". You have seen all the pictures in the books and all the documentaries but now, you are there ...

Eventually the Norit team members turned their minds towards the journey down to Camp Four. Pemba said he would go ahead to check the ropes and anchors. He was soon followed by Ger and Wilco, with Cas close behind.

Just metres below the summit, they met Marco Confortola, the Italian being the last of 18 climbers to summit K2 that day. Marco had earlier fallen some distance behind; as he crossed the ridge beneath the summit, he had found it difficult to breathe. He passed a group of descending South Korean climbers as he approached the top and saluted them; they seemed oblivious to his greetings.

On meeting the four Norit team members, Marco said, 'Quick, somebody has to take pictures of me'. Cas obliged and captured a dazzled Marco holding his sponsors' flags aloft. The Italian looked drained; the flash from the camera catching the reflection from a strip of hi-visibility garb on Marco's suit and indicating the fading daylight. The photograph showed a darkening sky and the sun setting in the distance behind the Italian. Night was encroaching rapidly.

'This is my dream and I have realised it,' the Italian later wrote, 'at 18.45 on 1 August I have put my foot on the top of K2.'[109] Marco had fulfilled his ambition of repeating the achievement of his fellow Italians, Achille Compagnoni and Lino Lacadelli, who, 54 years earlier – almost to the day – had become the first mountaineers to reach the summit. Marco came from the same Italian valley as Compagnoni and now had even more in common with his climbing hero.

Wilco was exhausted but elated; he had overcome his Karakorum nemesis, everything had gone so well for his team and the omens for the remainder of the expedition were good:

> It's just a matter of four or five hours and we will be back in Camp Four and we will phone again [when] we are successful ... We knew almost for sure that it was just a matter of a few hours. And in a few days, we would have a big party with all the teams in the Base Camp. It couldn't go wrong.

Triumph Turns
to Tragedy

1 August – 2 August

Ger McDonnell slumped onto the snow beside Wilco van Rooijen. They had taken just a few dozen steps from the summit and extreme exhaustion, exacerbated by oxygen deprivation, was already tightening its noose. Cas was still at the summit photographing Marco and the Norit duo wanted to wait for their friend before continuing. But the chance of a few moments' rest was also relished.

The overwhelming joy of reaching the summit had quickly been replaced by a debilitating physical and mental fatigue, a chronic tiredness that had been subdued by adrenalin on the ascent, but which was now virulent and impossible to ignore. After over 18 hours of climbing without rest or proper sustenance, the realisation that they were only halfway through the climb preoccupied Ger and Wilco as they sat silently at 8,600 metres.

Standing beside them, Pemba Gyalje watched the sun dropping below the horizon – it was approaching 8pm and the most demanding and treacherous part of the climb had begun. Contrary to what he had hoped, descent would now take place without the benefit of daylight, causing the hazards of the path back to Camp Four to multiply.

Ger and Wilco said little; they had long since run out of water and snacks and would need to dig deep into their physical and mental reserves to continue. Pemba recognised the impact of the Death Zone on his colleagues, a stranglehold that climbers could not fight with chocolate or sugary drinks:

> Even if they had some bars in their pockets that they could eat, that is not sufficient. Two chocolate bars is not enough energy to come a long way down ... they must think, "I have to go down", they have to generate energy naturally from the mind – not from chocolate, not from little drinks, but if they don't have strong mental state then – phuw!

Pemba glanced back towards the now-deserted summit; Cas was approaching, with Marco following some distance behind. Thirty metres below along the ridge, the distinctive South Korean team down suits were clearly visible. Pemba was puzzled; Mr Kim and his colleagues had left the summit almost an hour before – how had they only progressed some 45 metres in such a space of time?

Pemba realised that they were trying to negotiate the perilous ice face that had delayed so many on the ascent and they seemed to be making little progress. 'I have to go down,' Pemba told Ger and Wilco. They barely nodded. 'I have to see if Jumik has placed the rope in this section. We will need it to descend,' he said. Pemba trudged across the snow. 'Follow me as soon as possible,' he shouted back to the others.

Rolf Bae clipped his carabiner onto the fixed line just minutes before darkness enveloped the mountain. On rejoining him 100 metres above the top anchor, Lars and Cecilie had embraced their team-mate with tears in their eyes. Their summit achievement was tinged with disappointment that Rolf had been unable to join them at the top but, nonetheless, this was a success for the team.

Rolf had begun to shiver while he sat waiting in the plummeting temperatures and now he was anxious to get going. Lars quickly retrieved the spare rope he had left behind a rock on his ascent and they headed towards the top anchor and the safety that the ropes below it would bring. Their relief at reaching the security of the fixed ropes was palpable. Lars moved off first, abseiling down to a small ledge near the top of the Traverse where he paused for a few moments, glancing below and above him.

The rugged mountainous horizon, so distracting and captivating in the sunset, had now disappeared. The darkness was impenetrable save for the 50-metre arcing glow cast by his head torch. Lars found himself face to face with the Serac once more. It looked so different in the dark, its giant expanse less evident but its menacing presence more potent. Any trickling flows in its deep crevasses had begun to re-freeze in the bitter cold. The groaning noises it emitted sounded like the 'poing' from a catapult and every sound caused his heart to skip a beat.

He stopped for breath and waited for Cecilie and Rolf to catch up, listening to the rhythmic hack of their ice axes and the kick of their crampons as they moved towards him. The lights on their foreheads illuminated the tiny splinters of ice displaced by their axes. Lars found the conditions demanding and recognised the debilitating impact of the high-altitude environment:

The ropes were quite thin at the top of the Traverse so we were abseiling on a knot, it's called the Italian hitch. If you are a little dizzy because of the altitude it's not that easy to make that, you know. So Rolf wanted me and Cecilie to co-operate and help each other with this knot. So me and Cecilie on every stance, on every lay, we started out together. I was helping her with her knot and she was helping me.

Cecilie's head torch flickered on and off as the batteries began to expire and she fiddled with it, pressing the battery cover into place to try to revive the light. She stopped to retrieve spare batteries from her rucksack. Kicking her crampons deep into the crystallised surface to maintain a grip, she could feel the bitter cold now sheathing the mountain. It was a stark contrast to the heat of the day which had bathed all of the climbers' bodies near the spot where she had nearly fallen almost a dozen hours before. She thought of Dren Mandic, still not sure if the Serb had survived.

Lars asked whether he would continue further ahead, but Rolf decided to move down and lead the way across the Traverse to the top of the Bottleneck. 'I will go first. You look after my wife,' he told Lars, as he moved several metres ahead of them.

It sounded like thunder: Lars heard the sudden whoosh of ice falling, sliding and grating along the slopes, but he was unable to figure out whether the fall was happening nearby or further down the mountain. The creaking and scraping reverberated as if the side of the mountain itself was about to collapse into the void. Icy debris fell from above him and he pressed his body to the face of the mountain to avoid the shards.

Cecilie shuddered at the displacement from above, the force of the icefall causing her to be knocked downwards until her jumar activated. She turned to locate Rolf:

I don't know if I heard anything but I felt it ... like this earthquake shaking. The ground underneath me was shaking and I slipped and I lost my light because it was not very stable and because of the movement I lost my head torch again, but ... the last thing I saw was Rolf's head torch moving and then it was dark.

Lars heard Cecilie scream and moved quickly towards her: 'There had been some shaking on the rope and she had been pulled off balance. She had lost her head torch in the fall and was quite upset. And she recognised that Rolf's head torch was gone.' Climbing around and past her, Lars moved further down to try to locate his companion. Cecilie screamed Rolf's name and her voice echoed unanswered around the Bottleneck: 'I don't think I wanted to understand. Lars came and I think I was screaming Rolf's name a few times and I said to Lars that he's not answering, I don't know where he is.'

Lars had moved about 15 metres to an ice screw where one of the South Koreans' empty oxygen bottles still hung 'and on the other side ... the rope was cut like with a knife just 10 centimetres after the ice screw'. The rope had been severed by the massive icefall that had just blasted Rolf down the mountainside. The realisation of what had happened came quickly to Lars, his brain instinctively shutting out the emotion as he tried to focus on a solution:

> There had been a really big, big icefall and at that moment I understood that Rolf had disappeared and died. Rationally I had understood what had happened but emotionally it didn't affect me at all at that moment. And I don't know why I reacted like that, but quite fast I took the decision that we had to continue descending and that there was no hope of finding Rolf at all.

Cecilie was in shock. Looking down into the silent darkness, she screamed Rolf's name several times, her cries barely penetrating the icy emptiness. There was no light, no sound, no evidence that Rolf had survived. Lars clambered across and rejoined her, recognising that his job now was to bring Cecilie down the mountain:

> We didn't speak that much. We were standing there for a couple of minutes, just trying to take in the fact... but then I took the decision that we have to continue, we have to get down. We will not survive if we stay here for many hours. If we have to stay the whole night up here we will probably not survive.

Lars pulled the spare rope from his rucksack and began to fix it to the nearby anchor, hoping it would be long enough to get them across the Traverse and onto the Bottleneck. Cecilie wanted to stay, to search for Rolf. 'She didn't see any meaning in continuing,' said Lars. Calmly, he told her to wait as he watched her frantic breaths envelop the light from his head torch. Tears streamed from her eyes. 'I will find a way down,' he told her as he began his descent.

Abseiling slowly, he reached the top of the Bottleneck, recognising the walls of rock which enclosed it. All traces from the climbers' ascent, any footprints or climbing gear left behind, had been swept away in the avalanche. The rope Lars had soon ran out; they would have to descend much of the couloir without a fixed line. Once he had found a firm foothold, Lars called out to Cecilie to follow. Hearing his yell from below, she thought that Lars had found Rolf; it snapped her out of a paralysing shock and spurred her on:

> He was yelling up to me, "Ok, Cecilie, come down here, hurry up", like in a very positive way and in my head then he had found Rolf and everything was good and the three of us, we're going to go back to camp together. And I rappelled down and I remember I was so relieved that of course he'd found Rolf ... but he wasn't there and I was like, "Oh you tricked me down here". But Lars was so good. He was very, very strict, but very clear and he did absolutely all the right things. He understood what happened but he said we have to go down.

The grim reality began to seize Cecilie. The descent through the gulley became a blur and she no longer wanted to continue. But then she heard a voice, faint at first but then stronger, as she climbed down the Bottleneck; it was Rolf:

> And then I heard, and it's crazy ... I could hear his voice and it was so strong and it was saying, "You have to get down, you have to go on the fixed lines and you have to go down". And when I was on the fixed lines I could hear his voice saying, "Ok, have you checked? Have you fixed? Have you locked your carabiner? Have you done everything?" He was checking me all the time if I had done the right things; "Have you done it now?" and after a while ... I got angry. I was like, "Why are you asking me all the time? Come here and do it for me". But his voice was so clear; it was like he was there. And I know if I heard someone say this I wouldn't believe it and I would think you are crazy, but it was so clear.

Lars guided her across the Shoulder; they hardly spoke. A strobe light planted in the snow by one of the other climbers helped them find the way to their tents at Camp Four. There was no sign of life there and Cecilie went straight to her tent, the absence of Rolf and the sight of his empty sleeping bag hitting her like a body blow. She collapsed onto her sleeping mat in grief.

Lars found their team-mate, Oystein, in his tent and broke the devastating news. He then went to comfort Cecilie who began to weep uncontrollably:

> I wasn't angry then ... I slowly kind of understood what had just happened. And I felt so bad that I could go into the tent without him. How could I do that? But I did. And Lars asked me if I wanted him to stay in my tent

and I said yes, so he stayed. I don't even think we took our crampons off, I can't remember. But then I woke up and … he said, "Tomorrow when it's light we're going to look for Rolf. We can't do it now, it's too dark. We have to sleep". And the next day we didn't look for him … Me and Rolf, we shared dreams and we thought … that we were going to share a future. So I didn't only lose my husband but I lost … my best friend and my partner and my future like I was hoping it would be.

As the final gleams of sunlight disappeared from the sky, 11 exhausted and increasingly incoherent climbers struggled to find the right path to the Traverse and the fixed ropes hundreds of metres below. Along with the five South Korean expedition members and Wilco, Ger and Cas from the Norit team were Hugues D'Aubarède and his guide, Karim Meherban, as well as Marco Confortola. With them were four Nepalese Sherpas – Pemba Gyalje, Chhiring Dorje, and cousins Pasang Lama and Jumik Bhote, each of whom was becoming increasingly concerned about the capacity of the other climbers to cope with the demands of the darkness and the crippling altitude.

The heat of the sun and the brightness of daylight had inspired the climbers to take each step higher and higher even when another centimetre forward seemed impossible. But the encroachment of darkness was now compelling their bodies to relax and succumb to fatigue, causing a dangerous lethargy and carelessness. As the summiteers struggled across the snow plains at 8,500 metres in the dusk of 1 August, they were overcome with the same chronic debilitation and weariness that marathon runners feel when they hit the metaphorical wall.

Throughout the ascent, any thoughts of the hazardous journey down were suppressed, the focus remaining solely on taking the next steps towards the fulfilment of their summit dreams. Now, on the descent, the climbers' bodies, deprived of adequate sleep for days on end, began to relax into a melancholy stupor akin to a depressed drunkenness or a drug-induced sedation.

The terrain, swathed in darkness, began to look alien and uniform, making it incredibly difficult to find the trail back to the point where the descent could begin towards the Shoulder below. 'Down climbing is more difficult,' said Pemba, 'if there is not a proper fixed line, it is more difficult than climbing up. When you are climbing up, you can observe, you can explore, you can see clearly where is the handhold and foothold but for the down climbing you can't see that much.'

Everything looked different from the hours before; there were no reference points from which to get a bearing, just a sameness stretching before them into the blackness of night. In the same way as the darkness causes the body to slip into sleep mode in everyday life, the internal body clock in the mountaineer directs the limbs and the organs to slacken and ease up when night falls. The body is saying, 'Stop, slow down, you need to take a break, sit down and rest', which is precisely what many of the climbers on K2 did within a short time of leaving its summit.

Cas re-joined Ger and Wilco where they sat on the snow. Cas was tired but felt strong enough to make it safely back to Camp Four. He was not apprehensive about his own ability to descend in the dark but he feared for the rest of his team. He noticed how disjointed the group had become, any semblance of co-ordination and cohesion seeming to disintegrate in the darkness. The others were uncommunicative, Cas noticed, almost too exhausted to talk. They were no longer functioning as a unit, now overcome by the individual need to survive:

> One moment you are not walking all together anymore. Also you are a little bit separated, a few metres between you and when it is dark, everybody is just descending. You see some lights at the back of you and in front of you and also ... you are a little bit "I cannot make mistakes, where is the ropes, is everything ok?". So you are very much fixed to that.

When he got to the top of the steep icy section below the summit, Pemba could see that Jumik, Pasang and the South Korean team had made it down the slope. They were now huddled below the ridge, motionless, most of them sitting in silence on the snow. Pemba had asked Jumik to use the rope he had brought from Camp Four to create a temporary fixed line here but there was no sign of it.

Jumik and Pasang had roped the steep incline for Mr Kim and his team but had removed the rope as they climbed down; Pasang's ice axe, which had been used as an anchor point, was left behind, jutting out of the snow. The climbers still en route from the summit would have to down climb without the benefit of a temporary fixed line. Pemba caught up with Chhiring Dorje above the cliff and warned him of the dangers:

There was no rope and the others were coming down from the summit above the steep section and we talked. There is no rope, be careful and down climb slowly. And then me and Chhiring, we descended there and we waited almost one hour ... the Koreans were sitting below us and then Hugues, Marco, Wilco, Cas, Gerard were descending very slowly in this part, down climbing very slowly. They used their axes but they were too tired.

Observing the South Koreans, Pemba realised just how drained they now were. Apart from being unfocussed and fatigued, the group was unable to find the trail to the Traverse, unsure which way to go. The snowy topography looked the same in every direction. Some of the climbers were standing around, taking a long time to do something as simple as strap on their head torches. A manoeuvre which would take seconds at Base Camp could take several minutes at this altitude, the messages from the brain through the neurons slower to travel to the oxygen-deprived outer extremities of the body.

Pemba watched as cold fingers fumbled with the straps and batteries, further evidence that a successful descent was seriously compromised:

They took a long time to get their lights out – at altitude it takes a long time to do things. It takes exhausted people more than 20 minutes to do a simple thing like put on their headlights when they are at altitude. I put on my head torch before leaving the summit but they were totally crazy; when we were taking pictures on the summit I had already a headlamp on my head because I was already prepared ... I know it's going to be getting dark after one hour and I have to prepare here on the top, on the easy terrain so I don't have to do it on the way down. I told the other guys the same thing, but they didn't listen.

The bulbs of the head torches were now the only light source against a backdrop of moonless black. Pasang Lama approached his expedition leader, Mr Kim, who was sitting with his team on the snow. The South Korean climber tapped the side of his oxygen cylinder where the gauge was showing 'empty'. Mr Kim was hardly able to speak, panting in the still air, but Pasang knew what was required of him. Unquestioningly, he detached his own cylinder and handed it over, replenishing Kim's supply.[110]

The other South Koreans had already flopped onto the snow, their breathing laboured, their faces expressionless, with not a word from their mouths. They were waiting for guidance, to be marshalled towards the Serac.

The Norit team members, as well as Marco, Hugues and Karim, had taken a long time to descend the short ice face and they now stood silent beside the others, looking at the ground, waiting for someone to speak, to take the lead, to tell them what to do.

Pemba called Chhiring Dorje, Jumik Bhote and Pasang Lama together. Nobody was co-ordinating the descent and nobody seemed to know the trail. In their deteriorating condition, the climbers would need to be corralled and shepherded towards the fixed lines. If they weren't, they could drift away in the wrong direction and fall to their deaths. The rope which Jumik had just stored away was called upon again; it had been retained for an emergency and such a moment had now arrived.

Pemba and his fellow Sherpas decided to create a simple moving rope system which would allow the climbers to use their carabiners to affix their harnesses onto a temporary line with which the Sherpas could lead them in the direction of the Traverse. The rope was not fixed to any point but, rather, was tied to each of the four members of the impromptu rescue team who would act as moving anchor points at either end. Every climber would be clipped onto the rope so that none could go astray.

It was a system which would not work on very steep ground but here the gradient was suitable enough to try it, Pemba thought. The four Sherpas hoped they could lead the climbers towards the top anchor point and the security of the fixed lines. For Pemba, it seemed the only solution:

> We talked together and said that the majority of the people are already too exhausted and they have started to sit down but it is too dangerous here. The people were starting to move in different directions and that is very dangerous in that condition because there was very soft snow there and there was an avalanche risk. So we say now everybody has to connect on the rope and everybody clip on the rope; everybody has a personal safety sling and they clip on the rope. We decided to use a moving rope system because we had about 80 to 100 metres of static rope for emergencies. Then we had to put all climbers on this rope, two of us would go in front and two of us would stay at the back and then we would descend together in a running relay system. Otherwise people cannot descend because they wanted to sit down.

The initiative of Pemba and his colleagues, who were coping much better than the other climbers with the hazards of the Death Zone, was in stark contrast to the inability of the expedition leaders to guide their teams out of their life-threatening predicament.

The teams had become largely rudderless, adrift in a sea of snow, lost in the haze of oxygen deprivation. Exhausted and unable to think straight, they had been rendered punch-drunk by the rigours of spending so many hours in the Death Zone. Only the four Sherpas seemed coherent and focussed enough to do what was needed to steer the climbers towards safety.

———————————

Pasang and Jumik went with the rope to the front of the queue of hapless climbers, corralling them into line as they went. Pasang looked for his ice axe to hold the line in place while he helped the others to clip on. But he had left it further up at the ice bank and it wasn't feasible to retrieve it; he could borrow one if necessary, he thought. Pemba and Chhiring moved to the back of the line, shouting at the others to attach onto the rope. Some of the climbers had to be manhandled into position and helped to clip on.

Of the climbers fumbling with their carabiners on the line, only Cas and Marco seemed reasonably coherent: 'Okay Pemba,' Marco said, 'let's put everyone together.' Cas moved ahead of the others, more surefooted and collected. Though the trail left by the climbers in the snow on the ascent was visible to Pemba and the other Sherpas, it seemed beyond the radar and comprehension of the majority of the climbers:

> There was a big track, a very big track, but the majority of people could not see that big track because they already had a hallucinating problem. Even though I saw there was a big track, they could not see it. They were sometimes moving on the right trail but then immediately they changed the track, sometimes left and then right. But they could not see the big trail in front of them.

The problems with the moving rope system became apparent almost immediately. Most of the climbers on the line needed a lot of encouragement even to stand, let alone walk. Though the terrain was not very steep, the climbers acted as though they were being forced to climb a vertical face, every step a painful chore. As soon as one climber would clip on, they would sit down again after just two steps, bringing everyone to a halt, exposing the inbuilt flaw in the system – for anyone to move, everyone needed to move. Pemba and the others kept barracking them to concentrate, to keep walking:

They were not talking but they were sitting down; they always wanted to sit down. So we forced them to keep moving; then next two steps and they want to sit down again. Then another two steps and they want to sit down again. We say, "No, keep moving. No sliding; you have to stand up".

Increasingly listless and silent, the climbers stumbled forward only as fast as the slowest-moving member of the makeshift team. Any wait along the line for those ahead of them to move on triggered an involuntary reflex to sit, to doze, to succumb to the effects of a depleted oxygen supply to the brain. Steps became laboured, each attempt at securing a proper foothold foiled as boots sank into the soft snow. As the snow rose to the knee in places, it became so easy to sit, to take a moment to recuperate, even to close eyes and shut out the impenetrable night.

It was after 10pm and most of those now stumbling around in the darkness had been awake for almost 24 hours at an altitude at which human life is quickly rendered unviable. Pemba came to a grim realisation: 'I felt very sad because now we have a problem on the mountain. I understood that many people could not descend; they could not reach High Camp tonight.'

The moving rope system had been in operation for an hour and progress was agonisingly slow. The snow was like sugar, like crumbled Styrofoam and, on a gradient of 30 to 40 degrees, it was likely to shift at any time like a sand dune in a desert. One climber walking awry could set off a snowfall or a slab avalanche in which a massive wall of snow would yield to the forces of gravity, sweeping away everything in its path.

Where they now stood was simply too dangerous a place to delay but, infuriatingly, the climbers kept sitting down or falling to their knees, their bodies screaming for more oxygen. Pemba understood why:

> The Death Zone is a different world, naturally. If I want to help other people, if I see something wrong, if I want to give help to others, I cannot do that physically in the Death Zone ... People decide for themselves before they go into the Death Zone that we cannot guide each other, we cannot convince each other.

Pemba and the other Sherpas needed to be sure they were going in the right direction; if the semi-comatose climbers stumbled too close to the edge above the Traverse, they could fall in an instant, carrying everyone else with them. When the moving rope system eventually ground to a complete halt, Pemba hiked down to the front of the line.

Pasang and Jumik were unable to find the right route, fearful that they might lead everyone astray. The terrain looked alien to the pair, their head torches casting an arc stretching only 50 metres and they were unable to detect any landmarks or reference points that might lead them to the anchored ropes.

With Chhiring, the three regrouped while the weary climbers availed of the break to sit and doze. The Sherpas knew that the system was no longer working. Chhiring worried that the weight of so many people on the one unanchored rope would cause them all to slide, especially in the knee-deep snow which had not compacted. By the time he had moved down to confer with Pemba, Jumik and Pasang, some climbers had begun to detach themselves from the line and they scattered again. They seemed ungovernable and beyond instruction.

Recognising his navigational abilities, the other Sherpas urged Pemba to go ahead to try to find the beginning of the fixed ropes, with Pasang accompanying him. The plan was that Chhiring and Jumik would stay behind, and once the first anchor point was located they would lead the others to the Traverse. Pemba hoped that news of finding the ropes would rouse the climbers from their stupor, raise their spirits and encourage them to move on, re-energised.

Pemba and Pasang descended slowly, making good but trepidatious progress towards the Traverse:

> We felt that we were very close above the Serac edge. Now we had to carefully detect the anchor on the edge of the Serac because when we are looking down from the mountain it is a completely different terrain to when we are looking up the mountain. Very carefully we had to detect the top anchor. If we were unable to do that it would make a big problem for everybody.

The pair said little, their minds preoccupied by the task at hand. The gradient increased in places and Pemba worried again about the risk of a slab avalanche. They soon located the ridge of the Serac and, just over its edge, the anchor jutting out of the ice and tied to the rope which would lead them to safety at the end of the Bottleneck.

Pemba called out to Chhiring and Jumik but they were too far away and out of earshot. Now, without functioning radios – whose batteries had expired – the Sherpas had to resort to using their head torches to signal messages in a high-altitude version of Morse code. Pemba flashed his light on and off to tell

Chhiring that the line had been found, hoping that, somehow, those still above would be able to follow his trail.

At eight and a half kilometres above sea level and in the searing cold of the Karakorum mountains, Pemba turned to his fellow Sherpa: 'Okay, Pasang, you have to stay here and keep blinking your light for them. Follow me when you can.' They were standing at the precipice above the Serac, all of the other climbers still stalled above them, only a spattering of lights now visible against the outline of the towering summit.

Pemba needed to be sure that the rope and the anchors below were still secure; given the condition of the climbers, a securely fixed line to the Bottleneck was more necessary than ever. He clipped onto the line and began to rappel down into the darkness. Pasang disappeared from his view as he plunged over the ledge.

The Serac loomed large but, for now, it remained silent and stable. Temperatures had plummeted but it was calm and clear in the sky above. Halfway across the rope – the older rope from a previous expedition on which the climbers had ascended that morning – Pemba reached the second anchor jutting out of the ice face and catching the reflection of his head torch. Some of the rope was buried in the ice and Pemba was not satisfied with the reliability of the anchor – it would need to bear the weight of almost a dozen climbers who were now more likely to slip or fall in a trance-like inertia.

He used one of his own ice screws to forge a stronger anchor point. He paused, looking back up the line. Pasang was out of sight above the Serac. Why was he not descending? Was he helping Chhiring and Jumik to guide the other climbers towards the Traverse? Pemba waited in the ghostly stillness of the dark night.

It was 11pm and the climbers on the snowfields were showing no signs of movement. Pasang decided he would descend to Pemba and help him to chart the route to the Bottleneck. He had left his ice axe behind but thought he could achieve a secure descent with his carabiner and the fixed rope. He moved below the ridge and onto the line, using only the sling from his harness, his crampons and his gloved hands to inch his way along the face.

The light on his head torch began to flicker on and off as he battled to find a grip on the unyielding ice. He slipped several times, his fingertips providing little by way of security:

> By the help of eight fingers, I was coming down and I did not feel difficulty. But when I came down on the diagonal couloir my headlamp was also very dimmed and then I could not see very well. I found the rope and I clipped my safety and then immediately I slipped and that made me very afraid until the next anchor. I slipped [again] and I was totally out of it.

Several minutes later, Pemba's head torch appeared out of the darkness and Pasang rappelled quickly to join him on a narrow ledge. 'They are not coming,' he told Pemba. 'I cannot wait any longer. It is getting cold. I need to get down.' There were no lights visible anywhere above, no sound, just a hollow emptiness around them on the rock-hard face.

'We must continue,' Pemba told him as he picked his way quickly across the line. His weight jerked Pasang momentarily on the rope, knocking him off balance: 'He [Pemba] thought I was ready, and due to his weight I swung by the rope and it hit my hands, my side gloves fell down. I felt like there could have been a great accident, that all my luck was gone, [but it was] just a small hurt in my hand.'

Pemba edged onwards towards the next anchor. But something was amiss; he was shocked to discover a rope hanging freely down the vertical face. The rope was flaccid, untethered to another ice screw. It had been cut, displaced, by what he was not sure:

> There was no fixed line – it was totally cut, no fixed line there. And I observed everything here; with my light I explored the section over to the Bottleneck, I looked around and observed – this was a very technical part – and then finally I looked straight up and I found that the huge Serac had collapsed down ... and then I found, wow, there was an avalanche and everything was finished in the Bottleneck section. The rope was hanging there somewhere but I didn't know how long this rope was. I talked with Pasang and said be careful, everything is gone, there has been an avalanche, and I kept rappelling, we have to rappel with this rope but we don't know for how long. It was loose rope, very slack.

For the first time on K2, Pemba Gyalje was truly afraid: 'Now I was 100 per cent sure we had a problem.'

At 8,400 metres, Chhiring Dorje and Jumik Bhote waited with the stricken climbers. Everyone was stationary and quiet and even Chhiring found it difficult not to succumb to the desire for sleep. He sat on the soft snow, trying to detect light from Camp Four or any sign that they were on the right route.

Soon after they had disappeared over the horizon, he feared that Pemba and Pasang may have been swept away in an avalanche; there had been no sign of them for an hour, though it seemed like much longer. Chhiring dozed and found his mind drifting away from the desolation around him to his family back in Kathmandu:

> When I opened my eyes ... the only thing that came to my mind was my family. I remembered the tears in my wife's eye before I left for the K2 expedition. My daughters, my brother – that gave me strength to climb back ... What I thought was I don't have an option ... [if] I stay on the mountain I die, even if I descend I die, but if I fall while descending death would be easier.

Chhiring stood and moved slowly towards the Traverse. The other climbers behind him were non-responsive, many were sleeping, a few plodded around aimlessly. He decided that most of them could not or would not progress any further; those that managed to find the ropes had a chance of descending, those that couldn't muster the strength to do so would spend the night above the Serac and would have to climb down at first light. He and Jumik would not be able to steer the other climbers to safety alone.

Chhiring walked towards where he had last seen Pemba and Pasang. A short distance above the anchor, he slipped and slid several metres before arresting his fall with his axe. He was shocked but unharmed. On reaching the beginning of the line, he clipped onto the fixed rope and began to move across the Traverse. He could feel a tension on the line; the weight of the other Sherpas below him was evident. A distant light shimmering through the blackness from Camp Four on the tip of the Shoulder was the only evidence of life beneath the Bottleneck.

Pasang Lama had managed to find a foothold on the ledge on which he and Pemba now rested. Pasang felt faint and noticed blood trickling down his face; his head had rammed into the ice when he slipped half an hour before. Chhiring emerged from the gloom. There was no sign of any of the other climbers. 'Fuck, they are finished,' Chhiring told them, 'they sit down and there is no way to help them because they are not moving.' Pemba told him that the rope through the Bottleneck had been severed by an icefall and the route ahead was highly dangerous. He said he would climb across the ice in search of a way forward.

As he descended, the dimensions and features of the Bottleneck finally became familiar. He shouted to Chhiring and Pasang to follow; he had found the path through the gulley. Continuing to kick and hack his way downward without the aid of fixed ropes, Pemba felt the perspiration inside his down suit and admitted to himself that he was scared:

> I could see so many things – crampons, some jackets, pieces of clothes on the route and then I also found Wilco's rucksack that he dumped on the way up. I did a 15- to 20-metre fast down climb with no rope, and waited there to show light for Chhiring and Pasang because they had to come there. I had to give direction. I was descending fast because I wanted to get out of the Bottleneck because of avalanche danger. I was not confident with the Serac condition. When I saw that part of the Serac had collapsed, I was very worried about the Norwegians; I thought they had been killed, all of them.

Chhiring and Pasang would have to climb down without rope into the darkness, their dexterity and mountaineering proficiency their only weapons against a possible fall. Chhiring watched as Pemba's head torch moved down the slope and out of view. He heard his calls: 'This way, come down.'

Chhiring noticed the dread in Pasang's eyes as he gripped the ice; he would not make it through the Bottleneck without rope and an ice axe. It would be reckless in the extreme to climb backwards through the most lethal gulley on K2 with just crampons and freezing fingertips for grips. Trying to bring Pasang with him – two climbers relying on just one ice axe – was fraught with danger and could kill them both. Chhiring saw that Pasang was shivering and looking petrified:

> I thought if we stay there, we are going to be carried away by avalanche so we decided to descend in the alpine style. Pemba made his descent in alpine way and I told Pasang we have to go the same way. Pasang told me he didn't have his ice axe. I could see tears in his eyes. I felt it was humanity to save him and asked him to come as we will descend with one ice axe. Pasang was scared. He told me, "What if we slip?". So I told him, "If we fall, we fall together".

Pemba continued to move down the gulley as quickly as he could, unaware that Pasang Lama had no ice axe and that he and Chhiring were facing even greater danger, reliant as they now were on each other for their very survival.

A death-defying journey began as Chhiring and Pasang followed Pemba through the Bottleneck. Chhiring tied a short sling between their harnesses; if he slipped, Pasang would be pulled to his death without any way of arresting his fall. If Pasang fell, Chhiring would not be able to anchor their combined weights on his axe for more than a few seconds. The pair lined up, side by side, facing the mountain, just a few metres apart.

Chhiring moved first while Pasang stayed in place. Carefully picking the points at which to hack his axe into the ice or jam in the teeth of his crampons, Chhiring looked regularly at his passenger to his left. When he descended a few metres and found a foothold, and when the rope between them became taut, he stopped and waited to allow Pasang to descend.

Pasang's only connections to the mountain were his hands and feet, and the rope between his harness and Chhiring's. The improvised belay demanded that Pasang take every step as if his life depended on it. He remembered that it was near here that the Sherpa, Nima Nurbu, had plunged to his death the previous year. The Bottleneck stretched downwards at a dizzying angle.

Without the security of his ice axe, Pasang discarded his gloves and punched his fists into the frozen ice face, scratching out a series of miniature ledges on which to place his fingertips, a slippery and unreliable safety net should his crampons lose hold. Fragments of ice plunged unpredictably downwards as the Serac intermittently showered all beneath it. It was tempting to descend much faster. But if the two interdependent climbers moved too quickly, they could jeopardise whatever limited security their relay system now provided.

Pasang tried not to look down, suppressing his worst fears. But, mentally, he was preparing to die. He thought he was going to faint. The simplest of errors could be fatal. High above, the mountain rumbled, but any icefall passed mercifully over them, dropping into the snow below. Inching their way lower, Chhiring and Pasang sometimes held hands in the narrower sections of the Bottleneck.

Another rumble from above, and Pasang felt gravity sucking him inexorably towards death. Chhiring had been knocked from his perch and was frantically trying to self-arrest. He plunged downwards, carrying Pasang with him. After 30 metres or maybe more, Chhiring hacked his axe against the blue ice but it ricocheted as it struggled to hold the weight of two men.

They plunged metre after metre, limbs clattering off rocks and frozen snow. Another swing of the axe; this time it held and Chhiring almost catapulted back up the slope, the rope yanking tightly on his harness. Pasang jerked to a halt metres below and did not register that he had stopped for a few moments. He hung lifelessly on the rope, panting loudly, Chhiring now bearing the full weight of his companion. More icy rubble scattered past them.

The Serac was active, spewing its fragments down the Bottleneck at breakneck speed. But Pasang noticed that, for the first time since they had started their hellish journey through the Bottleneck, he could almost stand, the gradient having levelled out. Miraculously, they were close to the bottom. It had worked; they had made it.

Sometime before midnight, the radio crackled to life in the American team's tent on the Shoulder. Fredrik Sträng pressed the receiver. He, Eric Meyer and Chris Klinke had been resting, unable to sleep, waiting for the climbers to return. Fredrik recognised Chhiring Dorje's voice, whose tone was one of fear and concern: there had been an icefall in the Bottleneck, he told Fredrik, and the ropes were missing, the gear was missing, people had been taken away in the fall.

Fredrik and his team-mates had spent the previous hours monitoring their radios and the slopes above. As the hours passed and darkness fell, they had become more and more anxious about the welfare of the climbers above the Traverse whose head torches appeared stationary, apart from one or two lights which seemed to be shifting incrementally across and beneath the Serac. 'I started feeling hopeless,' said Fredrik, 'because it was dark and we couldn't go out in the dark trying to find our way up. All we could do was stay in Camp Four which we did, just waiting for people to come in and help them as much as we could with medicine, water. We boiled as much as we could and filled up all the bottles to serve people with water and support them with food that we had.'

The Serb team had left the camp a few hours earlier, anxious to get to Base Camp as quickly as possible after the loss of their team member, Dren Mandic. The Singaporean expedition had held back at Camp Three when news of the first fatalities filtered down the mountain.

Only a handful of the second wave South Korean team remained. Stepping outside his tent once more, Chris Klinke scanned the mountain. A handful of lights were still visible. The majority, however, remained worryingly motionless above the Serac.

Pemba waited for Chhiring and Pasang at the foot of the Bottleneck, watching their head torches bobbing and weaving in turn. It had taken him about 50 minutes to descend and, observing all the debris at the bottom of the gulley, he was anxious to move away as quickly as possible from what he considered to be an area fraught with objective dangers:

> I felt I was still in the danger zone and I had to get out very fast to a safe place. Chhiring and Pasang were still coming down very slowly and I kept flashing my light. I reached the safe zone and stopped and waited for them.

In that safer area, about 50 metres away from the bottom of the Bottleneck and where there was a better perspective of the upper mountain, Pemba noticed a smattering of lights higher on the Traverse.

Chhiring and Pasang walked slowly towards him, slumping beside him on the snow, partly out of fatigue but also in disbelief that they had survived an unthinkable descent. Almost immediately, however, Chhiring's thoughts turned to those still above them, struggling to comprehend what was happening:

> We came to safety and there Pemba was waiting for us. If the climbers on the mountain had done the same, they would have been safe. Why did they stay back? They were capable climbers, strong – then why did they stay there?

The three rested for half an hour, barely talking, fixed on the light twinkling at Camp Four. Chhiring and Pemba tried to radio those above, moving through the frequencies on their walkie-talkies. They wanted to alert Jumik about the severed rope in the Bottleneck but there was only static; either the radio batteries were dead or the climbers were too disorientated to hear.

Chhiring had last seen Jumik over an hour earlier and he was worried that he was lost with the others somewhere beneath the summit. He managed to talk to his team at Camp Four who encouraged Chhiring to keep descending; there was little he could do to help the others.

Pemba tried to gather his thoughts. How had it come to this? Strong, experienced climbers – for the most part – had forgotten the fundamentals of climbing, seemed incapable of rational thought and had become victims of the power of Wyss-Dunant's 'Fatal Zone':

> There were still people there just above the top anchor, we could see many lights but they were not moving, they had completely stopped ... if they are lucky some can climb down the next day but the majority cannot do that ... I was now 100 per cent sure that 80 per cent of the people will now be dead, they cannot come down and next day we cannot go up the Bottleneck to fix the lines again because we don't have rope, there is not enough manpower in High Camp. Now I was thinking that many good people were going to die.

The discontinuation of the moving rope system had left the climbers above the Serac devoid of direction and leadership. Those that did not sit down, wearied by oxygen starvation, throbbing headaches and aching limbs, drifted elsewhere in thought and in body, their minds numbed against any normal decision making and any attempt at productive navigation. Teamwork had evaporated; individuals were left to their own devices.

The Death Zone was wreaking havoc on bodies already racked by fatigue and any thoughts that formulated were now governed by a new emotion – fear.

Karim Meherban moved awkwardly across the snow. The lights of the other head torches were scattered around and away from him in a frigid haze. The 31-year-old Pakistani, who had embraced his client, Hugues D'Aubarède, just four hours earlier on the summit, was unable to find his team leader. Other summiteers had noted that both men were suffering from altitude sickness when they celebrated on the summit; they were vocal and mobile but appeared to lack lucidity or purpose.

When the four Sherpas had terminated the moving rope system, Pasang Lama saw Karim drift away from the group in what seemed to be the wrong direction. Everything around Karim was now a blur. Without a reference point with which to find direction, the ground before him looked monotonous and hostile. Karim's knees buckled and he slumped onto the snow: the handrail to Camp Four which the fixed line provided eluded him.

The members of the Flying Jump expedition had begun to disperse at 8,400 metres. So focussed were they on each step and the regulation of their oxygen supplies that Mr Kim's team had become separated and disjointed. Mr Kim and Ms Go were not prepared to wait any longer and pressed ahead towards the Traverse. If he could locate the top anchor, the South Korean expedition leader could direct his team members towards it.

The darkness was almost impenetrable but soon the edge of the Serac was found and the two began to descend. From the top of the Traverse, there was no sign of Jumik Bhote, 'Little' Kim Hyo-gyeong, Hwang Dong-jin or Park Kyeong-hyo. Mr Kim decided that they needed to be rescued. He would summon help once he reached Camp Four.

Marco Confortola had fallen behind the others but he could see Ger and the South Koreans ahead of him. Every fibre of Marco's being told him to stop; there was no point in continuing if the ropes could not be found in the dark. His body was buckling under the strain of the fruitless zigzagging across the dark expanse. A couple of steps in the wrong direction could send him plunging into a crevasse or, worse still, over the edge of the Serac.

He implored Ger to wait with him until daylight returned. They knew there was only one dreadful option: they would have to remain in the Death Zone until first light. Resigned to their fate, the pair began to dig out two small holes in the snow – one to sit in and one in which to place their feet.

Having established their meagre resting place, Ger and Marco suddenly heard a noise like an explosion interrupting the enormous silence of the night; to Marco's ears it sounded like thunder:

> I don't know what it is – it might be an avalanche – soon after we hear some voices and shouting but we can't make out what they are saying. They sound far away, the sounds seem to be coming from beneath the Serac and then there is a terrifying silence. I keep saying, "Stay here, we can't do something foolish".[111]

Marco thought that other climbers had fallen. Had some of them been swept away in an avalanche? Had they tumbled over the edge of the Serac? He could see a light at Camp Four: 'See, Jesus, there is Camp Four,' he told Ger. Fear gripped the Italian; he wanted reassurance and advice. Retrieving his satellite phone from his down suit, he called Roberto Manni at Camp Four. 'If you sleep, you die,' Roberto told him, 'don't forget your feet and hands.' He was right, thought Marco; it was vital to keep moving their limbs:

> It is the end if you fall asleep. It is a huge task for myself and Jesus. We are at 8,400 metres in the dark, without a tent, without a sleeping sac, no protection and without food or drink ... the cold is icy cold, we must stay awake, we can't sleep. Me and Jesus fight hard to keep our eyes open and to not fall asleep. The sky is black like tar, there is a terrible silence, we hear nothing.[112]

Marco switched off his phone and tried to focus on staying alive. Time became meaningless for the two men as they struggled to remain awake. The most terrible thing of all was the silence; interminable and deafening. Marco worried about his companion and tried to prevent him from falling asleep. He started to sing 'La Montanara', a song about the mountains that his father had taught him as a child. Ger seemed to respond, joining in and humming the song. 'Keep moving, clap your hands and feet, don't stop, don't stop, Jesus, don't stop,' Marco told him.[113]

The Italian had no idea how much time had passed when he saw a light approaching from a few dozen metres away:

> I say to Jesus, "Come on, they are coming to help us", even though I think
> it is very hard for anyone to come from High Camp in the dark to help us.
> I think that maybe they are indicating the route down.[114]

Wilco van Rooijen could not believe that the fixed ropes were evading him, but, despite his fatigue, he refused to panic. He had trudged to and fro trying to find the way but, by midnight, he was confronting the possibility that his descent would have to await the dawn. Wilco had many questions tormenting him. How was this possible? Where was the rope? Where was everybody? He scoured the surrounding terrain but nothing looked familiar:

> You are so exhausted and everybody is going down at his own speed. You
> are not that concentrated that you say, "Hey! Wait for me because I am
> losing you". You are going down because you will find the fixed ropes and
> if you find the fixed ropes, you will go down, follow the lines and there is
> Camp Four.

Having traversed the snow plain several times, dangerously close to the edge, Wilco collapsed onto the snow. It seemed impossible. He thought that they had ended up on the wrong side of the mountain. Were they now descending towards China? Wilco heard familiar voices above him and to his right, one of them singing: it was Ger and Marco. They were sitting huddled together, clapping their hands to keep warm.

Wilco approached, the hopelessness evident on his face. Marco mumbled something about seeing people fall, head torches disappearing out of sight. Wilco suspected he was hallucinating. 'We can't find this fucking trail,' Marco told him. Maybe just one more attempt, Wilco thought; there might still be time.

Marco pulled Ger up off the snow; the three of them would make one last effort to find the route. They split up and descended slowly in different directions, fanning out across the snow. Wilco peered over what seemed like a gaping void; the edge of the Serac perhaps? But it was unfamiliar and dizzyingly dangerous. Inside, he raged against their inability to progress. Marco begged Wilco to stop; to continue would be suicidal.

'At that moment the panic started a little,' said Wilco, 'because we were thinking what to do now, which way to go. Because there was no sign at all which way to go; no rope.' Wilco quickly realised that, at that altitude, with no tent, no stove, no food and drink and no sleeping bag, the only option for him also was a makeshift bivouac. He moved about 40 metres below Ger and Marco and scooped out a bucket seat for the hours ahead.

The Dutchman was stunned that it had come to this so soon after the ecstasy of the hours before: 'The contrast is enormous. The blissful feeling on the summit; you switch a button, and the next moment you are back in the hard reality of small ledges, slippery, black rocks, treacherous snow and immense ice masses.'[115] Alone with his thoughts, he tried to prepare mentally for a five-hour wait in the freezing, dry air, 8,400 metres above sea level.

<hr>

In the Netherlands, waiting for news of her husband's safe descent, Wilco's wife, Heleen, kept her phone nearby and was scanning the internet for information from the mountain. Like so many other spouses, partners and family members, she knew that the most dangerous part of the climb was under way, as a passage from her diary that 1 August illustrates:

> People call to congratulate me that the summit has been reached. My response is shallow, modest. People just don't understand. More than half the battle is getting down. The summit is only halfway home. I tell them that the team has to safely reach Base Camp and then we celebrate.[116]

Her fears were not unique. In Alaska, Ger McDonnell's partner, Annie Starkey, was becoming anxious too. She hadn't heard from Ger since he reached the summit. That was nothing unusual; it might take him four or five hours to reach Camp Four. The 14-hour time difference between Alaska and Pakistan forced her to continually calibrate the approximate time on K2.

At 5am Alaskan time, she had emailed the Norit team webmaster, Maarten van Eck, to say Ger had called her from the summit and that she was hoping to hear from him again in five or six hours. By lunchtime in Anchorage, however, Annie had become increasingly concerned:

> ... the phone rang when I was at lunch and I thought it was him, but it was another friend who was calling and she said, "Have you heard?". I don't know if she was on the internet. "Have you heard from Gerard yet?", and I said no, I hadn't and I was really worried. And then I went home from lunch and got immediately on the internet ...

The Norit expedition website flickered on the screen; its newest headline shocking Annie to the core: 'Major Problems on K2!'

Cas van de Gevel's only focus was survival: 'Above 8,000 metres, you are a little bit fixed on your own descending ... I was so much fixed in the descending that I didn't know who was in front of me or back of me.' Cas had found the top anchor and the fixed lines after midnight. Clipping onto the rope, he forced concerns about other climbers from his mind; his team-mates were experienced mountaineers and would surely find the way down, he hoped.

But he had not seen Ger McDonnell for at least two hours, not since they had all descended the ice face beneath the summit. Whether Pemba was ahead of him or behind, he could not tell. Wilco was nowhere to be seen.

Cas made steady progress along the rope, using his ice axe and crampons, every hack and kick a closely co-ordinated physical effort in the face of the biting cold niggling at his fingers and toes. A light shimmered further along the rope. Before he knew it, he was almost face to face with Hugues D'Aubarède. Hugues' high-altitude worker, Karim, was nowhere to be seen and the Frenchman had come to a complete halt, his forehead pressed against the ice as he gasped for oxygen.

Though Hugues looked tired, Cas was not overly concerned about him, thinking that he was now at least on the roped route to camp. 'You go past, you are quicker than me,' Cas heard him say. Cas unclipped momentarily and stepped around Hugues, continuing his descent as the Frenchman's head torch faded out of view.

Just a few metres below, Cas was astonished to find the rope severed and frayed. A new rope, which he did not recognise, was tied from the nearby anchor and hanging vertically into the darkness. It must have been left there by another climber. But where was the original line? Nearby, debris and craggy furrows on the surface pointed to an avalanche and the movement of a mass of ice down the face.

Cas paused, trying to assess the terrain. He clipped onto the new rope but it ran for only a few dozen metres before coming to an end. From there he would have to climb down to Camp Four without any fixed line. The experienced Dutch climber did not dally and began to hack his crampons and ice axe into the steel-like surface.

Pausing every few minutes to look around him, Cas could see two head torches way above him on the Traverse. They were making their way downwards; perhaps it was Ger and Wilco? But where was Hugues? He could not be far behind. Seconds later, Cas heard a scratching noise above him, like skates on an ice rink. His light caught a yellow-suited form plummeting quickly down the side of the mountain to his left.

The body did not emit a single sound as it rocketed by, silently awaiting the end. Hugues D'Aubarède plunged deeper into the darkness. And then there was silence, except for Cas' laboured breaths. His stilted reaction surprised him:

> You have a little bit of a different reaction at 8,000 metres. Above 8,000
> metres, when you are there for a long time without oxygen, you think, "Oh
> no, he's falling", and then one moment, you don't really know what to do.

The second oldest person ever to have scaled the world's second highest mountain was dead.

Tsering Bhote and his cousin, 'Big' Pasang Bhote, left Camp Four at midnight and moved across the Shoulder towards the Bottleneck. Three hours before, the Flying Jump B team, of which they were members, had called off their summit bid, scheduled for the next day, as the scale of the problems on the slopes above became increasingly apparent.

But Tsering and 'Big' Pasang were particularly concerned; Tsering's brother, Jumik, was out there on the mountain, still unaccounted for. Jumik was also 'Big' Pasang's cousin. They wanted to find him and lead him and the other missing South Korean climbers back to camp. Equipped with food, water and a handful of oxygen cylinders, the pair set out into the blackness. They shared their disbelief at the human catastrophe unfolding in the Death Zone.

Tsering looked up to his cousin; a broad-shouldered mountain climber known for his strength and versatility, 'Big' Pasang's nickname was no accident; his agility and toughness were renowned. To Tsering, he exuded competence and ability. The more experienced 26-year-old was something of a mentor and advisor to Tsering and his other cousins on the mountain. Before Tsering, Jumik, Pasang Lama and the cook, Ngawang Bhote, had left for K2, 'Big' Pasang was consulted for his opinion and gave the expedition his stamp of approval.[117]

He ploughed through the snow on the Shoulder and seemed completely fixed on what lay ahead, urging Tsering to follow in his footsteps. At just 21 years of age, and with only a summiting of Lhotse under his belt, Tsering now found himself in the midst of a rescue mission on the world's most dangerous mountain. But he tried to remain focussed on Jumik. Back in Kathmandu, Jumik's wife, Dawa Sangmu, was heavily pregnant and about to give birth to a baby. Tsering wanted to bring the child's father home.

Halfway to the Bottleneck, Tsering and 'Big' Pasang met three Sherpas making their way back to Camp Four. Pemba Gyalje, Chhiring Dorje and Pasang Lama availed immediately of the tea and chocolate the Bhotes had brought with them. 'Where is Jumik?' they asked Pemba, 'have you seen him or the others from our expedition?' Pemba shook his head.

Looking towards the summit, he told the cousins how the other climbers had spent over 12 hours in the Death Zone and of how they seemed to be overwhelmed by the effects of hypoxia. He told of the late time most of the climbers had summited, the disintegration of their attempts to lead the others towards the fixed ropes and the worsening condition of the climbers above the Serac. Tsering and 'Big' Pasang were incredulous, Pemba noted:

> They were very angry with us, the three of us. They said, "Why are you guys so late, why didn't you turn back? You are mad". They were totally angry with us. They asked where are the others and we said that they sat down, they are not coming down, and then they asked where is Jumik and we say he is also behind. They were angry with everybody, fucking Koreans, fucking everybody. "Why did you keep climbing?" The two men, they were crying and screaming, they were angry with us.

Pemba found himself agreeing in part with the Bhotes: the expeditions hadn't turned back when they could have or should have. The team leaders had said little or nothing to guide their teams when a series of crises emerged, nor had individual climbers shown the resolve needed to get down the mountain. The Sherpas also questioned why they themselves hadn't descended when they felt strongly that it was the right thing to do.

Collectively, the frustrations and setbacks of the day were finally brimming to the surface as the five Sherpas began to voice their criticisms: 'If they said quit, then everyone would have turned back down.' 'Why did those fucking people say nothing?' 'The snow was too deep to go on.' Pemba's experience, however, had taught him that all the logistical planning, physical preparation and leadership skills were rarely a match for the savagery and ferocity of the Death Zone.

Eric Meyer and Fredrik Sträng had tea ready for Pemba, Chhiring and Pasang when they made it back to Camp Four around 1.30am. A saddened Chhiring told his team-mates about the severed ropes in the Bottleneck, how he and Pasang had survived the descent and how so many climbers had been crushed physically and mentally in the hours after reaching the summit.

Eric, in turn, told him of the deaths of Dren Mandic, Jehan Baig and Rolf Bae: three climbers were now confirmed dead. Camp Four was also rife with rumours that other climbers, including Ms Go, had fallen from the Bottleneck.

Pemba was drained, thinking only of recuperation. If his team-mates had not descended by morning, they would need to be rescued and he would need all his strength to find them. He vomited several times. Eric gave him two anti-inflammatory dexamethasone tablets and he went to the tent he had shared with Ger.

The Irishman's sleeping bag and belongings had not been touched since he had left for the summit almost 24 hours earlier. All Pemba could hope for was that his friend had the resilience and tenacity to make it through the night in the Death Zone. He left their tent and went to Marco's, which was also empty, and decided to sleep there. 'I tried to rehydrate well when I was inside the tent. I felt very, very sad.' Pemba closed his eyes and drifted into sleep.

Marco Confortola, Ger McDonnell and, some metres away, Wilco van Rooijen, were perched on a gradient of 45 degrees in their improvised dais overlooking the bleak and empty darkness below. Sleep could precipitate a tumble into the abyss. But trying to remain awake was an almost impossible struggle. When they weren't dozing, Ger and Marco thumped each other's arms and legs to help encourage the capillaries to feed the limbs and outer extremities.

The extreme cold was having a traumatic effect on their bodies as the blood supply and any remaining warmth retreated to the core, leaving the peripheries vulnerable to the worst repercussions of exposure to subzero temperatures. At such altitudes and as the temperature plummets, the body begins to shut down and any remaining heat moves to shield key organs such as the heart and lungs; they must be protected to ensure survival.

Strangely, the transition into that shutdown, that surrendering of the outer extremities and the limbs to the frost, can be quite serene and peaceful. Fatigue takes hold of the mind as well as the body and, for a time, the encroachment of hypothermia and frostbite are almost forgotten, suppressed in the subconscious. The brain also reminds the body that if it can withstand the cold of the darkness for a few hours, so, too, will it respond to the heat of the daylight which dawn will bring.

Fitful sleep provides a refuge from thoughts of home but they are never far away – in the stillness and silence, and, at their lowest ebb, climbers cannot avoid thinking of their loved ones. They want the night to be over, to get down, to get home. Rocking to and fro, the climber whispers, 'I don't want to die, I don't want to die'.

As Cas completed his descent through the Bottleneck, he occasionally turned to cast the light from his head torch over the snow and ice to his left. Perhaps he would see Hugues? He had barely reacted to the fall, his brain struggling to take it all in, the impact of oxygen deprivation almost anaesthetising him against the shock of death on the slopes. There was no sign of a body or any track it had made across the snow.

Using his radio at the foot of the Bottleneck, Cas managed to get through to Roeland van Oss of the Norit team at Base Camp, telling him all he knew about who hadn't yet descended and those who had already perished; he did not know where his team-mates were, other than they were most likely way above him in the Death Zone. He was on the way to Camp Four and would radio any further updates.

Two lights emerged from the gloom below him as Cas walked along the Shoulder. It was the two Sherpas from the Flying Jump B team, whom he recognised from Base Camp. Tsering and 'Big' Pasang seemed uninterested in Cas' appeal to them to look for Hugues, and he continued downwards, his body begging for rest and his throat gasping for a warm drink. On reaching Camp Four, he spoke to no-one and fell into his sleeping bag at 2am, a full 24 hours after he had last left it.

In the pitch blackness and frigidity of the night, Tsering and 'Big' Pasang continued their trek across the Shoulder. They were still carrying food and water for anyone else they might meet. High above, something bright caught Tsering's eye: two lights plunging simultaneously, one down the south face of the mountain to the left of the Bottleneck, the other to the east on the couloir's right side. He could not be sure if they were stars falling from the sky or lights from the head torches of falling climbers. Was it Jumik or one of the South Koreans? Tsering could not be sure. Maybe it was an illusion.

Minutes later, the Bhotes caught a glimpse of yet another climber shuffling towards them along the ridge of the Shoulder. It was their expedition leader, Mr Kim, and he was alone, not another of his team members in sight. Mr Kim showed all the signs of having been without sleep and sustenance for the previous 15 hours. His oxygen supply had expired.

Gulping the water he was offered, he told Tsering and 'Big' Pasang that Ms Go was still out there. She had been descending behind him as they left the snowfields above the Serac but they had become separated. 'Ms Go is coming down. Help her and serve her with water,' Mr Kim told them. He continued towards Camp Four.

A voice cried out from the wilderness above, a distressed appeal for help. Tsering and 'Big' Pasang had been searching near to where they thought one of the mysterious lights had fallen from higher on the slopes. They knew the cries had to be those of the only woman now left above High Camp.

Ms Go had gone off course just below the Bottleneck, straying onto a rocky outcrop, and was unable to find her way in the black night. 'Didi?' 'Big' Pasang called, using the name the Sherpas had given the 41-year-old adventurer. Perhaps, Tsering thought, she had been one of the falling lights he had witnessed just minutes before:

> We heard her yell and we reached the place. We saw Ms Go. She was stuck in a rock, trapped as she could not move. She was sitting there shouting. So we went there and rescued her by clamping Ms Go to 'Big' Pasang's safety ... we didn't talk with the girl, she was not in the state of communicating, most probably because of energy loss.

The three set out for Camp Four, arriving there at 4.30am. They took Ms Go to Mr Kim's tent; the South Korean superstar had been saved.

'Dutch K2 Norit expedition webmaster, Maarten van Eck, reports that a big chunk of ice has fallen below the summit, taking a large part of the fixed lines with it,' read the new posting on the ExplorersWeb blog late on 1 August. 'About 12 people, including possibly Wilco, Gerard, Marco and Korean climbers are stuck before either the Traverse or the Bottleneck. Cas and Pemba down climbed to C4 [Camp Four] without fixed ropes. Dutch Norit Base Camp manager, Roeland, is in the Korean expedition tent organising a joint rescue effort.'[118]

Through the power of the internet, the world was beginning to learn that something had gone drastically wrong in K2's Death Zone.

Chapter five

Trapped in the
Death Zone

2 August – 3 August

Ger McDonnell's ice-encrusted eyelids fluttered repeatedly against the brightening glow before he opened them. Though sitting awkwardly and uncomfortably on the cold snow at a life-sapping altitude, his brain and body begged him to remain asleep. However, a nourishing warmth had begun to permeate his hypothermic frame, the light of the rising sun soothing his stiffened and throbbing muscles. It was a welcome release from what had been a seemingly endless and psychologically harrowing night, exposed to the remorseless and inhospitable middle reaches of the troposphere.

Ger allowed his eyes to crack open, letting in the brilliant rays which were lighting up the jagged peaks on the horizon. Another perfect dawn had broken over the Karakorum mountains to reveal three stranded climbers hunched over in semi-foetal positions in their improvised bucket seats high above the infamous Serac.

Attempts to remain awake in the cold blackness of the night had yielded to fitful sleep as Ger – and alongside him Marco Confortola and, further down, Wilco van Rooijen – succumbed intermittently to slumber during almost five hours on the freezing snow. First light brought rejuvenation and the prospect of escape from the clutches of the Death Zone.

Rousing each other, the trio stamped their feet and pummelled themselves to re-activate the blood flow to their limbs. The rising sun re-energised them, raising the core temperature in their bodies and boosting their confidence that they would find the route to the fixed ropes. As Wilco stood, he tried again to discount the notion that they had somehow ended up on the wrong side of the mountain. He was on his feet after 5am as the first shafts of light reached the slopes around him: 'Now the surviving started because we were not in control anymore.'

He knew the ropes were close by and that they would surely become visible in the morning sun. He began walking in one direction, Ger and Marco going the other way, their eyes peeled, every step carefully considered. But the terrain was still unfamiliar to Wilco, even in the long-awaited daylight, and there was no sign of any rope. After almost an hour, he became exasperated, every look over the edge of the Serac yielding nothing.

As he traversed to and fro, the rays of the sun ricocheting from the white snow into his eyes, Wilco started to experience a blurring of his vision and a searing headache – the first signs of snow blindness. Having experienced the condition before during polar expeditions, he immediately recognised the symptoms – a feeling of grittiness in the eyes, a loss of peripheral vision, and a burning sensation at the back of the eyeballs as the retinas became scorched by the ultraviolet light.

The otherwise phlegmatic Dutchman began to panic. He was also likely experiencing the creeping effects of cerebral oedema, a debilitating accumulation of fluid around the brain at high altitude which affected vision but, whatever the diagnosis, the treatment was clear: Wilco had to descend. Lower altitude would ease the symptoms.

Though he did not know precisely where he was, or what exactly lay below, Wilco knew he was somewhere close to the Traverse. He could make it down to a lower altitude without rope. Perhaps if he free-climbed downwards he would find the line across the Traverse; he was a skilled and professional mountaineer, used to navigating his way out of danger.

Staying with Ger and Marco was not an option. If his sight deteriorated any further, he would be unable to move at all. Finding the fixed ropes quickly became secondary; Wilco would make his descent directly downwards and as quickly as possible:

> ... then I was getting more in a panic because I knew, fuck, when I start getting snow-blind at this altitude, it's finished. No helicopter is coming, the guys can't do something with a body of 80 kilos so I said, "Listen guys, I have to go down. I have to go down". So I started just going down without thinking anymore, just going down ... we all knew we were in big shit now ...

By 6am, Wilco was back climbing into the unknown, with no safety rope, no climbing companions and no way of alleviating his burning eyes. He was extremely dehydrated. Resisting the temptation to melt snow in his mouth, which would only further lower his core temperature, he continued. The gradient was incredibly steep and Wilco risked falling if his descent became too speedy, too careless.

He rarely glanced downwards and, when he did, he struggled to see; the sun now his enemy rather than his ally. He instructed himself verbally on what to do and settled into a robotic routine, straining to maintain three points of contact with the ice at all times. One wrong move could send him plunging to certain death. Ger and Marco were soon out of sight and earshot as they continued their quest for the top anchor point.

So engrossed was he in concentrating on each step, the shocking scene which caught Wilco's eye took a few moments to register. On the blood-stained snow lay a climber hanging from a rope around his waist, his eyes shut, apparently unconscious. His head was cut and badly bruised, the snow around him an incongruous deep red.

Just below him, tethered to the same rope, was another climber hanging almost upside down, moaning softly as if in severe pain. A third climber, also trapped on the rope and further to Wilco's left, was hunched over, staring ahead in a trance; he had no gloves and had lost a boot in the fall. His skin had turned a waxy grey as frostbite took hold.

The three climbers were caught up in a web of ropes which were tied to some fixed point higher up on the ice face. Wiclo found a foothold and moved closer to the most alert of the trio. From the colour of their suits, he knew that they were members of the South Korean team.

Stretching out his exposed hands, the lowest hanging of the climbers whispered to Wilco: 'Gloves, gloves,' he implored. It was Jumik Bhote, the South Korean team sirdar. Wilco retrieved a spare pair from his backpack and handed them to him. He did not ask what had happened.

How they had come to be there, Wilco had no idea. He had not heard anyone fall on his own descent nor had he heard any screams. But they had evidently been hanging there for several hours and must have fallen during the night:

> At that point in time I didn't realise what had happened. But the night before Marco spoke about lamps suddenly disappearing into the depth. These lamps must have belonged to the Koreans and the Sherpa Jumik.[119]

Wilco believed that there was no way he could free the trapped climbers on his own. They were bound in an intricate mesh of ropes which would require the untangling skills of a number of rescuers working in unison. There was no sign of Ger and Marco. Cutting ropes to ease the tension on the line and give the climbers some comfort would almost certainly send the three to their deaths. Wilco felt helpless.

One of the climbers seemed barely alive; another only partially conscious. 'Help is on the way,' Jumik told him; perhaps their team-mate, 'Little' Kim, ahead of them on the descent the previous night, had witnessed their fall but was unable to free them, and continued to descend believing that the second Flying Jump team could come to their aid.

'I have to go down, I am snow blind,' Wilco told Jumik. He hesitated again, yielding to the burning sensation in his eye sockets. The climbers would have to await help. He could do nothing more for them. Within minutes, Wilco continued his painstaking descent, sure neither of his direction nor his ability to climb down to safety.

Chhiring Dorje had slept little since returning to his tent in the early hours of the morning. At 4.30am a restless Pasang Lama had come to his tent in search of gas for his stove. He told Chhiring that Tsering Bhote and 'Big' Pasang Bhote had brought Ms Go back to camp and they were planning to head out again to find Jumik and the other South Korean climbers who were still missing. As the sun rose, Pemba joined Chhiring in his tent. 'Wilco and Ger have not returned,' Pemba told him, 'and only Cas is here.'

Chhiring felt too exhausted to join any rescue attempt: 'I thought if I go to rescue there are avalanches and my physical stamina would not allow me to climb. I was really worried.' As he lay in his sleeping bag, listening to the multilingual mutterings of climbers outside his tent, Chhiring was puzzled as to how the various expeditions had crumbled so spectacularly in the Death Zone, while just a handful of climbers had prevailed:

> Marco is an international mountain guide, why didn't he climb back? Even Gerard? The girl? Hwang, our co-ordinator? I am amazed why he didn't climb back. Jumik? The Pakistani guide? Everyone strong and capable. Who decided to stay back? It was the same risk that we faced; if we made it to safety they could have done the same.

As dawn broke at Camp Four, the full horror of what was happening on the mountain was filtering through. A veil of silence and disbelief rested over the climbers who gazed towards the Traverse, waiting and worrying. The few climbers who had made it back to camp had brought crumbs of news; ice had fallen and killed at least one climber in the Bottleneck and severed essential ropes but there was no definitive explanation why so many climbers were still trapped above the Serac.

Cecilie Skog lay in her sleeping bag, racked by grief and replaying the events of the night over and over in her head. She and her team-mates had not slept a wink. Cecilie wanted to get away from K2 as quickly as possible but seemed unable to rouse her insensate body. Other climbers, just hearing the news of Rolf's death for the first time, were shocked. When she emerged from her tent they embraced her. She was speechless and distraught.

Accompanied by Lars, she went to the American team tent just after 7am to tell them about what had happened to Rolf. Cecilie seemed inconsolable. Fredrik approached her to sympathise, offering her his team's oxygen and satellite phone. She told Fredrik she wanted to go back out on the snow to search for her husband but he cautioned against any attempt to recover the body: 'I said to her, with the memory of Jehan Baig fresh in my mind, "Please go down, go down now. Don't think about it, he is gone. He is gone".' Cecilie turned to Oystein and Lars and they prepared to descend to Camp Three, gathering what personal effects of Rolf's they could carry.

An exhausted Pemba had got little rest in Marco's tent and he wakened to fresh despondency as flashbacks of the previous day and night flooded his mind. He heard the grief-stricken cries of Cecilie Skog; it was only then that Pemba learned Rolf Bae was dead. He went to the Americans' tent to talk with them. Fredrik Sträng's camcorder captured the Sherpa's disillusioned description of a frenetic and chaotic night on the mountain:

> There was nothing, no ice anchor, no rope anchor, no fixed line, nothing. Then I tried to contact the Korean Sherpas but I couldn't get them on the radio, because nobody switched on the radio. It was a big problem.[120]

He checked all the other tents to see who had returned during the hours he had slept. He found only Cas, who told him about the fall and likely death of

Hugues D'Aubarède. Cas told Pemba how quickly the Frenchman had fallen through the Bottleneck: 'It was like throwing a stone, it was in seconds; you cannot see it was so fast.'

Norit team member, Mark Sheen, was still at Camp Four. He had been contemplating a summit bid with the second wave of climbers but, when he learned of the human devastation of the previous hours, the realisation quickly dawned that too many climbers were either lost or missing on the mountain to allow for any new summit attempt.

The vibration of his cell-phone woke Bjorn Sekkesaeter from his slumber. It was 2.30am high in the Norwegian mountains where the experienced mountain guide and adventurer was leading a training course. Bjorn was the webmaster and media spokesperson for the Norwegian expedition and he had gone to bed having read an inaccurate report that his friends, Rolf and Cecilie, had summited K2.

He anticipated a call full of joy and excitement and started to congratulate Cecilie when he heard her voice. It was a few moments before he realised that she was crying. Bjorn's was the only number Cecilie could remember. Between the tears she repeated again and again the tragic news:

> I was completely shocked. She kept on saying that Rolf was gone and I finally realised what had happened. She had borrowed a sat phone from one of the other teams. She was in Camp Four when she made the phone call. She had to hang up because she had borrowed the phone and had to call me later. They had to get down. The only phone number she remembered was mine so she called me to help her to get Rolf's parents' numbers. She couldn't remember them.[121]

The line went dead but Cecilie called Bjorn again and he gave her the Baes' phone number. She was very anxious to talk with Rolf's parents but, such was her grief and distress, Bjorn became increasingly worried about her ability to descend the mountain safely:

> I understood how serious the situation was because I knew they were still high up on the mountain. I realised they were not down at Base Camp. She

had to get down so I told her I wanted her and Lars to get safely down ... Immediately when I gave her the numbers, I began to think about what to do and I thought maybe the best thing to do was to call Rolf's parents so they were prepared for what was coming. And they would know what her situation was so they could tell her they wanted her to come down, so they could support her.[122]

Bjorn decided that, in light of Cecilie's trauma and in the best interest of trying to ensure all three team members came safely off the mountain, he would make one of the most difficult phone calls of his life. He dialled Rolf's parents' number:

I had to tell Rolf's father and he took that message really hard but he understood the situation. We spoke calmly and we said time was of the essence. I told him, "Jacob you have to tell her to get down because I am afraid for her", and he immediately supported me in that.[123]

The hiss of gas from the stove filled the cold emptiness in the tent at Camp Three on the Abruzzi spur where Alberto Zerain had spent the night. There were slim pickings for breakfast at the camp which was home to just the Spaniard and a team from Singapore. One of the Singaporeans told Alberto snippets of information from higher on the mountain which pointed to several more deaths:

So from that I knew, okay, I better get down. A tragedy was developing. I didn't have a telephone. I didn't have anything. I knew that my colleagues from Broad Peak would be nervous because they knew that I was doing the ascent ... So I went down as quickly as I could to the Base Camp.

The expedition from Singapore, which had been planning a 2 August summit bid, had stalled at Camp Three on their ascent as news filtered through from above that lives had been lost. Base Camp had asked Robert Goh and his climbers to remain there and to gather food, fuel and oxygen for those who would need it on their descent. The Singaporean webmaster posted a grim update:

They [the Singaporean team] are in contact with BC every two hours, standing by to help rescue if needed. They will be spending a third night at Camp Three which will surely leave their bodies even more debilitated. Their expedition now hangs in the balance, but that is the last thing on their minds, as lives are at stake. If you are so inclined, please pray for everyone on the mountain.[124]

Elsewhere, climbers from other teams moved downwards from the lower camps on the Abruzzi route; there was nothing they could do. Staying at the higher camps would only serve to drain what limited resources each depot had to treat and rejuvenate any of those who might yet descend safely. But two climbers from the second wave of would-be summiteers had not turned.

Tsering Bhote and 'Big' Pasang Bhote were about to leave Camp Four. They had spent an exhausting night searching for missing team members and had eventually brought Ms Go to safety. However, their family member, Jumik, still had not returned and, convinced that he was now in serious danger, the two men set out once more into the Death Zone.

Ger and Marco continued the search for the top anchor long after Wilco had dropped out of sight. They moved around the snow with an increased sense of urgency; spending any more time in the Death Zone would be catastrophic. They needed food and water quickly.

Traversing along the Serac ridge, it finally appeared; an ice screw, around which was wound the familiar rope which had led them towards the summit the previous day, protruded from the snow. Their relief was palpable and the pair wasted no time in affixing their harnesses before easing themselves onto the line. The gradient was steep, the terrain on the early part of the descent difficult to navigate.

After scaling downwards 100 metres or so, they came across the same shocking spectacle that had so astounded Wilco an hour earlier. It was a mess of bodies and ropes. Marco thought he recognised one of the South Koreans – the expedition's deputy leader, Hwang Dong-jin, who had a German Rolleiflex camera hanging from his neck. Marco knew the camera from Base Camp, where Hwang had spent much time photographing the mountain.

The second man was Park Kyeong-hyo, the South Korean climbing leader, his face swollen and purple, his eyes shut. He seemed to be in the worst condition, unable to move and unresponsive. In his many years as a mountain rescuer in Italy, Marco had never come across such a scene of entangled and beaten bodies:

I don't know how long they have been like that. A little bit down from them is another climber, sitting down in a strange way. He is a Nepalese Sherpa [Jumik]. He is out of his head, he has a terrorised expression. He has lost a boot, probably during the fall. He has his thick socks on but is missing one boot. He is sitting in an abnormal position and doesn't say anything.[125]

Moving immediately to assist the afflicted, Ger unclipped from the fixed line and moved across several metres towards Hwang. He lifted Hwang's head to help him breathe more easily and tried to unravel the rope that was forcing the injured climber into an almost-fully upside down posture. With Marco, Ger tried to lift Jumik into a more comfortable position. Marco shuddered to think what they must have endured during the bitterly cold night.

A few metres down the slope, he could see a backpack and some oxygen cylinders. He climbed down in the hope of finding oxygen masks; without them, the cylinders were useless. He couldn't find any; the injured climbers would have to survive without the essential gas.

Ger and Marco did all they could to make the listless climbers more comfortable, Ger whispering to the injured that they would be okay, help was here. Every move was carefully co-ordinated as they tried a number of manoeuvres to ease the pressure on the hanging men. Though they could not cut the rope for fear the climbers would plunge to their deaths, they tried to relieve the tension on the line.

The rope was so taut, however, it was virtually impossible. Marco took a knife from Park's suit and cut about 10 metres of old rope which lay on the snow nearby. He sank his axe into the ice and tied Park to it, easing the pressure from the fixed rope. He placed a ski pole under Jumik's shoulder to help him to remain upright and give him some relief. But the situation, Marco thought, seemed hopeless without more manpower to help.

Wilco had descended a short distance before becoming disorientated and completely lost. His tongue and throat begged for water. His blurred vision deceived him as he tried to figure out where he was. Back climbing downwards several times, he hit unnavigable ridges, surrounded by rock on both sides and below, forcing him upwards again to re-trace his steps:

I was so thirsty and knew I was getting crazy in a few hours because when you don't have water at that altitude for such a long time, you won't survive it. So I had to go down, down, down and I couldn't go down anymore so the only thing I could do was go climbing up again. Of course I was exhausted but there was no other way, I had to do it. So two, three, four steps and I was bending over my ice axe, I was falling asleep. I got some black things in front of my eyes because I was so exhausted and then I woke up and I think, "Oh shit, I have to go up again", so I climbed again and finally I looked up and I saw that Marco and Gerard were also with those Korean guys. But I couldn't reach them because I was too exhausted and I was shouting but they didn't answer me. I was asking, "Listen guys, where do I have to go? To the left or to the right? I can't go down". But they didn't answer.

After over two hours with Jumik and the South Koreans, Marco paused to assess his own condition and that of the climbers who hung motionless, suspended like puppets on a string. It was around 9am and he and Ger had done everything possible to make them more comfortable but it would take more than two fatigued, oxygen-deprived and dehydrated climbers to get them safely down the mountain. Marco's mountain rescue experience had prompted him to do all he could to help those in need, but that same experience also told him that there was no more he could do.

Suddenly, above him, he saw Ger climbing back up above the entangled climbers. What was he doing and where was he going, a baffled Marco wondered:

> In that moment I look up and I see Jesus [Ger] gradually putting the climber gently against the vertical face. Jesus starts hiking higher up; I shout up to him, "What the fuck are you doing?". No answer, he doesn't turn back. Jesus continues walking in the high part of the Serac. I call him once more but in vain. I think that maybe he is going to take pictures to document what we are attempting to do – it is the only explanation. In one second he goes out of my sight. I give one big shout. Nothing. Jesus is gone and I am on my own.[126]

In disbelief and near despair – and unaware that Ger had given his camera to Pemba when they were on the summit – Marco returned to the task at hand and slowly lowered Hwang about 10 metres so that he was beside his team-mate. Park seemed more lucid but his physical condition and the bruising to his face worried Marco. His mouth and eyes were swollen.

The Italian could wait no longer. Tending to the stricken climbers had sapped more of his limited energy reserves and it was still a long climb to Camp Four. Removing one of his gloves, Marco tugged it onto Jumik's exposed and frostbitten foot 'to give us both a bit of hope'.[127]

When he turned around to take stock of the downward journey facing him, two things caught Marco's attention. Wilco was about 100 metres below; he seemed unsure of his direction and unable to move downwards. Marco yelled Wilco's name but the Dutchman was out of earshot. The second thing Marco spotted was a microphone in Jumik's jacket; this prompted him to look for the radio, which he found 50 metres below on the snow.[128]

Having carefully retrieved the radio, Marco immediately turned it on in the hope of alerting someone further down the mountain to the need for help. He spoke into the receiver and he heard a voice, the dialect alien to him:

> I spoke with someone. I don't know who it was who was listening. I said, "I don't speak English. I speak Tarzan English. I am Marco, I am at the Serac, there is a problem. Somebody has to come up, I am tired".

There was no reply. Every muscle in the Italian's body ached and his dehydration and light-headedness were needling him to descend. He looked back at the three stricken climbers as he left: 'All I could think about was leaving, surviving. I had to survive.'[129]

A rope lying on the snow suddenly caught Wilco's eye. Somehow, he had managed to locate the fixed ropes on the Traverse under the Serac and clipped onto the lifeline in relief. The ropes gave him a renewed hope and he made his way painstakingly across the diagonal and towards the Bottleneck. But soon the rope ended, inexplicably severed, and Wilco tried to suppress his desperate sense of helplessness. The sun burned his retinas and his head pounded as snow blindness intensified.

He tried to breathe through his nose to avoid moisture loss; the thirst was driving him insane. The snow and ice, laden with water, were irresistible, but even a palmful of snowmelt would further lower his body temperature, turning his saliva to a repulsive glutinous paste and causing his throat to contract.

He continued to climb downwards, without fixed lines once more, hoping he was in the Bottleneck but, for much of the time, Wilco had no idea where he was. Time, as well as his vision, continued to blur. He stopped and groaned. Neither his body nor his mind seemed able to advance another step: 'I look at the sun, which is beating down on me. I stare straight at the sun and ask: is this the end?'[130]

In between preparing provisions for anyone else who might return to Camp Four, Fredrik Sträng and Eric Meyer maintained constant surveillance of the Traverse. Above the Bottleneck, the weather was almost as clear as the day before, although cloud had started to move intermittently across the Shoulder. They could see coloured dots that looked like several climbers near the top of the Traverse, a short distance from where the fixed ropes should have ended.

By mid-morning something above the Serac and to the right of the summit snowfields caught Fredrik's eye; it was a moving form, clearly well off route and seemingly lost:

> We could see one climber traversing, strangely enough, on top of the Serac towards China/Tibet ... I told Eric and the other guys he must be mad, he must be hallucinating because ... he was going wrong ... he didn't start at one point and go right, he went up the mountain and then started traversing right. And there was snow to his knees; probably to his waist.

Karim Meherban had spent a long, lonely night adrift high above the Traverse. Crushed in the vice-like embrace of the Death Zone, he had become separated from the other climbers once the moving rope system had been abandoned in the hours before midnight.

As he ploughed through unfamiliar snow, the head lights of the other climbers had dimmed and finally disappeared until he was alone with his own thoughts and paralysed limbs, unable to move further, submitting himself to a night exposed and alone on the mountain.

On rising after dawn, the terrain remained foreign to Karim as he trudged to and fro above the cliff that plunged downwards into the Bottleneck, a safe passage to the fixed lines eluding him. Around 10am, photographs taken by Pemba from Camp Four on Ger McDonnell's camera showed a lone figure moving slowly between higher and lower altitudes along the snow above the Serac.

Pemba was perplexed – at one point it seemed as if he was climbing towards the Chinese side of the mountain. The climber was beyond rescue; unless he could make it to the top anchor of his own accord, and quickly, he would surely perish.

At Camp Four, discussion turned to a possible rescue attempt, something not undertaken lightly at such an altitude. Pemba knew that a rescue effort would be fraught with danger and that anyone attempting it would have to feel strong enough, both physically and psychologically. Taking everything into account, the general consensus was that mounting a rescue wasn't a good idea. Pemba was in agreement:

> Visibility became very poor. Everybody knew the Bottleneck was very dangerous because multi times the Serac fell down. The majority said it was now impossible to go and rescue because the Bottleneck was still very dangerous. The westerners and Koreans were 100 per cent sure they were not going for rescue on the Bottleneck; the Pakistanis were definitely not going and we were only a few Sherpas ... and also we didn't have equipment, we didn't have enough rope, protections, oxygen – we had nothing ... even if we wanted it was impossible because we had no manpower and no equipment. Also, I didn't want more disaster on the mountain.

Notwithstanding the hazards and following confirmation that several of his team members were still unaccounted for, Mr Kim planned to send another rescue team back up the Bottleneck to search for Hwang, Park, 'Little' Kim and their expedition sirdar, Jumik Bhote. Members of the Flying Jump B team were still present at Camp Four and would be commandeered for the rescue effort.

Pemba warned Mr Kim about the treacherous conditions which now prevailed in the Bottleneck; after the displacement of so much ice overnight, both the terrain and the risk of further avalanches presented acute dangers.

During the early hours of the morning, the weather around and above Camp Four continued to deteriorate, convincing the majority at the camp that descent was the most sensible option. Pemba concurred:

> So we discussed all that and we decided that everybody will go down. The weather was also becoming bad – cloudy, blizzard. We discussed a lot that we will descend the Abruzzi route safely together ... the American team decided to go down, they said we cannot do anything because we do not have enough manpower and physically we are also weak. Now we had to go down.

There was constant contact with Base Camp and, by late morning, the remaining members of the American expedition were getting ready for their descent. Whatever limited provisions and supplies remained at Camp Four would be required for any survivors. Fredrik Sträng believed they had little choice but to go down:

> ... we had spent too much time there already. If we didn't go down now that means that we wouldn't have any water. The food and water we had was at Camp Three. So we couldn't eat the food and water that was being used to keep people alive on that platform on Camp Four. We had to go down before further incidents would happen and we actually communicated this to Base Camp. We wanted to stay there and help with the rescues but they said with a strong voice, "You guys get the hell out of there. You go down now! You are not staying up there. That is not an option. Go down now, that is an order".

Throughout the morning's discussions Pemba had kept Ger's satellite phone – which the Irishman had given him at the summit – switched on, repeatedly dialling Wilco's number, which was sometimes ringing and often failing to connect, but Wilco never answered. Shortly before the group was ready to descend, however, Pemba got a call from Roeland van Oss at Base Camp: he had just spoken to Wilco. Finally, Pemba was also able to make direct contact with his expedition leader:

> Wilco made contact on the satellite phone before the Americans descended. If Wilco had not been on the phone, then definitely me and Cas and Mark Sheen would have descended with the Americans on the Abruzzi. Then Wilco came on the phone and me and Cas thought in a different way. We just had a short talk on the phone. I asked where are you,

can you explain your points, and he said, "I can't see because I am getting a kind of blur. I am trying to descend but am at about 8,000 metres". He told me nothing about anyone else and I didn't ask.

Based on his own information, it was estimated that Wilco was about 100 metres above Camp Four, but he was nowhere to be seen. For an hour, Cas and Pemba circled a large radius around the camp in an attempt to spot their team leader through the haze. Visibility had worsened. Wilco could not be far away but he remained elusive and invisible to his would-be rescuers.

Pemba used Ger's satellite phone to call his wife in Nepal. Da Jangmu picked up immediately. She was relieved to hear his voice. She had been watching CNN which was already reporting news of problems and fatalities on K2. Pemba told her he was fine and that he was going to remain at Camp Four for at least a few more hours to help in the rescue effort and await the safe arrival of his team-mates.

The majority of climbers had left Camp Four and he was happier now that they were descending as it meant there would be fewer climbers exposed to the dangers of high altitude. Ger, Wilco and the others had already survived over 36 hours in the Death Zone and, though that was incredible, it was not impossible. Pemba believed there was still time and there was still hope:

> I saw people survive four or five days above 8,000 metres in Cho Oyu even though they got deep frostbite, without shelter, without eating, drinking, oxygen, without bivouac – some lucky people. That is why I think on the mountain if some people are missing, I think we have to wait if conditions are favourable. They were still alive. That is why we didn't quit the next morning; if conditions were favourable we keep searching for them.

Pemba also feared for Jumik Bhote whom he had gotten to know at Base Camp and who was the only one of the four climbers who operated the moving rope system beneath the summit the previous night who had not yet returned to Camp Four. As he contemplated how Jumik and the other stranded climbers might be helped, he recalled a troubling conversation he had with the Sherpa just a few weeks earlier at Base Camp:

Jumik was exhausted from another expedition from before K2, and we talked a lot about that in Base Camp. Jumik told me he had come back from Lhotse expedition and had just spent two days in Kathmandu and then came here to K2. I said, "Oh fuck, why did you do that? I came here for K2 and didn't climb a big mountain for a while, I was training, training, training, but you came here after climbing Lhotse. It is 8,500-something metres". I thought this was crazy. I talked a lot about K2 – the training, the mentality and the preparation. It was his first time to K2. He felt tired ... he was exhausted from Lhotse and we said it is really not a good idea within one climbing season to climb two 8,000-metre mountains including K2. It is stupid. He was laughing; he agreed with me but he was still going to try and do it.

The effort of helping the injured climbers had taken a huge physical toll on Marco Confortola. He inched his way slowly across the Traverse, trying to ignore the gigantic and glistening danger of the Serac just over his head and resisting the temptation to look towards the Shoulder and the awaiting sanctuary of Camp Four.

After a 100-metre traverse, Marco made the shocking discovery that had so dumbfounded Cas, Pemba and the others who had made it to camp overnight: the fixed ropes had been cut. The evidence of a large icefall was immediately apparent to the Italian. He shuddered. Below lay the deadly Bottleneck, perilous and un-roped. Marco had left his ice axe behind with the South Koreans; he had just one ski pole and one glove. He felt the energy ebbing from his body. He breathed heavily and shut his eyes, begging for salvation.

Wilco felt a welcome sensation beneath his feet: it was flatter ground. For the first time in hours, he was able to stand without the aid of an ice axe or crampon points. He flexed his burning calves. It was a relief. But his physical condition was deteriorating. His tongue felt swollen for want of a drink. His peripheral vision was non-existent and his eyes felt like they were full of sand. Had he made it through the Bottleneck?

The terrain seemed unfamiliar and Wilco could see nothing that identified it as the route he had travelled a day earlier on the way to the summit. A thick fog prevented him from getting his bearings: 'There was a cloud hanging ... I couldn't see anything, I didn't know where to go.' There was no sign of Camp Four. In the whiteout, he felt completely lost.

Wilco retrieved his satellite phone, which still had charge; due to his snow blindness he could no longer find the correct buttons to access the pre-programmed numbers. He manually dialled the only number he could remember. His wife, Heleen, picked up immediately. There was no time for small talk: 'I am lost. You have to make contact with Base Camp. Ask them if they can start a search and rescue for me because I think I must be near Camp Four.'

Wilco tried to suppress the emotional intensity he felt on hearing his wife's voice. He needed to be matter of fact and practical. He needed help and needed it quickly. He told Heleen to contact Maarten in Utrecht and Roeland in Base Camp. He hung up and sat on the snow, cursing himself for being so blunt with Heleen; he hadn't even asked about his baby son, Teun. But there was no room for sentimentality, just concentration on survival.[131]

In the distance, he thought he saw two shadows moving across the snow, but Wilco did not trust his eyes. He continued to plod his way downwards; towards where, he could not tell.

Cecilie, Lars and Oystein eventually arrived at Camp Three on the Abruzzi route. The mountain seemed to make Cecilie claustrophobic. She gathered her emotions and retrieved a satellite phone the team had stowed in one of the tents. She punched in the number Bjorn had given her.

Primed for the tragic news, Jacob Bae remained calm on the other end of the line as he comforted and consoled his daughter-in-law. Cecilie's dread was defused by Jacob's supportive encouragement:

> ... I was so scared to make that phone call; that he was going to be mad at me for not looking after his son but instead he said, "You have to get off the mountain, you have to come home, you have to come home to us".

Jacob Bae's selfless stoicism was essential in bringing Cecilie down from the mountain and was all the more remarkable in the circumstances; 33-year-old Rolf was the Baes' only child.

Bjorn was conscious of the need to prepare a press release for the Norwegian media. It was still the middle of the night in northern Europe but once the newspapers and TV and radio stations in Norway sprang to life the following morning, the media pressure on the team members and their families would become intense.

Bjorn tapped out on his laptop what thoughts he could muster; he then phoned Jacob Bae to go through the details of the press release with him. They both agreed that it would contain as little information as possible: Rolf Bae was reported missing on K2. It was a holding statement; it would give everyone some space to prepare themselves for the inevitable media frenzy that would accompany news of the death of the husband of one of the best-known adventurers in the country:

> There were several reasons for this. It was partly that we were still hoping for something magical to happen and also because we wanted to buy ourselves some time. It would be disastrous if we said that he was dead and if later it turned out that he wasn't. So it was partly to check the story with more sources and get to talk to Cecilie again and to tell her what we were doing, because it would affect her because she was his wife.[132]

Bjorn rechecked the details and clicked the send button.

By mid-morning on 2 August, the ExplorersWeb homepage relayed to the outside world the snippets of information it had gleaned about the dramatic developments on K2:

> ... Wilco and Marco have reportedly left their bivouac just above the Serac
> ... All involved, such as Roeland in BC and the Dutch K2 Norit expedition webmaster Maarten van Eck have been awake for at least 48 hours non-stop by now. Maarten urges people to please not jam satellite phones, emails or other communication with general messages. The ground team works feverishly to assist the stranded climbers. Weather at present seems to be holding, although winds tend to pick up briefly early morning on 8,000ers. K2 also suffers wind gusts from China on the upper slopes. Free-climbing the steep, icy sections of the Traverse and the Bottleneck

229

is possible but highly risky as the mountaineers now have spent almost 48 hours in the K2 summit push, most without oxygen support.[133]

The wider world was already learning about the unfolding tragedy on K2 and, bizarrely, the news was being relayed from around the globe back to some climbers who were en route down to Base Camp. Nick Rice had descended from Camp Four on the afternoon of 1 August, his dream of summiting K2 dashed. He spent the night at Camp Three on the Cesen route with Jelle Staleman of the Norit team.

At Camp Two, they stopped to rest and rehydrate, largely unaware of the overnight chaos on the peak above. But when Nick turned on his satellite phone, news of what was happening higher up on K2's slopes flooded his inbox. One of the messages, from thousands of kilometres away in the United States, was from his mother: fixed lines had been cut by a big icefall from the Serac, climbers were stranded above the Bottleneck and lives had been lost.[134]

Marco stepped his way laboriously and agonisingly through the gulley, his ski pole a poor substitute for an ice axe. Moving each limb was an enormous undertaking; he wanted to stop, to sleep, to await rescue. But he had to go on and remnants of old fixed rope that he came across in the Bottleneck provided brief reprieve. However, the ominous rumblings of the mountain, which signalled the imminent displacement of rock, ice and snow, had begun above him.

Just 100 metres from the end of the Bottleneck, the Serac disgorged another mass of ice and snow in the direction of the desperate climber. Marco struggled to pin himself closer to the rock face as the avalanche funnelled furiously downwards. The snowfall stopped just 10 metres from him and a dreadful silence returned. Looking around, he shuddered at what he saw:

> I see some yellow in the snow – they are the boots of Jesus. I can't even cry. I want to but I don't have the energy to do it. Like a flash I can see his face and see him laughing when I called him 'Jesus' and also when he was singing a popular Irish song in Base Camp. I can see his eyes again – his blue eyes. I feel like I will collapse; it's like having no more energy. I feel all the work of these days. I've no energy anymore and I don't care. I go on my knees and collapse into the snow but it is only for a split second and I stop myself. In a short time I am up again … With my last energy I start

going down again. The snow is up to my knees, the wind is lashing my face. I don't think of that, I don't even think of Gerard, not of K2 – I just go blank; I only want to go home.[135]

As he moved downward, Marco's journey through nightmare terrain continued unabated: he saw a dark patch in the snow and moved closer, identifying body parts. Any belief that he had control over his own destiny dissolved:

At a certain point I see a dark patch, I don't know what it is. I get near to it and it is blood. I look closer and beside it are some body parts. I can't stop. I don't know where I am or how long it is to Camp 4, I just know that I have to keep going. I start walking for a never-ending time. I fall and get up, fall and get up, then I give up.[136]

Karim Meherban was also wearing yellow boots and a suit not dissimilar to Ger's. From the time he rose at dawn, those boots had failed again to lead Karim to the top anchor. Instead they had ploughed into some loose snow hundreds of metres above Marco, the powdery surface collapsing under his weight.

In his wretched oxygen-deprived stupor, the Pakistani followed his friend and client, Hugues D'Aubarède, to his death, forced downwards at such a high speed and from such a height that his wearied body was smashed onto the rocks and strewn across the mountainside below. No Shimshal Valley native had ever died on K2, he had told his father before the expedition.[137] The mountain had just claimed its second Shimshali in as many days.

By midday on 2 August, most of the climbers at Camp Four were about to leave, with only those who chose to, or who felt obligated to do so, remaining in the hope of bringing to safety even one of the missing climbers. Pemba had spent over an hour moving between the radio frequencies on his walkie-talkie in an attempt to contact the climbers still unaccounted for on the mountain, but there was no response.

He did a quick tally: either still missing or presumed dead were Karim Meherban, Jumik Bhote, Park Kyeong-hyo, Hwang Dong-jin, Kim Hyo-gyeong, Wilco van Rooijen, Ger McDonnell, and Marco Confortola.

The only communication Pemba did receive was from Tsering and 'Big' Pasang Bhote who were moving slowly across the Shoulder once more, trying to locate the missing Flying Jump team members. They favoured Pemba as a point of contact ahead of their own leader: 'We used the same frequency. They did not want to talk with the Korean leader; only with me because they believed me.'

The Sherpas reported dangerous climbing conditions to Pemba as they approached the Bottleneck – there was a lot of icy debris that had fallen from above; the Serac was volatile and had already unleashed significant quantities of ice and rock. The Bhotes feared a more substantial avalanche. In the distance and amid the cloud, Tsering thought he saw a figure sliding at speed across the lower part of the Bottleneck.

Minutes later, 'Big' Pasang radioed Pemba again. He and Tsering were at exactly 8,000 metres and had found someone who had crawled towards them on all fours 'like a horse' before collapsing in front of them on the snow. The zip of his down suit was undone and one of his gloves was missing. The exhausted climber was a stranger to the Bhote cousins but Pemba recognised the description of his green down suit immediately: it was Marco Confortola. He implored Tsering and 'Big' Pasang to help Marco back to camp:

> I told them they cannot go further up, they have to bring Marco down to High Camp. After a few minutes they called me again because Kim was not agreeing with this ... and said they have to go further up and they are now going to start to climb on the Bottleneck. I did not say anything then but wished them a safe climb.

In his delirium, Marco mumbled something to Tsering and 'Big' Pasang about Jumik and the South Koreans whom he said were still trapped on ropes further up the mountain: 'You go up [and] help Korean people and Jumik, you go, continue up,' he told the Sherpas. Tsering's relief on hearing that his brother Jumik was alive was quickly followed by the realisation that he and the South Koreans were in urgent need of rescue.

Tsering told Marco that he and 'Big' Pasang had to go and find the others. 'Help is on the way,' he said, 'wait here.' Alone once more, Marco could go no further:

> I have no more energy and am at my limits. So I lie in the snow with my belly up and my hands behind my head inside my hat and that is the

only way I can heat my hands. Finally I feel better, I relax. The snow is falling softly on my face and I am thinking, "Don't fall asleep", and then it becomes dark.[138]

The news that a climber was still alive filled Pemba with a renewed energy and sense of purpose; something positive could be salvaged from this doom-laden day. If the Bhotes could not help Marco, another rescue party would have to go from Camp Four. Marco might be hypoxic, immobile or even unconscious so Pemba began to search the tents at Camp Four for spare oxygen. From 'Big' Pasang's description, Pemba figured that Marco would need it to complete his descent.

In the Italian's tent, Pemba discovered a coil of rope lying amid the climbing paraphernalia. He was perplexed: where had this rope come from? The realisation was almost as swift as the discovery: Pemba had found what he assumed was the 100 metres of rope the Italian team's high-altitude worker, Mohammad Ali, had been given as a member of the trail-breaking team. It was the same rope that could not be accounted for when the lines were being fixed on the Traverse.

Pemba confronted a confused and embarrassed Mohammad: 'He told me, "I took this rope on the mountain yesterday but then I bring down. I don't know – here is rope inside my back pack but I don't know". That means the Pakistani had an altitude problem. I think this was the problem, otherwise, why didn't he know that he was carrying rope?'

Pemba asked the climbers still at High Camp to assist in the rescue of Marco but they declined, citing the dangers of avalanches and the conditions below the Bottleneck. Only Cas offered to help, although he looked truly deflated. The pair moved a short distance from camp before Cas stalled, unable to take another step.

Despite his desire to help Marco, the Dutchman buckled under the fatigue of the previous days. 'I am too tired,' he told Pemba, 'I will stay here and be some kind of lighthouse waiting for you. We will stay in touch by radio.' Pemba placed the spare oxygen in his rucksack and left Cas about 100 metres from camp. Cas admired the Sherpa's tenacity and resilience: 'Pemba was having the leading in the rescuing, in the searching for the other people.'

In Utrecht in the Netherlands, Maarten van Eck had a growing sense of foreboding. He found himself inundated with calls and emails from relatives and friends of those still unaccounted for on the mountain. To create effective channels of communication with them, he identified and began to correspond with one nominated person per expedition or individual climber. He provided them with a private email address and phone number on which they could contact him directly.

Maarten also worked on a communications strategy with Bjorn Sekkesaeter, the Norwegian team spokesperson, and Tom and Tina Sjogren of ExplorersWeb:

> We made an agreement that we were not going to publish names of climbers who died. First we had to be sure and have confirmation from eyewitnesses and after that we made sure we would first contact family members to prepare them for the worst. This became the modus operandi … and one of the reasons I used the phrase 'Status Unknown' … I had to beg people not to phone or text to sat phones because they were jamming these important ways of communicating.[139]

Roeland van Oss had passed on whatever information he could piece together at Base Camp but, by midday on 2 August, the whereabouts of two of the members of the Norit team were still unknown; Wilco had made contact with his team but Ger had not been seen. Pemba had the latter's satellite phone, making contact with the Irishman impossible. Maarten updated the expedition website with what information he had to hand:

> STATUS AS FAR AS WE KNOW:
> ROELAND in K2BC
> CAS and PEMBA in C4
> WILCO left Bivouac, whereabouts unknown
> MARCO left Bivouac, whereabouts unknown
> MARK in C4 and will move up with CAS to Bottleneck!
> JELLE on his way down to K2BC
> GERARD unknown
> HUGUES unknown[140]

Maarten added a footnote for the family and friends of Ger McDonnell:

GERARD'S SAT PHONE IS NOT WITH HIM. Pemba carried some stuff down from the summit. In it is GER's sat phone. PEMBA is using Ger's sat phone during the rescue. PLEASE STOP SENDING MESSAGES!!! to that sat phone. TO GER's family: This would explain why we are not able to contact him or why he is not able to contact you.[141]

'Big' Pasang powered ahead of Tsering towards the Bottleneck. He remained in regular radio contact with Pemba – now en route towards Marco – and Pasang Lama who was still at Camp Four, updating them on his progress. Dense cloud put 'Big' Pasang out of sight of Tsering at times and, as they became further separated, the pair shouted to each other to check on their positions on the mountain. The foggier conditions, obscuring the route ahead, worried Tsering; though they now had daylight, the terrain seemed alien and malevolent.

He moved towards the foot of the couloir, gathering pieces of rope, the detritus of the previous day's climb, which might be needed later. Tsering craned his neck; he could see 'Big' Pasang just above the top of the Bottleneck at the start of the Traverse. Blinking in disbelief, Tsering spotted other climbers with his cousin. Who was with him? Had he found Jumik? Had he survived?

Exhilarated, Tsering clambered onto and up the Bottleneck. He shouted towards 'Big' Pasang but the latter was out of earshot.

Pasang Lama had held his radio close as he waited at Camp Four for news. He had rested for a few hours in his tent but still felt exhausted; his terrifying descent through the Bottleneck with Chhiring Dorje the night before tormenting his mind as he had tried to sleep. The ecstasy of his summit achievement the previous day seemed a lifetime away now; he feared for his cousins and Jumik in particular.

Pasang had last seen Jumik before he descended the Traverse in the darkness, leaving him to tend to the remaining members of the South Korean team. He struggled to comprehend why they had not made it back to camp and, with every hour that passed, his anxiety became more acute.

It was 1pm and, from Camp Four, the Bottleneck and the Serac remained hidden behind a blanket of cloud. Over the radio, Pasang Lama recognised 'Big' Pasang's voice once more. His tone had changed; he sounded excited. Shortly after 'Big' Pasang had started to cross the Traverse he met Jumik and other climbers descending towards him. 'Every one of us will meet now,' he said.

Immediately, Pasang Lama grabbed his rucksack and headed out from camp with two of the South Korean climbers from the second summit team. Visibility was poor but Pasang Lama made steady progress across the Shoulder. He and his fellow Sherpas were now in almost constant communication, spearheading the rescue attempt, co-ordinating and in control. Pemba was up there somewhere with Marco and could not be far away.

Another radio call from 'Big' Pasang signalled that he and the other climbers were descending the Bottleneck. Over the radio, Pasang Lama could hear Jumik speaking to their cousin, Ngawang, at Base Camp; Jumik was able to climb but his feet and hands were badly frostbitten and he would need an airlift to Islamabad.

Several metres on, Pasang Lama paused, unsure of his direction in the fog and fearful of the terrain. He tried to radio 'Big' Pasang once more but his calls went unanswered. Instinctively he knew something was wrong. He grabbed an oxygen cylinder from one of the South Koreans standing beside him, pressing onwards and leaving them behind.

Between breaks in the fog, Tsering Bhote peered upwards as he edged his way higher through the Bottleneck. One of the other climbers was finally visible and immediately familiar: it was Jumik. Tsering struggled to maintain his composure. He could also see two other climbers, the red colour of their down suits convincing him they were members of the South Korean team, although he could not identify them through the gloom.

Finally, 'Big' Pasang's voice was audible through the fog. 'Jumik is with me, we are coming down. Climb up to meet us,' Tsering heard him roar. The 21-year-old stepped onto a rocky outcrop halfway up the Bottleneck. Elated at Jumik's rescue, he paused for breath. His brother was coming down; they were only 100 metres apart.

Pemba remained in radio contact with the Bhotes as they ascended ahead of him. The weather conditions had worsened again and it was becoming increasingly difficult to see what was happening on the slopes above. At 1.30pm Pemba found Marco Confortola exactly where Tsering and 'Big' Pasang said he would be. A motionless and bedraggled human form lay the snow. Pemba checked for a pulse; Marco was alive. The unkempt Italian looked as though he had fallen or slid down the Bottleneck:

> He was completely dismantled, his harness was below his knees and his suit was completely open, no hat, no gloves ... Climbers who descend by sliding, sometimes their suits are off ... I think he was not able to think very well because when I first saw him on the debris, he was almost finished. If I did not have oxygen I would not have been able to bring him down because I was unable to carry him.

Unpacking the oxygen supply, Pemba placed the mask over Marco's nose and mouth, opening the valve to the maximum. The gas hissed through the tube and flowed through the Italian's lungs and veins. There was little hope of getting Marco to descend without an infusion of oxygen to rejuvenate him but, in his derangement, Marco flailed against the mask. He spluttered and gagged, Pemba imploring him to breathe and stay calm.

Within 10 minutes, the oxygen was having the desired effect: 'At that time he didn't like the oxygen and he became angry with me. "Who are you?" he said. "I am Sherpa Pemba." There was no answer.' Marco felt someone trying to rouse him from his slumber; it felt otherworldly and surreal: 'Pemba protected me. He held me like a mother.'

It was 2pm and, as Pemba knelt over Marco, his radio crackled again. It was 'Big' Pasang. He was near the top of the Bottleneck. 'Go ahead Pasang,' Pemba said, Marco remaining listless beside him on the snow. 'I am here with Jumik and the others,' came the reply, 'they are alive, they've got frostbite. We are trying to come down slowly. Tsering is below on the rocks somewhere, and now we are descending and we need a helicopter from Base Camp.' 'Come down,' Pemba replied,' I am here with the Italian and I am taking him down.'

Pemba looked up but could see nothing through the murkiness. He was astonished but relieved that at least some of the missing climbers had been found and were now descending with 'Big' Pasang. Immediately he thought about Ger, his friend and team-mate. He pressed the talk button once more: 'Is there anyone else there, Pasang?' he asked. 'There was one other climber,' came the reply, 'but he was hit by ice and fell.' Pemba shivered, fearing the worst. 'What was the colour of his down suit?'

After a moment came the dreaded response: 'Red and black.' Pemba shuddered, gasping in horror.

Annie Starkey's hard drive crashed several times as she frantically sought any update on Ger's status from whatever source she could find. Ger hadn't called since he stood on the summit. Every possible media source was analysed repeatedly. It was the middle of the night in Ireland and she didn't want to call Ger's family, in case of arousing unnecessary concern. Annie found herself bombarded by conflicting information from a plethora of online dispatches:

> I was just going back and forth between all these websites trying to figure out what was going on. Everything that would come out ... what does that mean, does that mean this or does that mean that? What do they know? ... You would hear they are going to send a rescue up and then you would wait to see that. Then you would hear that so and so is heading down – why are they heading down? What do they know that I don't know? It was just craziness.

Annie managed to make contact by email with Tom Sjogren of ExplorersWeb which was closely monitoring all the expedition websites and blogs for updates. Tom told her that it was early days, communications were difficult, and that she should not give up hope. He did suggest, however, that she take a look at Nick Rice's blog. Annie found the Californian's update for 2 August. What she read both astonished and frightened her:

> The Italian, Marco, and Irish, Gerard, had apparently made a bivouac, and then in the morning, had headed in the opposite direction from each other. Marco made it back down to Camp IV with severe frostbite on his hands and feet. Gerard had been sighted heading toward the Chinese side of the summit.[142]

The increasingly unpredictable snow and ice of the Serac gave Pemba little time to dwell on what might have happened to Ger. He had to focus on what was now taking place just below the Bottleneck. He would have to get Marco back to camp and wait there for the descending climbers who faced a perilous journey to Camp Four.

Almost on cue, a crack, sounding like a gunshot, echoed from above as pre-avalanche rubble ricocheted down the Bottleneck. A cloud of soft, powdery snow enveloped Pemba and a still semi-conscious Marco as bullet-like pieces of rock and ice sped past. Pemba heard metallic noises, like the scratching of crampons and the clash of adzes on ice on the surface around him. In the blizzard he caught a glimpse of bodies being thrown across the Shoulder in the full force of the avalanche, with items of climbing equipment strewn around the snow.

He crouched over Marco to protect him but the snowfall and powerful wind pushed the still spread-eagled Italian away from him. Pemba grabbed his down suit in an instant, preventing Marco from being swept further down the mountain. For several seconds, they waited, huddled against the wind and braced for more while the mountain vented its spleen.

As he prepared to ascend further and embrace his brother, Tsering heard what sounded like an explosion. He hugged the rocky face as the mountain spewed ice and snow towards him at high speed. He winced and held his breath as the avalanche plunged past. The bodies of several climbers caught his eye as they plummeted past him in the snowfall. Tsering thought he was going to die and waited for the final, fatal blow. The avalanche seemed to last for several minutes and he prayed to be spared as bodies were shunted past him in the blizzard:

> They had been on the descent in the couloir ... they tried to come down but the Serac ice fell, then all the people were gone. I saw immediately some bodies fly very close [to me] maybe 20 or 30 metres and they were flying down.

Tsering breathed heavily in shocked relief as the tempest abated. He called out for 'Big' Pasang but there was no reply. Instinct told him that his cousin and those he was leading to safety would have been unable to avoid the force of the falling snow and ice, funnelling all in their path at high speed through the gulley, though he hoped that they somehow might have survived the fall:

> I didn't think I would lose them. Somewhere in my heart I felt I would meet them down [below] because the storm was not big and the sound from their fall was also not that big. So I thought they will have slight fracture[s], nothing worse than that.

He unclipped from the short length of rope still in place in the Bottleneck and made his way slowly downwards, screaming 'Big' Pasang and Jumik's names.

It took several minutes for the spindrift to settle and for Pemba to feel confident the avalanche was at an end. He stood beside a barely lucid Marco. A short distance away a mass of mangled remains lay on the snow. Approaching the human wreckage, Pemba couldn't make out their faces through the web of ropes, torn down suits and contorted limbs. A gloveless hand lay open on the snow.

Though unable to identify them, Pemba knew immediately that they were dead. It was 'Big' Pasang and his cousin, Jumik; they lay head to foot, trussed up tightly in a macabre embrace, bruised and bloodied after the catastrophic fall. Using Ger's camera to record what evidence he could about who had died, he photographed the remains; the mechanical click of the shutter now the only sound in the desolate wilderness.

Through the haziness of the spindrift and fog, two more bodies were visible in the distance beyond the dead Sherpas. Pemba could see that the climbers were wearing red down suits, similar to those worn by Hwang, Park and 'Little' Kim of the South Korean team, but also like the red and black down suits worn by Ger McDonnell and Karim Meherban. He couldn't be sure who they were but was in no doubt that the two climbers were also dead.

Pemba now needed to get himself and Marco out of this area of extreme danger; the Serac was at its most volatile and the fog was preventing speedy navigation through the snow. He returned to the Italian, determined to move down the mountain as quickly as possible, away from the risk of further exposure to the debilitating effects of high altitude, exhaustion, oxygen deprivation and the horror of more avalanches.

K2 was exacting a deadly toll and Pemba was beginning to doubt their chances of escaping from the mountain's increasingly frequent and merciless assaults.

Oblivious to the turmoil in the Bottleneck, Pasang Lama had stopped again, unsure of the route upwards. He heard someone call his name through the haze; it was Pemba. Marco was staggering beside him. The Italian seemed punch-drunk and completely shattered. 'There has been an avalanche,' Pemba told him, 'four climbers are dead. There are four bodies. I have to take Marco down.' In shock and disbelief, Pasang surged ahead immediately.

Tsering quickly hacked his way down the Bottleneck and onto the Shoulder. Arriving at the spot where two of the climbers lay, he was overwhelmed, realising instantly that the men were dead. Tsering recognised his brother Jumik tethered to 'Big' Pasang, their bodies frozen in time. He ran from the nightmare scene, reeling in horror.

Pasang Lama emerged from the gloom below. The Sherpa cousins embraced, dazed and dumbfounded at the destruction and death around them. 'What happened them?' Pasang Lama asked:

> I asked Tsering if they are dead and he said "Yes" ... I asked him, "Did you check?", and he said, "There is no life; [Big] Pasang has a cut in his head". I asked him where and he showed me right there [pointing to his own forehead] ... There was no chance to reach them so I contacted Base Camp and informed them about the incident.

Pasang Lama, still wary of the terrain, did not approach the remains, some 10 metres away in the snow. He radioed Mr Kim, telling him what he knew, as Tsering, kneeling in grief on the snow, struggled to comprehend the deaths. The South Korean expedition leader instructed them to return to Camp Four immediately. Pasang Lama burst into tears. A numbed Tsering felt disconsolate – he would return home without his older brother and his cousin. This expedition to K2 had brought only unspeakable anguish to his family.

An oxygen-revived Marco managed to walk slowly and unsteadily to Camp Four with Pemba's help. He had barely been able to assimilate what had happened; too dazed to comprehend the loss of life just metres from where he had collapsed. Frequently leaning on Pemba, he moved along the ridge of the Shoulder, the pair hardly speaking, regularly stopping to allow Marco rest. Pemba found him to be 'totally quiet':

> He was roped to me, I had a short rope about 10 metres and I used that, all the way down. Many times he fell down and I had to pull him up, that was difficult in some places but I was used to it as I have often done it on the mountain.

Calling ahead to the handful of climbers still at High Camp, Pemba asked them to tend to Marco; he was exhausted and too weak to help any further. Marco stumbled towards Mr Kim and Ms Go. They cried when he told him of his experience with their team-mates; Marco had done all he could. Bereft and exhausted, he fell through the door of his tent and crawled to his sleeping bag.

Pemba told Mr Kim what he had seen. Producing Ger's camera, he watched the seemingly unflappable expedition leader break down in grief as he looked at the image of two of his high-altitude workers, entangled in rope, their bodies broken:

> Kim and the other Koreans were screaming and crying. I said I took this a few hours ago and now they are dead; he saw the picture and he was crying.

It was after 3pm and Wilco van Rooijen was still lost on K2 but Pemba was not giving up hope. After a short break to rehydrate himself, he and Cas started to search the area around Camp Four for the Norit expedition leader, trying to avail of every remaining moment of daylight. The prospect of another night in the Death Zone was alarming but the thought of leaving their team leader alone and without shelter for the second night in a row appalled them.

As the sun sank over the horizon on 2 August, the mood at Base Camp was sombre. Every morsel of information which was relayed from Camp Four was devoured, the hope of another story of survival rising with each crackle of the radios. On his arrival at the bottom of the mountain earlier in the day, Alberto Zerain was struck by how their walkie-talkies seemed almost surgically attached to the palms of the climbers who remained there as they paced the moraine in anticipation of news, helpless and numbed in the face of the unfolding tragedy. His friends, who had come over from Broad Peak once word of the fatalities had reached them, embraced him. He immediately borrowed a phone to call his wife and reassure her that he was well.

Roeland and Jelle from the Norit team were watching the mountain, waiting and hoping for news of Wilco. Hoselito Bite had descended, as had Marco Confortola's climbing partner, Roberto Manni. The remaining American team members were making their descent. Alberto heard mixed mutterings about the extent of the fatalities on the mountain.

Confusion reigned: 'At first they thought there could have been more people who could have died, 12, 14, they were talking about up to 16 ... at first people were thinking there were Americans attempting the summit. I don't know who broadcast the news that some Americans had died but that wasn't the case.'

Alberto drank some welcome tea but declined to talk to others about his successful summiting; any individual achievement on the mountain had now been completely overtaken and overshadowed by subsequent events:

> I was perplexed seeing the whole camp destroyed ... I mean destroyed, completely affected, upset ... I saw people, everyone was really upset. It wasn't a time for celebration or anything ... Truth is when I arrived to Base Camp I couldn't talk much. People knew I had been to the summit but I hadn't seen anything strange. They were in continuous contact with people who were up there and it was more important to listen to people who were up there at that time than to listen to me or to what I had to tell.

Just before dusk, Cecilie, Lars and Oystein arrived at the Advanced Base Camp depot at the foot of the Abruzzi route. Her team-mates had said little as they shepherded their zombie-like colleague through the higher camps and towards the sanctuary of Base Camp. They had met other climbers at the various camps on the way down; some had already heard that Rolf was dead.

But they could go no further for now; Cecilie was exhausted and they decided to stay at the depot for the night. Lars had phoned his family on the descent; they told him the world's media was reporting a number of fatalities on the mountain. He hoped that Cecilie could be shielded from the media frenzy that had begun to unfold.

The ghostly quiet of Advanced Base Camp was matched only by the disappearance of the voice in Cecilie's head that had helped her to find the strength and courage to descend: '... it was quiet, Rolf didn't talk to me anymore and then I missed it'. She collapsed into a tent, praying that her stay on the mountain would not have to last much longer. She and Rolf had spoken many times about confronting death and its consequences on the polar plains and the world's highest peaks:

> We talked about that, what we did, that it can be dangerous, that we can die ... you had to know that when you expose yourself to danger something can happen, but I hadn't ever imagined coming home without him ... You can't do it, it's so strong, you can tell yourself that it can be like this ... but I never imagined coming home from an expedition without him.

Back in Norway, Bjorn's second press release had arrived in the inboxes of journalists. It carried the revelation that Rolf Bae had been killed by icefall on K2. His team-mates were well and were making their way down the mountain. As he dispatched a report he never envisaged writing, Bjorn reflected on the three goals his friends had set themselves on their expedition; to come back as better friends, to get someone to the summit, and to get everyone back safely to Norway: the most important of those goals could now never be fulfilled.

The mountain seemed ready to consume Wilco van Rooijen. He was coming to the end of his tether. He had already spent almost 48 hours at a life-crushingly high altitude. His throbbing throat fought with his increasingly frostbitten toes for his attention. He had reached deep into his reserves, physically, emotionally and psychologically:

> I am alone in a dull, ice-cold world of snow, mist and rocks, and suffering
> from poor vision. I clear my throat and cough several times. Tears well up
> in my eyes, but the sharp pain in the back of my throat brings me back to
> reality. Just one more step, careful. I imagine to myself that Valhalla lies
> below, and that is where I need to go.[143]

Completely unknown to Wilco, a complex and sophisticated international search effort was being initiated, drawing on satellite technology thousands of kilometres into outer space, as well as the nous and IT savvy of his expedition webmaster. Maarten van Eck, along with Tom Sjogren of ExplorersWeb in the United States, had set in train a series of phone calls and emails that would pinpoint the Dutchman's precise location on the mountain.

Though Wilco had left his GPS tracking device at Camp Four two nights earlier, his position could be approximately tracked by following the location of the phone calls he had made with his Thuraya satellite phone. The company that retained the longitude and latitude co-ordinates which were now required proved less than forthcoming with the data; it could only be released to the telephone user himself.

But when the Thuraya official received an outline of their customer's present location, and a mild barracking from Tom Sjogren, the GPS co-ordinates were released, allowing Maarten to map their position on a graphic of K2 in his high-tech hub in the boathouse that he hadn't left in three days.

Just as the sun began to set, Base Camp sprang into action, energised by the information Maarten had provided. The satellite data showed that Wilco had gone astray beneath the Bottleneck, scaling down the south side of the Cesen route, between Camps Three and Four. His most recent phone calls placed him at approximately 7,300 metres, 600 metres below the Shoulder. Binoculars and improvised telescopes were used to scan the mountain. Yes, he was there – his orange suit almost invisible in the gigantic expanse of K2 but clearly identifiable against the monotonous white backdrop.

A breathless Roeland van Oss radioed Pemba: 'Wilco is between you and Camp Three. He is moving.' They needed to find their team leader before night fell. The news filled Pemba with a renewed sense of hope. Now equipped with precise information about Wilco's whereabouts, Pemba and Cas were swiftly en route down the Cesen spur from Camp Four. If they searched the area to the west of the fixed line between Camps Three and Four, they would surely locate him.

In constant radio contact with Base Camp, Cas and Pemba descended on the fixed ropes, calling Wilco's name as they dropped lower and lower. Moving off the ropes and towards where they thought Wilco might be, Cas and Pemba became separated as darkness closed in. Cas began to struggle with the demands of the descent; his limbs still throbbed and he was more fatigued than he had realised. Before long, Pemba was out of sight.

With no sign of his rescuers and as the sun began to dip towards the jagged horizon, Wilco prepared to face the horrors of another night on the exposed flanks of K2. He dialled Maarten's number in the Netherlands, trying to describe his location, but there was nothing in the terrain that he recognised. Maarten assured him that help was on the way and asked him to resist the impulse to sleep. Buoyed by the conversation, Wilco walked a little further:

> I try to imagine how Heleen is sitting and waiting in our comfortable living room in the Netherlands. It pushes me to keep going and not give up. But, on the other hand, it also makes me angry. How could it have ever gotten this far? Didn't we take every imaginable precaution? What went wrong? I know these are useless thoughts and won't help me survive, but they appear spontaneously, I can do nothing about them.[144]

'Cas, Cas! Pemba, Pemba!' he yelled, but the effort pained his throat. There was no reply. Unable to resist any longer, he cupped some soft snow in his hand, melting it in his mouth, the effect like a droplet in a desert. It tasted wonderful but he could barely swallow. The ache in his throat had become unbearable, the numbness in his feet now, strangely, more tolerable.

Frostbite was gnawing at his toes, the subzero temperatures causing the muscles, tendons, blood vessels and nerves to freeze, destroying flesh in the process. Every step was a chore, his knees buckling under the tiredness that was engulfing him. Nothing was recognisable; nobody had ever been here before.

Wilco called Heleen again, trying to suppress his tears and being factual and almost blunt with his wife. She was in the midst of frenzied efforts to organise an outside rescue operation, calling the Dutch Ministry of Defence, officials in the Norit company and contacts in Pakistan. He gave her what information he could deduce from his surroundings, asking her to call Maarten again. The battery was failing and he hung up.

Every new descent or traverse came to naught. Eventually, Wilco found himself sitting beside human remains – a dead climber in a yellow suit, tied to another climber a few metres above. Unperturbed, he could not tell in the dusk whether they had been there for days or years. He had no head torch; it had fallen from inside his down suit the night before.

Wilco's energy was spent and his mood and the sun plunged lower in unison. Unlike the previous night, he would face long, black hours on his own with nobody to talk to, to help him stay warm, to encourage him to stay alive.

Cas had become frustrated and angry. Now well away from the fixed ropes, he found himself alone on a rocky ledge with no obvious route downwards. Darkness had fallen and he did not know where he was. His head torch was failing and flickered on and off. Radioing Pemba, Cas told him he was going to use his radio batteries to power the head torch but he was unable to tell him where he was. Cas fumbled with the batteries which escaped his frozen fingers and fell into the darkness. He cursed his folly.

He would not be able to find his way back to the fixed lines. Without radio contact or light, a grim realisation overcame the Dutchman: unfurling a sleeping bag he had brought, Cas prepared to spend the night in the open air. He called Wilco's name repeatedly. Wilco heard nothing; nor did Cas. The friends, who had achieved their goal of conquering K2 just a day earlier, were both lost and alone, oblivious to the fact that they were now sitting just 300 metres apart.

Heleen van Rooijen was struggling to contain her emotions but she had to, not least for her nine-month-old son, Teun. Her diary entry pointed to the turmoil that she and a dozen other families around the world were facing:

I take him in my arms and cry ... We look at Wilco's photo and say goodbye. I put Teun back in his cot. I cry and scream in my own bed, and scream in my sister's arms. So tired, so unreal, such sorrow. My thoughts unintentionally go to a memorial service that I want to hold to say my last goodbyes with the people I love around me.[145]

Shortly before midnight, Pemba found his way to Camp Three on the Cesen route. Why Wilco had not been found surprised and frustrated him. From the point where those at Base Camp had seen him just hours before, he could have made little progress in any direction. And there was no sign of Cas. Roeland radioed from Base Camp urging Pemba to stay put and wait for first light; a search in the dark for either of his team-mates would be illogical and potentially fatal.

Before he could rest, however, Pemba scoured the area immediately adjacent to the camp for signs of his expedition leader:

I traversed straight from Camp Three almost 200 metres across, it's a quite dangerous part of the mountain with high avalanche risk ... this was the main avalanche chute and I wanted to stop Wilco coming down this way. I wanted to intercept him because mentally he would not be good. I wanted to stop him because this section was impossible to climb down. I knew Cas was somewhere out there but we were not in communication.

Pemba lay against the steep face and reached for Ger's satellite phone once more. He pressed the redial button. A phone rang in the distance, but there was no answer. Could he keep dialling the number and follow the sound of the phone? Below Pemba, however, was a hanging glacier and he was unwilling to climb down such danger-ridden terrain:

The sound was about 150 metres away from me, and nobody answered the phone. I came back to Camp Three and took a rest for 10, 15 minutes and then I traversed again the same way and I tried to make another phone call. I heard the phone ringing again and still no answer but I couldn't go there because it was too dangerous and too dark so I came back to Camp Three.

It was just after 3.30am on 3 August and Pemba Gyalje resigned himself to another night high up on the mountain. Just four nights before, he had sat in the same tent as the storms battered Camp Three. Had it been some sort of omen, Pemba wondered. His unease at the time may have been justified. He lay in his sleeping bag and tried to rest before the search that would begin again at first light.

Survival and Rescue

3 August – 7 August

K2 stood tall and enduring in the stillness of the night, dwarfing its neighbouring peaks, its summit and the snow plains just below, free once more of human intrusion. The intermittent flickers of light at Base Camp and in the camps along its southern flanks were insignificant against the vast expanse of white snow, blue ice and black rock. Bodies, some intact, others dismembered, lay strewn across the slopes, most never to be seen again, entombed forever in the mountain's crevasses and gulleys.

The catastrophic loss of life over the course of just two days would lend further credibility to K2's reputation as the 'Killer Mountain.' In just 28 hours, 11 climbers had died in the inhospitable and merciless Death Zone. Sunrise was not far away but, for now, the mountain remained enveloped in a moonless darkness, impervious and unyielding.

———

While night had descended on the Karakorum mountains, it was daytime in other corners of the globe where dozens of relatives, friends and climbing companions battled with a suffocating sense of grief, helplessness and despair. Most still didn't know the exact fate of their loved ones; the frenetic search for more information, for new details, for an online update becoming all-consuming and often agonisingly fruitless.

At her home in Kathmandu, Chhiring Dorje's wife, Dawa Sherpani, did not have the luxury of an internet connection. For days, she and her family waited for news from the mountain. As time passed, Dawa could stand the tension no more. She wandered through internet cafés in the city, asking strangers to search for information about the expedition, for news of Chhiring. Some websites, she was told, indicated that Sherpas had been killed but failed to name-check the victims.[146] Dawa began to fear the worst.

In the south-west of Ireland, Ger McDonnell's mother and siblings had begun to keep a vigil around their computer, checking for any updates and praying for his safe descent. The Norit expedition website, as well as Irish and Worldwide Adventures, became their main sources of information.

In desperation, the family tried to use the Google Earth mapping system to see if lights were visible beneath the summit of K2; perhaps they could spot Ger? His sister, Denise, recalled how the family waited for news for what seemed an eternity:

> That's how we were finding out, looking at the internet ... And "Ger McDonnell unknown" were just the worst words that could be printed in front of your face because this is someone, this is our brother, this is our son.

A bottle of champagne to celebrate Ger's summit success lay in the fridge, still corked, to be opened only when he had returned safely to Base Camp.

In Alaska, Annie Starkey was still reeling from the suggestion that Ger had somehow begun to climb towards the Chinese side of the mountain. It just didn't make sense. Ger's brother, JJ, contacted the Department of Foreign Affairs in Dublin. He asked if the Chinese government could arrange an air search of that side of K2. If Ger was there, maybe he could be spotted from a plane. The family clung to every possible hope.

Annie emailed Nick Rice through his website, asking if he knew any more. A reply arrived from his mother, whom Annie thought was handling email correspondence for her son: Nick didn't have any further information about Ger. Someone at Base Camp had told him that Ger may have gone to the Chinese side; but it was just a rumour. Annie was numbed to the core:

> ... someone might throw out a comment on their blog about what they think might be happening or some rumour they heard, not realising, "Hey, we are waiting for our loved ones". We were waiting for Ger ... Wilco's family was waiting for him. Nobody really knows what is going on. Jumik's family; I don't even know if they would have the internet or any kind of way of communicating. We were all waiting anyway and you throw some comment out there. We were hanging on every single word and even how it was written to get some little clue as to what was going on.

Her mind was ablaze with questions as she packed her belongings for a flight to Ireland to be with Ger's family: 'When I heard at some point that Pemba was going down to Camp Three, that is when I thought he knows something. He knows something … I remember leaving the house and I said to my friend, "Is it crazy that I still have hope?" She said, "No it's not crazy". I still thought maybe he was down and had missed Camp Four.'

Marco Confortola resisted the temptation to remove his boots; he would see little anyway as it was not yet dawn. In his tent at Camp Four, he found sleep almost impossible. His feet felt as though they were encased in ice for all eternity, the awful pain of frostbite pointing to inevitable damage, but he tried not to dwell on that likelihood. Marco did not know if he could make it down the mountain without support. He was alone, the highest camp now deserted by those able to make good their escape.

Wilco struggled to remain calm in the freezing blackness. Unbeknownst to him, Pemba and Cas were just 300 metres away. Mentally, he was in turmoil and, physically, he had nothing more to give. He had no sensation in his toes. His tongue felt as though it was coated in sand. Like a parched sailor surrounded by sea water, Wilco was tempted by a frozen liquid which he could not drink, the negative consequences of doing so outweighing the benefits. But reason had now been set aside. He had not taken in fluids for almost two days and could resist no longer:

> I couldn't stand the pain in my throat anymore. So I start eating the snow which takes a lot of energy because you have to melt it from zero degrees to 30 degrees or whatever, and there is no energy in the snow so it's better off not eating the snow but I had to do it because of the pain … It was the most terrible night of my life, of course, because from half past seven in the evening 'til five o'clock the next morning, it's a long, long night. And I didn't have the guts to have a look at my watch because I knew when I look at my watch I am going to get frustrated because the time is moving [so] slowly.

'The guys are back in Base Camp, where the mood is sombre,' read the Singaporean expedition blog on the morning of Sunday, 3 August: "There is a taste of death in the air," Robert (Goh) said. Eleven deaths have been confirmed, including a couple of Sherpas with the Korean team.' The American expedition leader, Mike Farris, had waited at Camp One for his team-mates overnight and together they had made it back to base at 1.30am. For days, Farris' blog had received no updates as the sequence of deaths unfolded and on his return to Base Camp he was brief:

> August 3: Please excuse the brevity, but we are still very busy here. We arrived in BC at 1:30 last night. All members are now in BC, safe and sound (though tired). Chhiring summited K2, so we are very happy about that. Unfortunately, a beautiful day turned deadly and up to 11 climbers lost their lives. We are still involved in the rescue of two climbers; we think that both rescues are going well and the climbers should be in BC by tomorrow. More details later. Thanks for your support. Mike.[147]

From early morning, Chris Klinke was preoccupied with the ongoing search for Wilco. Before dawn he had left a voicemail for his sister, Amy, to say everyone on the American team was safely back at Base Camp.[148] Chris had stepped out of his tent as soon as the sun began to rise, hopeful that the daylight would throw up evidence of more survivors. At about 5.15am he spotted Wilco's orange down suit set against the white snow about 300 metres to the west of, and 100 metres above, Camp Three on the Cesen line.

Alongside Chris, looking through a telescope, Hoselito Bite could just make out Wilco sitting on the snow and, a short distance away, the lone and stationary figure of Cas van de Gevel. Hoselito prayed they were alive. He tried Pemba's radio but it was switched off.

A forlorn and frozen human form sat almost motionless but shivering at just over 7,000 metres above sea level. Wilco van Rooijen was still alive. He had somehow lived through a second night on the outer edges of the Death Zone without food, water or shelter. Between episodes of sleep, he looked repeatedly towards the horizon. Would the sun ever rise, he wondered, the hazy shafts of light seeming to tease him in his delirium:

> I was just sitting waiting ... I felt that I didn't have any feeling in my feet anymore but you are too tired and you are not that clear anymore that you think hey, listen, I take off my boot and start to rub my toes. You just think, just let it be. I will see tomorrow, you know ... Finally ... the sun was rising. It was five o'clock in the morning. I was thinking now I have to move on.

The first beams of sunlight roused a new energy from somewhere deep within and Wilco manoeuvred and hacked his way across the face, but the terrain was forbidding, strewn with small glacial overhangs and rocky ledges which did not lend themselves easily to the points of his ice axe or crampons. The phone vibrated inside his down suit. Remarkably, the battery still had charge. It was Heleen. 'Keep going, keep going,' she implored.[149]

A short distance away, Cas assessed the state of his fingers. He had inadvertently left his gloves off while he dozed, his chronic fatigue making him almost oblivious to the cold. The digits were an ominous white, indicating that frostbite had probably already burrowed into the capillaries and tendons. Daylight restored a clear view of the mountain beneath him and soon he was picking his way towards the tents which comprised Camp Three on the ridge of the Cesen.

Dislodging some rocks on his descent, Cas sent a large stone hurtling towards the tent where Pemba slept. The crash of the rock against the fabric woke the Nepali with a start. It was bright outside and he had slept for several hours. He switched on his radio. Another call from Base Camp told him that Wilco was on the move again; the orange dot was now within 200 metres of Camp Three.

Pemba poked his head out of the tent. 'I see Cas,' he told Roeland van Oss on the radio – he was just metres away. Pemba quickly melted some water and offered Cas a drink as he clambered into the tent. The Dutchman looked tired and dishevelled but Wilco was so close and they were determined to find him. 'Come on,' Pemba said, 'he is not far away. There is a hanging glacier and it is very steep.' He grabbed the oxygen he had brought from High Camp and the pair moved slowly across the rocks and ice.

'He's alive, he's alive!' an animated Hoselito yelled into the frosty morning air at Base Camp as the orange dot began to move. He ran to the Serb team tent to get a pair of binoculars: 'My wish was that it was Gerard ... that was my hope ... I had the best relationship with him, and that [hope] was natural.' Despite their disagreements and furious rows in previous weeks, Hoselito was overjoyed that Wilco was close to rescue. Maybe, he thought, something positive could be retrieved from the tragedy: 'For me it was not a question of who was there, it's Wilco or it's another person alive ... I felt a little like, if I will help somehow, that it will be my summit, I win, I win, not the mountain, I win.'

Through their radios, Hoselito and Roeland began to direct Pemba towards Wilco, asking Pemba and Cas to shout his name as they moved out from Camp Three. 'Wilco is down from your left side,' Hoselito told him. From thousands of metres away, Chris Klinke could see Wilco's reaction to the calls of his teammates:

> We ask them to start yelling Wilco's name and when they do we see Wilco respond by standing up. We start directing them to his location because they still are not in line of sight of each other. Wilco is proceeding across the snow slope above the [small overhanging] serac by punching his fists into the snow, and front pointing across the slope. He is moving in the direction of Cas who has started out across the snow slope.[150]

Wilco's feet began to weigh him down as though they were set in concrete. Any sensation of warmth in his toes was now a distant memory. He tried to suppress the realisation that irreversible frostbite was already doing permanent damage. Suddenly, two yellow tents seemed visible in the distance. His heart began to pound louder. Moments later, what looked like two shadows approached from a few hundred metres away.

Wilco could not figure out who or what was in the shimmering mirage set against the early morning sun. He didn't want to trust his eyes. He could hear voices but they were muffled. He thought it was a dream:

... I didn't realise it. Pemba was the only guy with a blue suit but I couldn't ... there was no sign for me in my brain, "Hey, shit, this is Pemba". I just saw two climbers. I just went over there and just 100 metres in front was Cas, then finally I recognised, "Fuck, it's Cas".

The embrace of the two Dutch friends was filled with tears and hoarse words. Wilco looked a shadow of the man they had last seen two days before, the searing rays and the bitter winds having ravaged his face and eyes, his stubble crusted over with frost and his lips blistered. Pemba watched as Cas and Wilco exchanged exultations in a foreign tongue. There was little time for celebration; they were perched on a dangerous gradient, away from the fixed lines.

Wilco was exhausted but mobile and Pemba was anxious to bring his expedition leader to the nearby tent to assess his condition. The three men were still over 2,000 vertical metres from Base Camp and the sustenance and crucial medical intervention that would bring. Pemba radioed Hoselito; they had found Wilco and would return first to Camp Three. The Serb was overjoyed:

When they got Wilco everybody in Base Camp was very happy ... 11 people had died ... that was too much, but there will not be 12 or 13, there will be 11 and that is it. This battle, little battle, we won, we lost 11 people, but we saved one.

The Norwegians hiked down from Advanced Base Camp just after dawn, every metre taking Cecilie a few steps further away from the site of the devastation the mountain had wreaked on her and her team. Despite its sobriety and funereal air, Base Camp had continued to focus on the rescue attempt kilometres above, the determination to rescue Wilco providing a welcome antidote to the death and destruction of the previous days.

The full extent of the death toll was not apparent to Lars until he reached Base Camp. Since Rolf's death, he, Cecilie and Oystein, stunned by their own grief, were fixated on their personal safety and well-being. Lars noticed how the co-ordination of the rescue mission helped to occupy the minds of those at the foot of the mountain:

It seemed to be well organised in Base Camp. There were a lot of people doing their best trying to save people on the mountain; especially the

Dutch team made a good effort and also the Americans did a lot. We saw that already on the way down ... Mike Farris was waiting for us in Camp Two. A Singaporean team in Camp Three, they were making us teas, just taking care of us, seeing if we were fine. And when we got back to Base Camp they were organising the rescue of Wilco and Marco.

As he prepared breakfast, one of the cooks in the kitchen area nearby heard Cecilie weep. He stepped into her tent. 'Ssshh,' he implored, as he knelt and helped her to remove her boots and socks. 'No cry, no cry,' he said as he gently massaged her freezing feet. Cecilie could hear smatterings of the hushed conversations outside the tent about rescue plans and the body count on the mountain. Part of her wanted to lead an attempt to find Rolf's remains but she also wanted to escape, to get away.

Wilco's body had stiffened in the cold and Pemba helped make him comfortable on a sleeping mat in a tent at Camp Three, knowing that the worst consequences of frostbite would be difficult to avoid for the Dutchman; the sooner they got back to Base Camp for medical treatment, the better. Wilco looked beaten, physically and mentally, and Pemba hoped he would be able to cope with the arduous descent, despite being plagued by frozen fingers and toes.

Wilco relished the oxygen his team-mate had brought from Camp Four. Cas boiled water for tea, the warm liquid was the first Wilco had imbibed in two and a half days. The three friends sat silently for a few moments, the emotional dam built up in the previous days now yielding uncontrollably to the awful reality of the breadth of the tragedy. Cas and Pemba relayed the events of the previous 36 hours.

'I saw Hugues fall,' said Cas. 'There were many avalanches.' Wilco shook his head in disbelief: 'I couldn't believe it because I was just going down those days and I hadn't seen any fallen ice, seracs falling, avalanches, or heard it even. So it all happened just in small moments, independent of each other.' 'Ger is missing,' said Cas.

Nobody wanted to say Ger was dead but, for the first time, Pemba accepted in his heart that there was no prospect of finding their team-mate and fellow-summiteer alive. In Wilco's pained face Pemba could see the same reluctant and unspoken acceptance of a terrible truth.

'He brought honour, not only to us, his family, but to the whole country, when he became the first Irishman to summit K2 on Friday': Ger McDonnell's brother-in-law, Damien O'Brien, struggled to maintain his composure as he read a prepared statement from the McDonnell family in the close-knit village of Kilcornan in south-west Ireland on Sunday, 3 August.

Just a day earlier, the Irish president, Mary McAleese, had issued a statement acclaiming the 37-year-old's historic achievement. Now Ger's death was being publicly acknowledged; his family had accepted the inevitable. During his expeditions, Ger would phone his mother at exactly eight o'clock every Sunday morning, to check in with her, to tell her that he was okay. That Sunday morning, the phone hadn't rung.[151]

The Irish media had descended on the small village, approaching locals going to morning Mass in an attempt to find out about Ger and what had happened to him. Most of the villagers didn't yet know about the tragedy and, in the hope that the media would give the family some privacy to grieve, the McDonnells had prepared a press release which was delivered to the assembled media later on Sunday. Damien concluded the statement by focussing on what Ger had brought to their lives:

> The last few days have been a roller-coaster of emotions as we celebrated with joy his historic achievement, and now we must try to come to terms with the untimely loss of a great son, brother and friend ... Above all we'll miss Ger's caring smile which brought light and warmth to all those who met him.[152]

After an hour's rest, Pemba convinced Cas and Wilco that it was time to get moving. The oxygen seemed to infuse Wilco with a renewed vigour but Cas moved incredibly slowly. Pemba raced ahead to Camp Two to prepare more hot drinks and waited almost two hours for his increasingly decrepit team-mates to join him. When they finally arrived, Cas lay spread-eagled in the tent, begging to be allowed spend the night there.

Pemba knew they had to press on – another night without proper medical intervention would be hugely detrimental for the injured Dutchmen. Reluctantly, the pair continued their descent behind Pemba, who was finding it more and more difficult to corral them towards Base Camp:

> I said, "No, we have to keep going". I said, "Okay, let's start", but they were sitting down. I said, "Okay, get ready and go", and they were still sitting and saying they wanted to stop here. I said, "No, we need to go down", and finally Wilco stood up and he started climbing down slowly and, then after, Cas.

———————————

Marco began the agonising descent towards the Abruzzi's Camp Three. He felt sluggish and nauseous as he moved down the fixed line. The camp was empty save for the remaining tents left behind by the other climbers who had already retreated from the ridge. It was silent and desolate and he felt as though the other peaks across the glacial valley were mocking him and his debilitation:

> I feel insignificant, alone and left alone. I want to shout at the mountain and to explain my feelings – all the rage that is inside me but I am too tired. I stop and stay for a night at Camp Three. I am lucky that Chhiring's tent is here. I am feeling very hungry; I have been two days without food. There is nothing in the tent. It makes me want to cry and I feel like collapsing. In the corner of the tent I see a red and yellow paper – it is an energy bar. I take it and tear the paper open but I can't eat it because it is frozen. I put it in my mouth and fall asleep.[153]

———————————

The thawing of ice between Camp One and the base of the mountain on the Cesen route had caused the fixed ropes to loosen or disappear. As temperatures rose in the early days of August, meltwater cascaded quickly and dangerously from the ridges. A Base Camp team, including Roeland and Jelle from the Norit team, along with Hoselito Bite and an American climber, Chris Warner, began to fix a few hundred metres of new lines towards Camp One to ensure that Cas, Wilco and Pemba could descend safely.

Separately, work had begun a short distance from Base Camp to create an improvised helipad. Eric Meyer, and even those without medical training, realised that Wilco, Cas and Marco would likely require helicopter evacuation to hospital; their frostbite injuries would make the trek back to Askole torturous for them.

By Sunday evening, the focus of attention at Base Camp had shifted to Marco Confortola. It was obvious to everyone that the Italian would require the assistance of fresher bodies to aid his passage to safety. Another American-led expedition at camp offered their assistance. Its leader, George Dijmarescu, and the team's Sherpas, Rinjing Sherpa and Mingma Tunduk Sherpa, agreed that on the following day they would climb the Abruzzi spur towards Marco, bringing food and oxygen.

Despite their relative inaccessibility and isolation from the outside world, the climbers at Base Camp found themselves unavoidably sucked into the media storm that was developing around the events that were unfolding on the world's second highest mountain. They were becoming the inevitable target for queries from an insatiable media trying to find out what was happening, who was dead and what was to blame.

In the hours and days after the summit attempt, Fredrik Sträng, Chris Klinke, Nick Rice and others at Base Camp began to field calls from journalists. It wasn't difficult to track them down – Fredrik and Nick's satellite phone numbers were on their websites, for example. By the afternoon of 3 August, the sound of phones ringing reverberated around the base of K2, with calls coming in from journalists across the globe. Fredrik soon found himself becoming the de facto public relations officer for the expeditions:

> We felt ... that we had the responsibility to go out and tell the world what had happened ... No one wanted to take that responsibility because everyone was sleep deprived, hypoxic. I was in a state of shock but somehow people had trust in me and we talked about this among us. Should we talk to BBC, should we talk to CNN, what should we say? And I didn't want to take the phone calls. You take it Chris, no you take it Fredrik, you can handle this better ... We had all the radio calls, we knew who had died, we knew who was missing etcetera and we had to break the news. We had to tell them what we knew for a fact.

Fredrik later faced criticism from his fellow climbers and some of the relatives of the deceased for appearing to overstate his role in the rescue effort. He told one interviewer how he had 'carried both the living and the dead down from the mountain,' a phrase that aggravated many.[154] Fredrik defended his media presence, however: 'Not in my wildest dreams did I think about, "Oh I'm trying to make myself famous here". Why would I do that? I came down, I was in a state of shock; friends had died on the mountain.'

Another climber who came to the attention of the world's press was Nick Rice. Despite the fact that he was not in the vicinity of the higher camps or the drama that unfolded beneath the summit in the days after 1 August, the American continued to play a key role in reporting to the outside world what was happening on the mountain, posting on his blog, in the words of one author, 'with the gusto of a society gossip columnist'.[155]

As soon as the first reports of the tragedy emerged in the international media, Nick's on-site reportage came to be in huge demand. Over the course of subsequent days his blog received almost two million hits and his commentary appeared in some 40 different newspapers.[156] Within days of his return to Base Camp, Nick found himself 'sorting through endless requests for interviews from news agencies all around the world'.[157]

His website had also become a critical point of information for the families seeking new information about their loved ones. But with the online posting of instantaneous information came the possibility that some of the details could be wrong. In a list of the deceased on his blog, Nick had included a reference to Ger McDonnell which further exacerbated the stress and grief of the Irishman's family:

> Irish – Gerard McDonnell – Confirmed Dead; Refused to descend because he was helping the others that were injured.[158]

Nick had previously suggested that Ger had gone to the Chinese side of the mountain; now there was another story suggesting that Ger refused to descend. Hugues D'Aubarède, Nick reported, had been, 'stuck above the traverse after Serac Fall cut the Fixed Lines', while their team-mate Karim Meherban 'Fell in Descent after Hugues Deceased'. Within his own messaging, the American seemed to signal that he recognised the inherent danger in publishing details that had not yet been confirmed or investigated: 'I can't guarantee that all the facts are present,' he blogged.[159] But these concerns weren't enough to deter him.

In many cases, the consequences of the speculative postings for the families involved would be profound and long-felt. As some blogs continued to fuel stories in the media, their authors began to take potshots at each other online. On his blog, Nick Rice accused others of spreading false information: 'Thanks to the internet, these lies and twisted rumours are being published as fact, and people are being given hope when none exists, or being misled to believe that their loved one is missing, when in fact they are safe in descent or in Base Camp.'[160]

Mike Farris condemned the spreading of misinformation and it was apparent to whom he was referring in his 7 August dispatch:

> It's incredible who the media interview about this tragedy. Any twit with a web page is considered an expert. Being on K2 doesn't make you a climber, or qualified to comment on the issues involved. I have a web page (obviously) but haven't been interviewed yet. I must be defective (or intelligent).[161]

The activities of bloggers and climbers quoted in the media from Base Camp in the early days of August 2008 prompted a debate within the climbing fraternity on the dangers of using or accepting contemporaneous reports from the scene of a tragedy. Some of the climbers earned a stinging rebuke from a hard-hitting editorial published on ExplorersWeb even before many of the survivors had left the mountain.

In her article on the widely-read website, co-editor Tina Sjogren castigated some for jumping the gun in releasing information about what had happened on the mountain. She went on to accuse climbers of engaging in a 'dance for scoops and fame on people's graves':

> To declare someone dead in normal life, you need a coroner's report or a judge. In the mountains, lacking proper authorities, you need an eyewitness or for sufficient time to have passed. Mountaineering history is filled with examples of "ghosts" walking into Base Camps. Only on K2 this weekend, one of the 11 "dead" climbers was found alive less than half a day ago. Several climbers are still reportedly coming down the Abruzzi ridge, their identities unknown. The summit push was early morning Friday August 1, today is Sunday August 3. There is a real possibility that the unlocated climbers have perished. But there's also a chance that some are still alive waiting for assistance that will not arrive, due to fellow climbers declaring them goners while busy in BC creating heroic stories about themselves ... In all our years of sleepless nights and phone calls with desperate relatives at ExplorersWeb, and through all our own climbs in the Himalayan mountains, we have never seen anything like it.[162]

Likewise, Maarten van Eck was dismayed by some of the blogs and information being articulated by those on the mountain:

> They [bloggers] would publish the strangest ideas and names without proper consideration. Some of the climbers already down in K2BC made that similar mistake. Some of the blog entries … and stupid remarks were infuriating for us and caused a lot of uncalled-for sadness and problems. I think it's stupid to make all kind of remarks in the middle of the rescue attempts that were organised.[163]

While the media storm closed in on Base Camp, Pemba remained focussed on bringing Cas and Wilco to safety. The painstaking descent continued slowly. It seemed that the nearer they came to Base Camp, the more stilted the progress became. From below Camp One, Pemba observed how the ice on the ridge was 'totally melting – it was very hot weather, sunny. In many places it was a waterfall. Water was pouring down on my head. All the ice that had been there three days earlier was gone'.

The Norit trio were grateful to discover the newly-fixed lines which made for a smoother descent toward the base of the mountain. The 2,000-metre climb from Camp Three to the glacier below had taken most of the day and Wilco and Cas were overcome with relief when they were finally able to stand, unaided by ropes, ice axes or crampons.

As they approached the bottom of the mountain, about 12 people climbed up to meet them, including Hoselito Bite, who asked Pemba about Ger. For the first time, Pemba was able to articulate what he knew to be true: Ger had died on the mountain; he would not be coming back. He name-checked all the others who had died. 'The best people at Base Camp,' Hoselito cried, 'they died on the mountain.' The three surviving Norit team members were supported by their fellow climbers on the hour-long walk to Base Camp as darkness fell once more over the Karakorum mountains: despair was temporarily mitigated by relief and joy at their safe return.

Eric Meyer had been on standby for several hours with a cocktail of drugs designed to arrest the ill effects of frostbite, hypoxia and snow blindness, among them a trial drug designed to combat tissue damage caused by frostbite. Soon the Dutch mess tent resembled a scene from a disaster zone with a series of improvised gurneys and intravenous drips held aloft. Cas and Wilco, propped against the inflatable couch left behind by the Norwegians, dipped their grey and waxen feet into pans of lukewarm water as other climbers gently massaged their digits.

Morphine helped somewhat to ease the pain. It was only while he rested, the warmth gradually returning to his limbs, that the full extent of the tragedy struck Wilco. He prodded his fellow climbers for the pieces of the jigsaw that he needed to put the full story together in his head. Rolf was dead, Hugues also, Karim too; 11 in total. He shook his head in disbelief. Eric examined Pemba. 'I am okay, I am okay,' he said. Pemba watched Wilco and Cas being treated; he noted their toes and hands and recognised the extent of Wilco's frostbite which was clearly extensive.

Pemba withdrew from the improvised hospital ward and joined some of the other Sherpas in one of the mess tents. In hushed tones they exchanged their stories of rescue and survival. Pemba felt unable to eat but sipped warm drinks. Chhiring Dorje told him he had already contacted home and asked his wife to phone Pemba's family with news of his safe return.

Seeking escape, Pemba walked back to his tent, unable to bring himself to visit Ger's: 'I hadn't slept for a long time, three or four nights, and it was a good sleep and I needed it. The mood at Base Camp was quiet and people were in shock.'

On reaching Base Camp, Pasang Lama and Tsering Bhote had also contacted home using Chhiring's phone; they learned that Jumik's wife, Dawa Sangmu, had given birth to a baby boy on the day the South Korean team had left Base Camp for the summit. Their cousin, Ngawang Bhote, had tried to radio the news from Base Camp to Camp Four while they and Jumik had been on the mountain but he was unable to get through.[164] Jumik had summited and died without knowing he had become a father.

Tsering was heartbroken but he would forever be a special uncle to Jumik's baby whom his mother had named Jen Jen. Pasang Lama, who had been living a dream from the moment he had left Kathmandu, struggled to comprehend the nightmare which had caused the deaths of his cousins and why he had been singled out for salvation:

I lost very close friends on the mountain. When I recall the Bottleneck, the climb, the danger in every instance ... we could have been carried away ... We were saved; God had his hand on our heads and he gave us another life. I feel that.

The morning of 4 August brought a familiar but somehow incongruous sound to the foot of K2. The rotor blades of two rescue helicopters blew the headgear from those ferrying a bespectacled Wilco and Cas on improvised stretchers towards their flying taxis. Eric had wrapped their feet in bandages and administered more drugs. He feared that Wilco's toes were beyond saving.

Just as Cas and Wilco left Base Camp by helicopter, Maarten van Eck published the first confirmation about the fate of their missing team-mate on the Norit expedition website:

> We are very sorry to inform you that our friend and climbing partner Gerard McDonnell died while descending from K2 Summit. We deeply sympathise with Ger's family in Ireland and his girlfriend Ann. Our friend Gerard will not return from K2.[165]

The loud whirr of helicopter blades hundreds of metres below seemed like an illusion to Marco Confortola. After another night of fitful sleep, he had managed to navigate the hazardous House's Chimney on the Abruzzi spur and had begun his descent towards Camp Two. It was a helicopter rising from below him, like a giant insect in the sky. He tried to avoid waving lest it send him plunging from the rope.

The chopper hovered a few hundred metres below him. Roberto Manni had managed to persuade one of the pilots to attempt an airlift of his climbing companion, but he was unable to see Marco and, at 6,000 metres – a dangerously high altitude for the aircraft – was unwilling to go any higher. Marco watched, clinging to the ice, as the helicopter dipped its blades and veered away to the south.

He wondered if he was being teased in some vicious game designed to force him into a mental breakdown. He rested his head against the rock, exasperated and forlorn. But help was not far away:

> I see shadows moving towards me. I don't know who they are. I am paralysed and can't do anything. I don't know if they are real or not. As they near, after a while, I can focus and I recognise them. They are two Sherpas, I don't remember their names but they are two brothers from Makalu, and George Dijmarescu, an American alpinist, is also with them. I know them from Base Camp. George smiles and says, "We are here for you"... I ask if they have a radio. George has and I ring Robby; I say, "It is me, I have made it". I don't know whether to laugh or to cry.[166]

In a vacant tent at Camp Two, Marco decided he could wait no longer. He slowly prised the boots from his numbed feet. He realised immediately that he was in trouble. His toes glowed violet and his feet were swollen. They felt as though they were not part of his body. The tendons around his ankles were frozen and inflexible. Marco fell backwards and onto a sleeping mat: 'The last thing I think before I fall asleep is that I cannot do this [climbing] anymore.'[167]

Pemba watched as Cecilie Skog said goodbye to her two remaining climbing companions. Lars and Oystein would stay behind at Base Camp for a few days to await their porters and pack their belongings. A final photograph with the pair showed Cecilie's vacant eyes sunken into her head, her braided hair unkempt, her shoulders slumped. She walked towards Concordia with a porter who helped with her equipment. It would be a long and lonely trek to Askole but she moved as quickly as her tired limbs allowed.

Bjorn Sekkesaeter was already on a flight to Islamabad and would meet Cecilie as soon as possible, hoping to shield her from the TV cameras and microphones. The death of one half of a well-known newlywed young couple would be like manna from heaven for a hungry media, and the rest of her team feared for Cecilie's well-being in the face of a media blitz.

As Base Camp began to empty, Pemba tried to focus on resting after the debilitating two and a half days he had spent in the Death Zone; he needed to recuperate for the long trek back to Askole. Mark, Jelle and Roeland set about breaking camp, putting aside Ger's personal items for his family. A surreal calm had descended on the camp as the climbers went silently about their final preparations for departure.

Pemba, slowly recovering from his ordeal, began to reflect on what had happened – the disparity between the indigenous climbers and those from other countries had been clearly evident as they approached the summit:

> Physiologically and naturally the Sherpa people are more capable, physically and mentally, to deal with extremely high altitudes and that is why we can still think and talk to each other and plan further until the end of the situation. Naturally, Sherpa people are much stronger and fitter than westerners.

During the ascent, Pemba had waited for direction from the various expedition leaders when Dren Mandic had fallen, when delays occurred and when the summit attempt was clearly behind time. But none was forthcoming: 'They were too optimistic for the summit ... If everybody turned back after the Serb fell down then I think there would only have been one casualty on the mountain instead of 11.'

However, in climbing, Hoselito Bite said, everyone took risks: 'Because in climbing ... every climber going up gambles with his life.' It was a gamble which had not paid off for so many of their peers. For Pemba, that was because many of them had failed to recognise and accept their own limitations:

> I am always saying high-altitude mountaineering is totally different. We cannot fight with the altitude; we cannot fight with the mountain. Everybody must be disciplined. People need good altitude experience for that kind of expedition, good technical experience, good physical condition. If my condition was not really good on K2, I have to quit. If some people feel like that, they have to quit. You have to keep trekking, hiking in a high-altitude environment, every season trying to reach a little bit higher and higher. You have to spend a long time – and after four or five years you can say my capacity is this much in this altitude.

'Base camp now seems to be like a cage that everyone wants to escape,' Nick Rice reported on 5 August.[168] He also noted how the area around their tents was deteriorating physically, as if the mountain was cleansing itself of the evidence of the most recent human presence along its slopes:

> Every evening, we hear cascades of rocks falling down the slopes around us; huge pieces of ice are crashing down in the icefall, and avalanches roar down the slopes of all the peaks around us daily. The routes up K2 mirror this decay, as rivers flow down where once consolidated snow was, and rockfall danger is exponentially higher as there is less snow and ice on the mountain. Those who remain and attempt to climb K2 will earn both my respect and disbelief, as she has proven herself to be quite deadly this year. These people must either just be insane or have a death wish.[169]

Even as the final climbers were descending from the higher camps, the logistics operation required to dismantle Base Camp and clear all of the remaining equipment and supplies was being put in train, as the same army of porters which had crossed the Baltoro and Godwin-Austen glaciers months before returned. Deconstructing and clearing a site which had, for several weeks, been home to 120 people, took time, but the porters from the valleys below were accustomed to clearing the otherwise unspoiled icescape of all evidence of human activity.

A few climbers lingered – including a couple of small expeditions which had recently arrived – and some were still considering a summit attempt. ExplorersWeb described the scene:

> The Americans, Dutch, Serb (Hoselito), and Norwegians are all waiting on porters to arrive so that they can head down. Very few people are considering staying and trying again. The Singaporeans, who arrived in base camp in mid-July, are reflecting within, and deciding whether to give K2 another try. Mike Farris, one of the Americans, is also considering staying in base camp, and seeing whether the conditions on the mountain improve.[170]

By Tuesday morning, 5 August, only Marco Confortola and those shepherding him towards safety still remained at a higher altitude. At Camp Two, it took

Marco an hour to get his boots back onto his feet. Taking them off had allowed the swelling to increase and the skin was fragile and brittle. The blood supply seemed to have long left his toes.

A few hours later, the rescue party was leading Marco towards the end of his horrendous journey. At Advanced Base Camp, a stretcher awaited him, along with refreshments in the form of salami and Coca Cola.[171] Within sight of his tent, further along the glacier, he rejected the offer of a stretcher and asked instead for two snow skis to propel him toward salvation. Mario Pancieri, a member of another Italian expedition which had not attempted the summit, approached his fellow countryman with tears in his eyes. 'Come on Marco, you're almost there,' he urged.

Marco noticed the surreal silence at Base Camp. With all eyes on him, he crumpled under the searing emotion of his return, stumbling towards the nearby chorten, a small Buddhist monument the Sherpas had erected, where he fell to his knees:

> I think of my grandfather, Loci, I talk to the mountain and I say, "Why did you do that?" and tears come to my cheeks. I ask Robby where are the other tents and climbers. He says, "They are dead". I say nothing. I go to my tent and sleep.[172]

Later that evening, Marco ate his first proper meal in almost a week in one of the mess tents, surrounded by climbers who were both exhilarated by his safe return from the summit and captivated by how he had survived.

Pemba opted not to join them and rested in his tent. As he lay prostrate, his eyes yielding to sleep, a shrill metallic tapping noise caught his attention. Across the camp, Hoselito Bite sat in the dim light, hunched over a set of aluminium dining plates, a small hammer in one hand and an improvised chisel in the other.

He was marking out a few short words on a plate that would be placed at the Gilkey Memorial, to sit alongside those of other climbers who, over almost a century, had lost their lives pursuing their passion and dreams. Hoselito checked the spelling and continued:

GERARD McDONNELL

20.01.1971 – 02.08.2008

LIMERICK

IRISH

Nameplates would be prepared for each of the climbers who had perished. Pemba listened, motionless in his sleeping bag, as the 'ting, ting, ting' resounded around the Godwin-Austen glacier like an improbable funeral dirge.

The sound of helicopter rotors echoed across Base Camp for the second time in three days on the morning of 6 August as Marco Confortola prepared to leave for Skardu and medical attention for his deadened feet. Marco had been a vivacious and fun-loving character at Base Camp and the other climbers gathered to wish him well. Jelle Staleman approached the Italian and shook his hand.

Marco spoke warmly about Ger, sympathising with Jelle on the loss of his team-mate. He told Jelle how he had seen Ger fall to his death from the mountain as he lay on the snow beneath the Bottleneck. He had seen 'two La Sportiva boots, the kind Ger was wearing, so it was probably him in the snow'.[173] He handed Jelle $800; 'Give this to Pemba for me, to thank him for all his help.'

Pemba had remained in his tent and was shocked at the offer. Jelle, Mark and Roeland told him he had to accept the money as a gift. Pemba shied away from seeing Marco again before he departed: 'I knew I would have to talk a lot and he was screaming, crying and I didn't want that because I wanted to take a rest. I didn't want to get caught up in the emotion of it.'

Marco was helped to walk the few hundred metres from Base Camp to a place on the moraine where the helicopter could land safely. As he was whizzed away towards Concordia, Pemba and some of the remaining climbers made the short pilgrimage to the Gilkey Memorial. Hoselito and others wanted to place the memorial plates they had made. Some of the plaques were hung from fishing line alongside flags, prayers and personal items.

Pemba had deliberately avoided going to the Gilkey before the summit bid; his visit now brought closure of sorts: 'We went there and we fixed the plates. We said, "It is over". The majority of people were upset there. I spent nearly one hour there. I read almost all the plates. It was a sad moment.' None of the remains of those who had died just days before were interred in the makeshift cemetery; their bodies lay where they fell, exposed to the vagaries that K2's weather and the passage of time would bring.

The Norit team members spent much of their final night at Base Camp with the American International Team. They were organising an 8 August departure, with only their expedition leader, Mike Farris, planning to stay behind for another possible summit bid; the route was still largely complete, all the camps were in place, he was still acclimatised and the weather was still reasonably good. On clearing up Ger's belongings, one of the climbers had found a bottle of beer; perhaps he had been planning to savour it on his return from the summit. Over dinner, it was used to toast the Irishman.

Pemba, Mark, Jelle, Roeland, and the American team members reflected on a traumatic week. Fredrik Sträng commented of the fragility of life in the face of nature's fiercest forces:

> I don't think there is anything romantic about dying in the mountains. I think that's just a picture that non-climbers put on us climbers. I'd rather die in a nice field of flowers when I'm 98 years old. You know, just lying down and just meditating and disappearing. That's more romantic to me ... They did what they did and sometimes things go wrong, you know, that's life. It's not a return ticket. Maybe we can learn something from the K2 accidents that we can take with us in our ordinary lives, that not everything is for certain and maybe we should live a bit more than just try to survive.

Tragedy Becomes
Controversy

7 August – 14 August

As Wilco, Cas and Marco departed Base Camp in their respective helicopters over the course of two days, they were flying not just to safety and urgently-required medical treatment, they were also flying into the epicentre of the one of the biggest media storms in mountaineering history. The extent of the carnage on K2 and stories of fatal mistakes on the mountain were continuing to gain worldwide media attention at a relatively quiet time of year when hard news stories were few and far between.

The allure of a story filled with death, delirium, extreme adventure and a part of the Earth's atmosphere dubbed the 'Death Zone' proved irresistible to the press. From the off, the coverage of events was controversial. Media interest in the early days gave a platform to commentators from the international mountaineering community to provide handy sound-bite critiques of the behaviour and attitudes of the climbers who had attempted to scale the world's second highest mountain on 1 August.

Until the survivors themselves could be interviewed and until the facts became clearer, expert comment was required by many media platforms to fill the vacuum, alongside colourful three-dimensional graphics of the Karakorum mountain range and mugshots of several of the climbers. TV studios filled up with climbers who were asked for their tuppence-worth.

By the time Wilco, Cas and Marco had been admitted to the Combined Military Hospital in Skardu, *Der Spiegel* newspaper in Germany, as well as New Zealand TV channel, NZTV, were carrying remarks from the renowned mountaineer, Reinhold Messner, who was highly critical of the climbers' 'inexperience' and 'pure stupidity' on K2 over the previous days, ever before any of those involved had been quizzed about what had happened.

Messner condemned the 'commercialism' of the expeditions to K2 and the penchant of wealthy but ill-equipped climbers for package deals to dangerous mountains, which, he said, were snapped up 'almost as if they were buying some all-inclusive trip to Bangkok'.[174] Messner's comments set the tone for much of the media fallout in the days after the climbers had left the mountain. Such stinging criticisms were coupled with a stream of misinformation and inaccuracies, which compounded the grief and trauma of family members searching for information and for the truth.

On 5 August, for example, *The Guardian* in the UK carried a report which referred to Ger McDonnell being last seen 'heading towards the Chinese border'.[175] A popular and usually reliable mountaineering website suggested that Jumik Bhote and the two South Korean climbers stranded on the ropes near the Traverse had died in a serac fall 'after reportedly refusing assistance from Dutch, Nepalese and Italian climbers'.[176]

Some media reported the deaths of Americans who had summited,[177] others misnamed the three climbers hanging from the ropes,[178] while yet another ran the headline 'K2 climbers froze to death hanging upside down on ropes'.[179]

An article on the front page of *The New York Times* on 6 August introduced yet another element to the contentious media debate that was now gathering around the tragedy. That news of the deaths of 11 climbers in the middle of Asia, no Americans among them, had made it onto the front page of one of the world's best known newspapers was significant in itself. The article, 'Chaos on the "Mountain that Invites Death"', by Graham Bowley and Andrea Kannapell, was pretty straightforward.

But the piece, which for a short time mistakenly carried a picture of Gasherbrum IV mountain rather than K2, prompted an outpouring of anonymous vitriol and condemnation of what was termed the greed, arrogance and carelessness of the climbers and the risks they had taken; criticisms that only compounded the distress of grieving families and friends. The online comment facility on the paper's website allowed anonymous posters to level a range of accusations at the climbers:

- Heroes, my ass. These egomaniacs should stay off mountains.
- Climbing K2 or Everest is a selfish stunt that benefits nothing.
- Just reckless irresponsible behaviour of selfish folks.[180]

Buried in the sea of condemnation was a message posted by Ger McDonnell's cousin, Fiona Hanley. She expressed her disappointment and shock at the hurtful comments about the climbers, reminding the faceless commentators that those involved were human beings with families and friends, left grieving and distraught:

Ger, along with the rest of the K2 both survivors and deceased, deserves respect, not the bitter tongue of people who continue to judge them for having a passion in life. Ger was a fantastic fella and anyone who had the pleasure of knowing him will know that. My condolences to all the families that have suffered loss due to the recent K2 disaster. I shall miss my brave HEROIC cousin. May he REST IN PEACE.[181]

As Cecilie Skog continued her long walk down the Baltoro valley towards Askole, a low-key but sophisticated logistical operation was in train to allow her to travel home away from the prying eyes of the media. Bjorn Sekkesaeter had taken a flight from Norway and had arrived in time to meet Cecilie in Skardu. They flew to Islamabad and from there to Norway via London. Bjorn succeeded in ensuring that Cecilie evaded the media at every turn:

> The media was trying to get to her but we managed to get them to talk to me instead. So I met journalists in Islamabad and in London and when they were waiting for us, we had made an arrangement that she was picked up at the airport and driven straight home. I dealt with the media in all the three airports. Oystein and Lars came home later. I think the media was after Cecilie and I don't remember Oystein and Lars telling me about any difficulties with media at all.[182]

Caught up in their own grief, the remaining team members were grateful for the space and time afforded them by being able to avoid telephone calls and requests for interviews from the media. Even on their return to Norway, Lars said, they shied away from interaction with the press:

> ... we avoided the media. Bjorn took care of that in Norway and we were really privileged to have a really sober guy like him doing it in Norway ... and also the other climbers which were talking to the media in Norway were really people with good attitudes ...

Cecilie did no interviews in the immediate aftermath of the K2 expedition. Instead, she completed a full debrief with Bjorn about what had happened and he briefed the press accordingly:

Cecilie told me everything that happened on the mountain and I took notes and I could bring facts down to the journalists. And when they had written their stories I went over to their hotel and we saw the story and we could proof-read it and make sure there was nothing wrong. Cecilie understood that no matter what happened the story would be told, with or without her influence. I think it was the best solution that she had been part of it and we wanted to kill the rumours because there had been a lot of rumours.[183]

Back in Skardu, the three hospitalised survivors found themselves surrounded by a barrage of cameras and reporters equipped with notebooks and dictaphones. As soon as it had become evident that a major tragedy was unfolding on K2, the international news agencies dispatched their reporters, already based in Islamabad and other parts of Pakistan, to the bedsides of the hospitalised. This was their only shot at speaking to the climbers in person and the reporters faced little difficulty in getting to the source.

In vivid contrast to hospital etiquette in other parts of the world, access to the wards where the bandaged and bruised patients lay was unhindered, the local health authorities dazzled by the cameras and hoping for some positive publicity from the care being afforded to their adventurer tourists in distress. Pictures and footage of the emaciated looking Wilco and Cas being treated by uniformed Pakistani military medics and of Marco on a gurney displaying his blackened toes were beamed across the globe.

There was no expedition co-ordinator or leadership figure on hand to protect the injured from a battery of recording devices and leading questions. They faced the cameras, dazzled, disorientated, fatigued, and alone. Neither Wilco, Cas nor Marco had any time to gather their thoughts after the most traumatic days of their lives. There had been no de-briefing, no sharing of information between the climbers who had survived K2, no common narrative among the survivors.

Instead, a mish-mash of hazy memories, disjointed analyses and stories fuelled by post-traumatic stress were devoured by a hungry media presence. Drugged up and having barely slept, the injured had little choice but to respond to journalists' queries in whatever way they could. And those responses were often laden with anger and accusations as the climbers lashed out in their trauma.

TV images of Marco being wheelchaired into hospital in Skardu and shots of his bandaged, frozen feet were accompanied by a voice-over which referred to comments by the Italian about an expedition 'plagued by inexperience and poor equipment'.[184]

An ABC news report from 5 August signalled not just Wilco's fatigue but also his pent-up frustration at what had transpired over the previous week:

> Lying in a hospital cot, a saline drip strapped to his arm, the leader of a Dutch team that lost three [sic] of 11 climbers who died on K2, has angrily recounted how tragedy unfolded on the world's second highest peak. "The biggest mistake we made was that we tried to make agreements," Wilco van Rooijen said, his face reddened by sun and snow burn after days on the unforgiving 8,611 metre mountain. "Everybody had his own responsibility and then some people did not do what they promised," the 40-year-old Dutchman said, singling out another team for only bringing half the length of rope they were supposed to have. "With such stupid things lives are endangered," Mr van Rooijen added.[185]

Like Wilco, Marco's comments to the media were heavily influenced by the impact of sleep deprivation and powerful painkillers. Much of what was reported about his tale of survival was innocuous but the media reported and repeatedly regurgitated his different versions of what had happened to Ger McDonnell, which continued to jar with the Irishman's family. In *The Independent* of London, one of those versions was carried, first in a news report and, three weeks later, in a more detailed news feature:

> It was at that moment, "for some strange reason", that McDonnell began to walk away. It was the last time Confortola would see his friend alive. Exhausted, he fell asleep, only to be woken by an ominous rumbling. "All of a sudden I saw an avalanche coming down. It was only 20 metres to my right. I saw the body of Gerard sweep past me," he says, covering his eyes once again. It was at the Bottleneck that calamity struck on the descent. An ice pillar broke off, snapping the ropes and causing an avalanche. Confortola recalls how McDonnell's body had been torn to shreds by the impact of the avalanche and all he could see were the separated parts tumbling down the mountainside. "Yes, it was very bad," he says quietly.[186]

However well-meaning and genuinely held the Italian climber's remembrances were – he was simply relating the story as he believed he had witnessed it – the suggestion that Ger had abandoned the rescue effort and was later dismembered in an avalanche that swept past Marco dismayed and infuriated Ger's family in equal measure. His brother-in-law, Damien O'Brien, knew there had to be more to the story:

> What Marco did on the mountain, nobody can take that away from him; he was a hero on the mountain. To this day, the [Ger's] family still say that Marco did what he could do, that he was a hero. But when we heard the stories, I mean, at this point, Marco was the last living witness to have seen Ger, so to hear these stories that Ger was out of his head, that he was hallucinating, that his body was splattered all over the mountain – this was heartbreaking for us.

It was the final straw for the McDonnells. There were too many unanswered questions, too many versions of the same story. Notwithstanding the extreme situation he found himself in, the suggestion that Ger had abandoned the three stricken climbers didn't ring true for the family as the actions of the compassionate and caring man they knew so well. They needed to find out more. Within days, several members of Ger's family were on a plane to Pakistan.

As the journalists filed their stories and prepared to leave Skardu, Pemba, the man with more first-hand information than most of the other climbers who had been on the mountain, was departing Base Camp and facing the trek back to civilisation. Mark Sheen, Jelle Staleman and Roeland van Oss had packed away Ger's belongings and the porters had returned from Askole to dismantle the tents and take away the gear and detritus left behind after a two-month stay on the Godwin-Austen glacier.

As they prepared to begin the walk south towards Concordia, Pemba met a group of American newcomers to Base Camp. They were planning to ski down from the summit, Pemba was told. The Americans asked if they could use the Norit tents at the higher camps; Pemba and the others assented, they would not be returning to dismantle their encampments on the Cesen ridge. Pemba had even left his climbing boots behind at Camp Two where he had changed into lighter footwear; there was no appetite for climbing again to retrieve personal items.

The members of the largest expedition on the mountain, the Flying Jump team from South Korea, walked from Base Camp to meet a helicopter which they had commandeered for their escape from K2 – at a cost of $14,000[187] – but which could only land safely at Broad Peak Base Camp. Before the South Koreans boarded the helicopter, they sent a final message back to friends at home. Three of the South Korean climbers expressed their awe about 'the mountain of the mountains' and 'the mountain that invites death'.[188]

Just as the remaining Norit team members reached the foot of Broad Peak, the South Koreans' helicopter arrived. Their liaison officer suggested to Pemba that he should ask for a ride on the helicopter to Skardu as he was still exhausted:

> His [Kim's] liaison officer convinced me; he said you are very tired and if you talk with Kim maybe you could go with us and that would be easier for you, otherwise it is a long way and you have been working very hard on the mountain ... There was no response from Kim. I don't know if there was room, so I continued.

Hoselito Bite was sorry to see Pemba leave Base Camp but he knew he would not be far behind. The Serb had got under the skin of a number of climbers for his naivety and ill-preparedness for a mountain like K2, but his exuberant behaviour and friendly manner had endeared him to others. As he had watched the death and destruction unfold from Base Camp, he found a revulsion growing within him:

> Now when I left the Base Camp, one American guy he told me, "Hey, you need to turn around and bless yourself to the mountain, to give respect", and I was just standing and looking and saying, "Fucking mountain". I was mad at the mountain, why did she do that ... I don't know, that mountain is beautiful, very beautiful still, but maybe I was mad, maybe at God, to let something like this happen on such a beautiful K2.

Hoselito's fellow nationals on the K2 Vojvodina Expedition visited the first police station they could find on their descent from the Baltoro glacier. They wanted to report the death of Dren Mandic. The police in Shigar, a short distance from Skardu, recorded the death of a Serb mountaineer in a climbing accident but no doctor could be found to issue a death certificate; they could not do so anyway without seeing a body.

It was left to the expedition leader, Milivoj Erdeljan, to contact the Serb Embassy in China. Officials there managed to obtain a document from the

Ministry of Foreign Affairs in Islamabad which confirmed that Dren had died on Pakistani soil. Only on the basis of that document was a death certificate issued on the team's return to Serbia.[189] But the team did not need a piece of paper to confirm their friend was dead; they tried to remember him as they knew him best – a smiling, young climber with a humble passion for high-altitude adventure.

A sombre blog update from the Singaporean team on 7 August announced the end of their expedition. Robert Goh, Edwin Siew Cheok Wai and their Sherpas planned to leave Base Camp within a week with 'great reluctance and heavy hearts'.

> The mountain is so near, yet so far,' said Goh, 'the tents and equipment are all up there ready for us. But with 11 climbers killed when the weather was perfect, it was just too shocking for words. We should not be angry at anyone. Each climber makes his or her own decision on the mountain whether or not to go up. You take the conditions as you find them and should not blame anyone. If there are problems on the way, you can always turn back. The challenge of the sport is not to summit at all odds. The challenge is to read the conditions, assess the risks, and be prepared physically and mentally to go up when conditions are right. But you must also know when to turn back ... the mountain will always be there.[190]

Pemba hiked along the moraine towards the beginning of the Baltoro glacier. The weather was still calm and the climbers, high-altitude workers and porters were quiet, lost in thought, desirous only of warm showers, meeting family and, notwithstanding everything that had occurred, planning the next expedition to another peak, a new challenge, another dice with death.

Before turning at Concordia, the team halted to take one last look at K2, reaching majestically into the sky, the swirls of cloud around it appearing to cleanse the summit of human invasion and carnage, waiting for the next incursion by daredevils and lovers of the invincibility of nature.

The mountain was returning to its pristine, untouched state, as it had been for thousands of years, eternal in a changing world. Pemba had come to K2 disputing the notion that it was a mountain of death, the 'Killer Mountain' or some sort of sinister and malignant force. Despite all that had happened to him and the various expeditions over the previous days, and despite losing a climbing friend and team-mate, nothing had happened to convince Pemba that he needed to revise his impressions of the mountain, its reputation and its magnetic allure:

> K2 is a beautiful mountain. People call it "Killer Mountain" when they are not well prepared, do not have enough experience, not enough manpower. Then something goes wrong on the mountain and they say "Mountain is killer, mountain is savage", or something like that. But it is not like that. K2 is a very beautiful mountain.

Wilco, Cas, Marco and all the journalists had left Skardu by the time Pemba, along with the three remaining Norit team members, Mark, Jelle and Roeland, arrived there on 11 August, after a four-day journey from Base Camp. After the silence of weeks on the mountain, the bustle of Skardu with the din of the mopeds, trucks and other vehicles zipping along its narrow streets, was an assault on the men's eardrums. The four weary climbers booked into a motel where beds and bathrooms were a welcome luxury.

Pemba went to visit the home of the cook from the Norit team who had become very ill and left Base Camp the morning before the climbers set out for the summit. He wasn't home but Pemba was told he had recovered fully from appendicitis. He left 2,000 rupees behind in gratitude for the cook's services to the expedition.

Later that day, a familiar face from K2 Base Camp turned up at the motel: Shaheen Baig, the Serb guide and previous K2 summiteer, had made the long and arduous journey back to Askole by mule, racked by nausea and vomiting. On his return to Skardu, he had learned from locals about the deaths of his Shimshal Valley friends and protégés, Karim Meherban and Jehan Baig. Shaheen was devastated.

Pemba noticed a sadness etched on the Pakistani's face; the tragic deaths and the illness which ravaged his body had aged him in a few short weeks:

> He was very upset. He said he was sorry that he couldn't make it to High Camp; that he had to leave the trail-breaking party because he got sick. He said I did a very good job and he asked about Karim and how he had died and how were the other Pakistanis. He was upset because so many had died on the mountain.

Pemba felt comfortable enough with the experienced mountaineer to vent his own frustration and misgivings about what had unfolded in the previous weeks. More than 60 per cent of those on the mountain did not have enough experience, he suggested; even some of the other Sherpas were ill-prepared. They had climbed only a few 8,000-metre peaks before attempting the world's most dangerous mountain and some had not even been to an altitude of 8,000 metres before.

Anger rose within him: many of the climbers had no technical climbing education, no training: 'Those people who are willing to get involved in this kind of activity, they should respect the mountain and they should respect their own physical and technical abilities. They should not try to climb beyond their own limits.' Shaheen nodded in agreement.

News of the K2 fatalities was everywhere in Skardu. Pemba found it impossible to avoid the media interest in the story and a short time in an internet café provided plenty of evidence of that. His email inbox was flooded with messages bearing good wishes and requests for information, including from a handful of journalists he had never heard of and from people he barely knew. He counted 500 unread messages; most of them went ignored.

A simple perusal of websites churned out by a search engine threw up sensational headlines of death and destruction on the 'Savage Mountain.' There were so many reports, with so many different versions of events, he thought, and much of the detail didn't tally with his own experiences.

From his motel, Pemba phoned his wife, Da Jangmu, in Kathmandu. It was the first time they had spoken since he had left Camp Four on the mountain. 'Gerard is dead,' he told her. She said, 'We have to go to the monastery to pray for him, you have to come back soon so we can do that'.

Seeking some spiritual release and anxious to clear his head, Pemba sourced a local guide to take him to visit an iconic mandala, a Buddhist painting on a large rock, near Skardu, dating from 800BC. From there he travelled to the picturesque and secluded Satpara Lake near the city. The trauma of the previous weeks abated somewhat in a place in which Pemba sought to cleanse his body and mind:

> I wanted to see green as much as possible and I wanted to stay as long as
> I could around green vegetation, that is why I went there, it was refreshing
> for myself and I spent almost a half day there. It is a very nice place, green
> with crystal clear water and a lot of green trees around the lake.

Annie Starkey, Ger's brother JJ and his girlfriend Céren, Ger's sister Denise, and her husband Damien O'Brien, landed in the searing heat and noisy congestion of Islamabad just over a week after Ger had perished on K2. JJ and Céren had been on holiday when word reached them that Ger was in trouble. The week since he left the Canary Islands had been an emotional rollercoaster, but JJ had heard too many different stories about what had happened on the mountain.

Apart from inconsistencies in Marco Confortola's evidence as reported in the media, the family had been told, among other things, that Ger had died with Rolf Bae. Another tale suggested that Ger had left the three stricken climbers on the ropes to take photographs of them from higher up the mountain.

There was no escaping the contradictions and confusion; on the evening before the McDonnells left Ireland, one of its national newspapers repeated a report on Marco's final hours with the Irish climber: 'It was at that moment, "for some strange reason", that McDonnell began to walk away. It was the last time Confortola would see his friend alive.'[191]

JJ and his siblings felt they owed it to their beloved brother to establish the truth. Their turmoil was exacerbated by the fact that nobody from the Norit expedition had phoned them to outline what had happened or how Ger had died. If the climbers did not come to them, the family would have to go to the climbers. Damien O'Brien felt torn by emotion when they landed in the Pakistani capital:

> It was really frightening because we didn't know what we were going in for and I guess half of me believed Ger was still alive and the other half didn't believe it. Because at that point we didn't have ... we still got no confirmation as to whether Ger was dead or not. I mean we got no phone call from Norit to say Ger was gone.

The McDonnells' quest began at the Italian consulate at a meeting facilitated by the Irish ambassador to Iran, Alan Cummins.[192] The Italian consul had spoken to Marco before the injured climber departed for Milan. The consul expressed concern for Marco's well-being and state of mind; he had been deeply traumatised by his experience, mentally drained and tormented by what he had experienced and seen. But Marco had reiterated his belief that Ger was very tired and that he went back up the mountain for reasons that Marco did not know or understand.

Cas and Wilco were nervous. How would Ger's family react? They were alive and, for a moment, felt guilty for it. The McDonnells were waiting for them at a house which had been arranged by diplomatic personnel in Ireland and Pakistan. Annie embraced Wilco and tears of helplessness and grief flowed. Wilco said there were no words for what had happened.

Just a year before, he had climbed Denali with Ger and Annie. Now Ger was gone, the circumstances of his death still a mystery. But Cas and Wilco had little to fear; Ger's mother, Gertie, told Damien and the others to treat Ger's team-mates with kindness:

> She wanted somebody to go out and meet the Norit team climbers coming off the mountain. And just to give them a hug, not to criticise them ... or not to push blame on anyone, just to go out and give them a hug and just to show the appreciation that the family had towards them because, obviously, Ger spent the last three months of his life with these guys, they were his friends, they were his family on the mountain.

The Dutch climbers looked ashen-faced and gaunt as discussions shifted to events on the mountain. Cas drew sketches of the area between Camp Four and the summit to try to illustrate as best he could where he and Wilco had been on the mountain. They had not spoken to Pemba since leaving K2. But they had spoken to Marco and he told them Ger had left him and ascended for no apparent reason.

'I'm sorry,' Denise told Wilco, 'I'm just totally in denial ... In my heart there is still hope, I know that sounds ridiculous.' Were they sure that Ger was dead, Damien asked. 'Yes, for sure,' said Wilco, 'because that is what Marco told us directly.'[193] Marco had been overwrought and emotional, Cas told them. He felt deeply moved, listening to their sobs and desperate pleas for more information:

> When you meet the family, you see how much broken hearts or tears you leave behind. Then of course it's horrible, one stupid sport ... even a little bit selfish. But it is the way Gerard always had been and all the climbers are. On the other hand, we can be happy that he chose ... that he was walking behind his dream. He really was doing the things he wanted to do and that Ger really was Ger ... He was very strong and passionate.

After an hour's discussion, the McDonnells hugged Wilco and Cas. They were none the wiser and were now pinning all their hopes of getting closer to the truth on Pemba Gyalje.

───────────────

Pemba and his three climbing companions arrived in Islamabad on 12 August. In a house in the city, owned by the Irish aid agency, Concern, the six remaining members of the Norit expedition met Annie Starkey and the McDonnell family.[194] Nervously, Mark Sheen handed Ger's passport and wallet to Annie. He shared a story about his time in a tent with Ger on Broad Peak. 'Ger's sense of humour is what I loved about the guy,' he said. The smiles and laughter helped to defuse the solemnity and sense of anticipation.

'My mother has heard all about you, Pemba,' Denise told him. Pemba shuffled awkwardly in his seat. Discussion moved quickly to what Pemba had seen and heard on K2 in the weeks before. The family had brought a camcorder to record footage that would be played and replayed countless times over the following months. They wondered if Pemba could fill any of the gaps in the story.

What he had to say took not just Ger's relatives by surprise, it also startled Cas and Wilco:

> *Pemba*: Two fresh Sherpas, forced up by Korean leader, reached the Koreans at the top section of the couloir and then they are descending together.
>
> *Cas*: I thought they were already dead, the three that were hanging there but probably they'd been moving then...
>
> *Pemba*: Then at the same time, three or four times the Serac fell down, multi times Serac fell down.[195]

If Ger had been behind the South Korean team as they descended towards the top of the Bottleneck, Pemba thought, perhaps he had freed Jumik from the entanglement of the fixed ropes. Somehow, the partially conscious climber, after a night hanging on the ropes in unforgiving conditions, had been roused from his exhaustion and propelled to continue downwards:

> I thought that after Marco descended that Ger was trying to release the Koreans, and maybe he climbed back again because he may have wanted

to reach the anchor to make the ropes more slack or something ... In my experience; some people get extra energy even after a long time being exhausted ... I guess that Ger could be descending behind them ... I thought that Ger had been hit by the avalanche ... I could not identify all those who died in the avalanche in the Bottleneck but Jumik and [Big] Pasang were definitely there.

Ger McDonnell had been known to come to the aid of others in trouble on the mountains. During a climb on Denali (Mount McKinley) in 1999, Ger and a climbing colleague had helped some Taiwanese and South African climbers who had got into difficulty. On another expedition to the same mountain he had held the hand of a dying climber and comforted him until he passed away. On Everest in 2003, along with Pemba Gyalje, Ger had come to the aid of their expedition leader who faced an almost-certain death just below the summit after succumbing to hypoxia and oedema.[196]

On his previous visit to K2, in 2006, prior to being seriously injured himself, Ger had been deeply upset at being unable to muster a rescue team to assist an Austrian expedition who sent out a distress call from beneath the summit. The Irishman's sincerely-held concern for the welfare of others had been evident, not only to others at Base Camp, but also to the Nepalese Sherpa whom he had asked to join him on K2 in 2008:

> He was 200 per cent always thinking about safety and security and health conditions. On K2 he was very worried about me, not himself ... before I left Kathmandu he was asking if my family was happy, in Islamabad he said to me, "You have to come back from the mountain in good condition for your daughter, for your wife". He said the same thing in Base Camp, "You have to come back home for your daughter, she is young" – something like that; he was always reminding me ... he was especially concerned about my family, and also for Wilco who had a young kid, he said the same about him.

The disparity between what they had heard earlier and what they were now hearing registered with the McDonnells immediately; Pemba had much more detail than they had gleaned from their original meeting with Cas and Wilco. Until then, Cas and Wilco had not had the opportunity to discuss with Pemba what he had witnessed. From the moment they were reunited at Camp Four, their focus had been on survival and rescue.

In the hospital in Skardu, Marco had told Cas that he had left the three hanging climbers for dead. The Dutchman had assumed the trio had died there and then. It soon became apparent that it had taken the determination of a grief-stricken family from Ireland to bring the Norit team together for the first time since they had left the mountain, and to create a more comprehensive and factual narrative about what had happened. The revelations continued:

> *Cas*: Did you see something Pemba? Did you see persons falling down?
>
> *Pemba*: Ah no. Only Sherpa ['Big' Pasang Bhote] before he fell down by Serac, talked to me on walkie-talkie, 'Ah, ok, Pemba, there is one member fell down on Traverse because hit by Serac'. The visibility was very poor ... I then ask Sherpa, 'Can you identify him?' And he told me red and black down suit. I'll say definitely Gerard.
>
> *Cas*: This is different here. Marco says that they were next to three Koreans hanging on ropes, then he says Gerard was going up and of course the only one there to see anything was Marco. We have been trying to figure out why Gerard would have gone up, but now we listen to your stories we know Marco has been telling more stories.[197]

Damien O'Brien felt dizzy as his head went into a spin: Pemba had been told Ger had fallen. Moments before 'Big' Pasang and the others died, Pemba had radioed him from below the Bottleneck. That this second radio conversation had taken place was new information; it was during this conversation that 'Big' Pasang told Pemba that a climber in a red and black down suit was descending behind him and the others but had been swept to his death by icefall.

Damien trusted what he was hearing absolutely. For the McDonnells, Pemba's testimony was the missing piece of the jigsaw.

Before going their separate ways, JJ McDonnell invited the members of the Norit expedition to travel to Ireland the following weekend. A memorial service was being arranged for Ger in his native village of Kilcornan, a funeral in all but name, though without a body or a coffin. Wilco nodded; of course they would be there. The relief on JJ's face was palpable; the McDonnells now had a complete picture of how their brother had perished on a mountain he had fallen in love with.

It was not quite closure; the family faced a long campaign to convince a media which would continue to peddle misinformation and mistruths about Ger's fate. But, for now, they had some solace and a greater understanding of what had happened to help salve their grief. Pemba declined the offer to travel to Ireland. He was anxious to get back to his family in Nepal: 'I will pray for Ger at the monastery near my home,' he said.

Back in the Nepali capital of Kathmandu, Pemba's wife had consulted with the lama who gave her the most auspicious dates on which to pray for the dead climbers. A couple of days after her husband returned home, the entire family visited the Big Maitreya Buddha monastery and Shree Guru monastery at the Buddhist site of Boudhanath where they offered prayers for the souls of the 11 climbers who would never return from K2.

Epilogue

The Summit

AUGUST 2008

The farms and families of the porters waited for them. Having lugged the tents, barrels and boxes of supplies and equipment – much lighter now – back across the Baltoro glacier, the men of Askole and the surrounding region returned to the toil of the land. The climbing season's earnings would sustain them through the winter, a welcome supplement to their meagre agrarian incomes.

The mood of the climbers and high-altitude workers on the journey away from K2 had been reflective and sombre. Gone was the excited anticipation of a few short months before. The porters whispered respectfully about horrific icefalls, dramatic rescues and violent deaths. Their clients did not delay in Askole; some left even before their gear had been collected, ready to be shipped back to the four corners of the world.

It was as though the mountaineers wanted to escape, for another year at least. But they would return, the porters knew, as they had done for generations, in search of the high-altitude holy grail that filled their daydreams.

As they walked back along the dusty dirt tracks to their homes, the men noticed the perennial changes in the landscape. Swathes of yellow corn had replaced barren fields. Tomatoes and apricots lay drying on the rocks. The weather had turned too. Autumn and winter were approaching and with them would come a quiet in the valleys and a return once more to solitary perfection on the snow-capped peaks.

LIST OF THE DEAD

Dren Mandic (Serbia)

Jehan Baig (Pakistan)

Rolf Bae (Norway)

Hugues D'Aubarède (France)

Karim Meherban (Pakistan)

Gerard McDonnell (Ireland)

'Big' Pasang Bhote (Nepal)

Jumik Bhote (Nepal)

Hwang Dong-jin (South Korea)

Park Kyeong-hyo (South Korea)

Kim Hyo-gyeong (South Korea)

POSTSCRIPT

Tsering Bhote stopped climbing after his experience on K2 in 2008 but returned to the mountains in 2013 with an expedition to Manaslu. Marco Confortola lost all of his toes to frostbite. He continues to climb and works as an alpine guide. The Italian Olympic Athletes Association awarded him a heroism medal following his return from K2.

Chhiring Dorje Sherpa has settled in the United States and has climbed Everest and Lhotse several times since 2008. He received the Tenzing Norgay Award for Heroism from the Explorers' Club in 2013. Pemba Gyalje Sherpa was named the National Geographic Society Adventurer of the Year 2008 and appeared on the front cover of the society's magazine. He continues to work as a guide and is president of the Nepal National Mountain Guide Association. He has not returned to K2.

Pasang Lama joined the South Korean Flying Jump team on an expedition to Manaslu, the world's eighth highest peak, two weeks after leaving K2. He continues to work as a mountain guide. Members of the American expedition are still climbing mountains, with Dr Eric Meyer regularly working as an expedition doctor. Fredrik Sträng continues to climb in the Himalaya and in 2009 became one of the first two Swedish climbers to reach the summit of Makalu.

Go Mi-sun (Ms Go) died in a fall on Nanga Parbat in Pakistan on 11 July 2009, having reached the summit. Kim Jae-soo (Mr Kim) succeeded in climbing all of the world's 14 8,000ers, dedicating the last of those climbs, in 2011, to Go Mi-sun.

Cecilie Skog continues in her polar adventures and completed an unassisted crossing of Antarctica in 2010. She also lectures and runs the adventure business, Fram, founded by her husband, Rolf Bae. Wilco van Rooijen had all of his toes amputated in stages within three months of leaving K2. He continues to climb the world's highest mountains and explore the polar regions.

NOTE ON THE SOURCES

The principal source material for this book comes from a series of extensive interviews conducted for the documentary film, *The Summit* (Image Now Films & Pat Falvey Productions, 2012). Quotations from those interviews which are used in this book are not individually referenced. All other quotations are individually referenced. Interviews were carried out with the various interviewees in the following locations:

- Wilco van Rooijen, Cas van de Gevel and Maarten van Eck in Utrecht, Netherlands, October 2008 – Pat Falvey and Nick Ryan.

- Pemba Gyalje Sherpa, County Kerry, Ireland, November 2008 – Pat Falvey and Nick Ryan.

- Chhiring Dorje Sherpa, Pasang Lama, Tsering Bhote and Pemba Gyalje in Kathmandu, Nepal, February 2009 – Pat Falvey and Nick Ryan.

- Marco Confortola, Bormio, Italy, March 2010 – Nick Ryan.

- Hoselito Bite, Subotica, Serbia July 2010 – Nick Ryan.

- Alberto Zerain, Vittoria, Spain, July 2010 – Nick Ryan.

- McDonnell Family (Gertie, Martha, Stephanie, Denise, JJ) – Limerick, Ireland, August 2010 – Nick Ryan.

- Annie Starkey, Limerick, Ireland, August 2010 – Nick Ryan.

- Damien O'Brien, Dublin, Ireland, September 2010 – Nick Ryan.

- Fredrik Sträng, Stockholm, Sweden, January 2011 – Nick Ryan.

- Lars Nessa, Oslo, Norway, January 2011 – Nick Ryan.

- Cecilie Skog, Oslo, Norway, January 2011 – Nick Ryan.

In-depth interviews with Pemba Gyalje Sherpa were also carried out by researchers Bridget McAuliffe and Owen O'Shea while this book was being compiled during a visit Pemba made to Ireland in April 2013.

Interviews were also conducted by phone with a number of climbers and others, including Bjorn Sekkesaeter, spokesperson for the Norwegian expedition (April 2013) and Shaheen Baig, a guide with the Serbian expedition (June 2013). Emails were exchanged with Maarten van Eck of the Norit expedition, Bjorn Sekkesaeter and Shaheen Baig.

The narrative draws on contemporaneous blogs, including those of Chris Klinke, Ger McDonnell, Hugues D'Aubarède, Nick Rice, and Mike Farris. It also draws on the online expedition updates and reports of the Norit (Dutch), Serbian and Singaporean expeditions. Reports from the ExplorersWeb website and the Norit expedition website were also used as sources.

BIBLIOGRAPHY

Articles

Wyss-Dunant, Edouard, 'Acclimatisation' in Kurz, Marcel (ed.), *The Mountain World* (George Allen & Unwin Ltd., 1953), pp 110-117.

Hallgren, Markus, 'Groupthink in the Death Zone: failure of temporary organizations' in *International Journal of Managing Projects in Business*, vol. 3, no. 1, 2010, pp 94-110.

Blogs

Nick Rice, www.nickrice.us

Ger McDonnell, www.humanedgtech.com/expedition/mcdonnell

Chris Klinke, www.k2klinke.blogspot.ie

Hugues D'Aubarède, www.pakistank2.blogspot.ie

Mike Farris, www.mfarris.net/blog

Books

Bowley, Graham, *No Way Down: Life and Death on K2*, Harper, New York, USA, 2010

Coffey, Maria, *Where the Mountain Casts its Shadow*, Hutchinson, London, UK, 2003

Confortola, Marco, *Giorni di ghiaccio*, Dalai editore, Milan, Italy, 2009

Falvey, Pat, *A Journey to Adventure*, The Collins Press, Cork, Ireland, 2007

Falvey, Pat with Dan Collins, *Reach for the Sky*, The Collins Press, Cork, Ireland, 1997

Jordan, Jennifer, *Savage Summit: True Stories of the Five Women who climbed K2*, William Morrow, New York, USA, 2005

Kaczynski, Richard, *Perdurabo: The Life of Aleister Crowley* (2nd edition), North Atlantic Books, Berkeley, CA, USA, 2010

O'Brien, Damien, *The Time Has Come: Ger McDonnell, His Life & His Death on K2*, The Collins Press, Cork, Ireland, 2012

Van Rooijen, Wilco, *Surviving K2*, G+J Publishing, Diemen, Netherlands, 2010

Viesturs, Ed with David Roberts, *K2: Life and Death on the World's Most Dangerous Mountain*, Broadway, New York, USA, 2009

Wilkinson, Freddie, *One Mountain, Thousand Summits*, New American Library, New York, USA, 2010

Zuckerman, Peter and Amanda Padoan, *Buried in the Sky*, Norton, New York, USA, 2012

DVDs

A Cry from the Top of the World, Demand DVD, 2009

Against the Sky, Falvey Film, 2005

Magazines

Rock and Ice Magazine

Outside Magazine

National Geographic

Newspapers

The New York Times

The Independent (London)

The Guardian (UK)

The Daily Telegraph (UK)

The Evening Herald (Ireland)

Websites

www.explorersweb.com

www.summitpost.org

www.k2climb.net

www.8000ers.com

www.patfalvey.com

ENDNOTES

[1] Richard Kaczynski, *Perdurabo: The Life of Aleister Crowley* (2nd edition), North Atlantic Books, 2010, p. 98 – 108

[2] Ed Viesturs with David Roberts, *K2: Life and Death on the World's Most Dangerous Mountain*, Broadway, 2009, p. 83

[3] On 9 August 1977, six Japanese climbers from an expedition led by Ichiro Yoshizawa made it to the summit and the following year, an American group of four led by James Whittaker reached the top (source: www.8000ers.com)

[4] *Daily Telegraph*, 13 May 2009 and *National Geographic*, September 2004

[5] www.8000ers.com

[6] Viesturs, p.9

[7] www.8000ers.com and www.adventurestats.com

[8] Wilco van Rooijen, *Surviving K2*, G+J Publishing CV, 2010, p. 17

[9] Ibid., p. 11

[10] Ibid., p. 14

[11] Ger McDonnell blog, 29 May 2008

[12] Ibid.

[13] Singaporean team expedition dispatches: www.singaporemountaineers.com

[14] 'Italia K2', Cineteca, Club Alpino Italian, Milan/*The Summit*, Image Now and Pat Falvey Productions, 2012

[15] Van Rooijen, p. 31

[16] Interview with Fredrik Sträng, *The Summit*, Image Now Films and Pat Falvey Productions, 2012

[17] Interview with Mick Murphy, April 2013

[18] Damien O'Brien, *The Time Has Come: Ger McDonnell – His Life and Death on K2*, The Collins Press, 2012, p. 131

[19] Ger McDonnell blog, 16 June 2008

[20] ExplorersWeb, 5 June 2008

[21] Known as the French TGW 2008 K2 Expedition, the group is not to be confused with another French-led expedition headed up by Hugues D'Aubarède. The latter is usually referred to in this book as the French team/expedition

[22] Ger McDonnell blog, 16 June 2008

23 Chris Klinke blog, 26 June 2008
24 Report of the Expedition Serbia K2 2008, www.planinari.org.rs/PDFFormat/K2english.pdf
25 Ibid.
26 Mike Farris blog, 26 June 2008
27 Ger McDonnell blog, 18 June 2008
28 *K2 – A Cry from the Top of the World*, Demand DVD, 2009
29 Nick Rice blog, 17 July 2008
30 Singaporean team expedition report: www.singaporemountaineers.com.
31 Ibid.
32 Mike Farris blog, 18 July 2008
33 Ger McDonnell blog, 16 June 2008
34 Hugues D'Aubarède blog, 24 June 2008
35 Ger McDonnell blog, 16 June 2008
36 Singaporean team blog, 17 July 2008
37 Chris Klinke blog, 3 July 2008
38 Ger McDonnell blog, 10 July 2008
39 Marco Confortola, *Giorni di ghiaccio*, Dalai editore, 2009, p. 22
40 Ger McDonnell blog, 18 June 2008
41 Mike Farris blog, 22 July 2008
42 Chris Klinke blog, 15 July 2008
43 Mike Farris blog, 11 July 2008
44 *Daily Telegraph* (UK), 13 January 2007
45 Ibid., 6 June 2010
46 Mike Farris blog, 5 July 2008
47 Of the 66 climbers who died on K2 prior to 2008, 28 had perished in August, 27 in July and 11 in June; source: www.8000ers.com
48 Nick Rice blog, 30 June 2008
49 Ibid., 20 July 2008
50 Ger McDonnell blog, 23 July 2008
51 Mike Farris blog, 22 July 2008
52 Ibid., 27 July 2008
53 Nick Rice posted a blog which referred to a seemingly cranky liaison officer:
'We had lunch, which was made quite unpleasant thanks to the foul demeanor of our Liaison Officer, Imran Ahmed. He refused to eat the food that was served and insisted that the cook prepare a completely different dish, which he, yet again, barely touched. It is a good thing that in the past I have had quite pleasant experiences with LO's, otherwise, I might come to the conclusion that all of the Pakistani military were pretentious, abusive, abrasive people who had no business being in the mountains. Thankfully, this is not the case, and I realize that this is an isolated case.' (Nick Rice blog, 20 June 2008)
54 Ibid., 22 July 2008
55 Freddie Wilkinson, *One Mountain, Thousand Summits*, New American Library, 2010, p. 171.

56 Ger Mc Donnell video/Fredrik Sträng video/*The Summit*, Image Now Films and Pat Falvey Productions, 2012

57 ExplorersWeb, 31 July 2008

58 Mike Farris blog, 4 July 2008

59 Louis Reichardt, an American climber, was the first to reach the summit without oxygen on 6 September 1978

60 Mike Farris blog, 18 July 2008

61 Hugues D'Aubarède blog, 27 July 2008

62 Nick Rice blog, 27 July 2008

63 Ger McDonnell blog, 25 July 2008

64 Ibid., 24 June 2008

65 Nick Rice blog, 28 July 2008

66 Ibid.

67 Singaporean team expedition report: www.singaporemountaineers.com

68 Van Rooijen, p. 102

69 www.K2climb.net

70 Source: Maarten van Eck/Ab Maas

71 Interview with Shaheen Baig

72 Wilco van Rooijen, 'K2 Expedition 2008, Triumph and Tragedy': www.youtube.com/watch?v=KaHr1_5ujoM

73 *The Summit*, Image Now Films and Pat Falvey Productions, 2012

74 Source: Maarten van Eck

75 Ibid.

76 *K2 – A Cry from the Top of the World*, Demand DVD, 2009

77 Ibid.

78 Nick Rice blog, 31 July 2008

79 Van Rooijen, p. 105

80 Wilco van Rooijen video/*The Summit*, Image Now Films and Pat Falvey Productions, 2012

81 Singaporean expedition report: www.singaporemountaineers.com

82 Mike Farris blog, 27 July 2008

83 Van Rooijen, p. 106

84 Named after the Khumbu region of Nepal, the Khumbu cough is usually caused by the very low humidity at high altitude which aggravates the bronchial tubes causing a dry, coarse coughing among climbers.

85 'Acclimatisation' by Edouard Wyss-Dunant in *The Mountain World*, edited by Marcel Kurz, George Allen & Unwin Ltd, 1953, pp 110 – 117.

86 'Perfect Chaos' by Freddie Wilkinson in *Rock and Ice Magazine*: www.rockandice.com

87 Interview with Shaheen Baig

88 Sources: Chris Warner (leader of the Shared Summits Expedition to K2 in 2007) and www.summitpost.org

89 Nick Rice blog, 1 August 2008

90 Ibid.

91 Viesturs, p. 1.

92 Ibid., p. 2.
93 *K2 – A Cry from the Top of the World*, Demand DVD, 2009
94 Van Rooijen, p. 108
95 Josef Rakoncaj (Czechoslovakia) in 1983 and 1986, Juanito Oiarzbal (Spain) in 1994 and 2004, and Sherpa Jangbu (Nepal) in 2000 and 2001
96 'Groupthink in the Death Zone: failure of temporary organizations' by Markus Hallgren in *International Journal of Managing Projects in Business*, Vol. 3, No. 1, 2010, pp. 94 – 110
97 Report of the Expedition Serbia K2 2008, www.planinari.org.rs/PDFFormat/K2english.pdf
98 *K2 – A Cry from the Top of the World*, Demand DVD, 2009
99 Peter Zuckerman and Amanda Padoan, *Buried in the Sky: The extraordinary story of the Sherpa climbers on K2's Deadliest Day*, W. W. Norton & Company, p. 88 and 225 – 226
100 Van Rooijen, p. 110
101 *K2 – A Cry from the Top of the World*, Demand DVD, 2009
102 Report of the Expedition Serbia K2 2008, www.planinari.org.rs/PDFFormat/K2english.pdf
103 Nick Rice blog, 1 August 2008
104 Wilco van Rooijen video/*The Summit*, Image Now Films and Pat Falvey Productions, 2012
105 Van Rooijen, p. 112
106 Ibid.
107 The oldest person to have climbed K2 is the Spaniard, Carlos Soria Fontán, who summited in 2004, aged 65
108 Van Rooijen, p. 114
109 Confortola, p. 110
110 Zuckerman and Padoan, p. 164
111 Confortola, p. 115
112 Ibid., p. 116
113 Ibid., p. 118
114 Ibid., p. 118 – 119
115 Van Rooijen, p. 117
116 Ibid., p. 115
117 Zuckerman and Padoan, p. 61 – 62
118 ExplorersWeb, 1 August 2008
119 Van Rooijen, p. 123
120 Fredrik Sträng video/*The Summit*, Image Now Films and Pat Falvey Productions, 2012
121 Interview with Bjorn Sekkesaeter
122 Ibid.
123 Ibid.
124 Singaporean team blog, 2 August 2008
125 Confortola, p. 121
126 Ibid., p. 122

[127] Ibid., p. 122
[128] Ibid., p. 123 – 124
[129] Ibid., p. 124
[130] Van Rooijen, p. 125
[131] Ibid., p. 128
[132] Interview with Bjorn Sekkesaeter
[133] ExplorersWeb, 2 August 2008
[134] Nick Rice blog, 2 August 2008
[135] Confortola, p. 125
[136] Ibid., p. 126
[137] Zuckerman and Padoan, p. 90
[138] Confortola, p. 126 127
[139] Source: Maarten van Eck
[140] Norit expedition website, 2 August 2008
[141] Ibid.
[142] Nick Rice blog, 2 August 2008
[143] Van Rooijen, p. 129
[144] Ibid., p. 132
[145] Ibid., p. 139
[146] Zuckerman and Padoan, p. 227
[147] Mike Farris blog, 3 August 2008
[148] Chris Klinke blog, 3 August 2008
[149] Van Rooijen, p. 141
[150] Chris Klinke blog, 3 August 2008
[151] O'Brien, p. 149
[152] Ibid., p. 150
[153] Confortola, p. 130 – 131
[154] www.thelocal.com, 3 August 2008
[155] Wilkinson, p. 44
[156] Zuckerman and Padoan, p. 96, and Nick Rice blog, 7 August 2008
[157] Nick Rice blog, 4 August 2008
[158] Ibid.
[159] Ibid.
[160] Ibid., 3 August 2008
[161] Mike Farris blog, 7 August 2008
[162] ExplorersWeb, 3 August 2008
[163] Source: Maarten van Eck
[164] Zuckerman and Padoan, p. 209
[165] Norit expedition website, 4 August 2008
[166] Confortola, p. 132
[167] Ibid., p 134
[168] ExplorersWeb, 6 August 2008
[169] Nick Rice blog, 5 August 2008

[170] ExplorersWeb, 6 August 2008

[171] Confortola, p. 134 – 135

[172] Ibid., p. 136

[173] O'Brien, p. 164

[174] TVNZ and *Der Spiegel*, 4 August 2008

[175] *The Guardian*, 5 August 2008

[176] www.alpinist.com, 7 August 2008

[177] Interview with Alberto Zerain

[178] 'A Few False Moves' by Michael Kodas in *Outside Magazine*, September 2008

[179] *The Daily Telegraph*, 5 August 2008

[180] *The New York Times*, 6 August 2008

[181] Ibid.

[182] Interview with Bjorn Sekkesaeter

[183] Ibid.

[184] Associated Press, 6 August 2008

[185] Reuters, 4 August 2008

[186] *The Independent* (UK), 9 and 27 August 2008

[187] Nick Rice blog, 6 August 2008

[188] The 'mountain that invites death' formed part of the headline in *The New York Times'* front page story on 6 August 2008

[189] Report of the Expedition Serbia K2 2008, www.planinari.org.rs/PDFFormat/K2english.pdf

[190] Singaporean expedition blog, 7 August 2008

[191] *Evening Herald*, 9 August 2008

[192] Ireland did not have an embassy in Pakistan at the time

[193] McDonnell family video/*The Summit*, Image Now Films and Pat Falvey Productions, 2012

[194] O'Brien, p. 163 – 169, McDonnell family video/*The Summit*, Image Now Films and Pat Falvey Productions, 2012

[195] McDonnell family video/*The Summit*, Image Now Films and Pat Falvey Productions, 2012

[196] During an ascent of Everest in 2003, the co-author of this book, Pat Falvey, ran into severe difficulty a short distance from the summit. He had changed his oxygen supply a few hours before but did not realise that the valve on the oxygen bottle had become obstructed by ice. He quickly began to experience hypoxia, pulmonary and cerebral oedema and a loss of peripheral vision, exacerbated by the fact that he had already spent two days in the Death Zone. Pat was within an hour of the summit when he decided to turn back. Ger McDonnell and Pemba Gyalje were returning from the summit and came across their expedition leader, who had begun to deteriorate rapidly. Ger and Pemba helped Pat to descend safely to High Camp despite his disorientation and he subsequently recovered.

[197] O'Brien, p. 167, McDonnell family video/*The Summit*, Image Now Films and Pat Falvey Productions, 2012

INDEX